MW01094240

Pakistan Traveller

Tim Blight

UrbanDuniya

UrbanDuniya.com
UrbanDuniya.com/PakistanTraveller

Dedicated to the wonderful people of Pakistan

© Tim Blight 2017
UrbanDuniya   Melbourne

Except as provided by the Copyright Act 1968, no part of this publication may be reproduced or communicated to the public without prior written permission of the publisher.

While every effort has been made to verify the information provided in this book, it is given in good faith, and to the authors' best knowledge was correct at the time of writing. Neither UrbanDuniya nor the writers can accept any liability for injury, loss or damage arising with respect to any of the information contained herein.

Foreword

Pakistan has been in the headlines a lot in recent years and unfortunately for all the wrong reasons. This has had the effect of deterring many would-be travellers to this beautiful, fascinating and rewarding destination. Many parts of Pakistan are undoubtedly dangerous for anybody, locals included. However there are still many areas of the country that are open for business, and attracting a handful of determined visitors.

The downturn in tourist numbers is the contributing factor in many publishers pulling out of the Pakistan guidebook market. Pakistan Traveller by UrbanDuniya aims to fill this gap in the market by providing basic, yet practical and relevant information relating to Pakistan's more stable regions.

It is our hope that the information will be of use to the small but steady stream of travellers in these parts of Pakistan, and will hopefully encourage more intrepid tourists to visit this remarkably hospitable but grossly misrepresented nation.

"in sha Allah"

How to use this guide

This guidebook is divided into five main sections;

- **Background Information** provides you an introduction to the nation - what makes it the place it is today, including history, society and culture.
- **Planning** is a summary of how to get to Pakistan, what to see when you're there, and when to visit.
- **Practical Information** includes useful details on how to prepare for your trip to Pakistan, and how to survive once there - information on everything from clothing and etiquette to toilets and internet access.
- **Regions of Pakistan** includes all the necessary on-the-ground information for local travel - details of attractions, hotels, places to eat and local transport.
- **Basic Urdu** includes the basic vocabulary and phrases you need to get around in Pakistan.

Unlike many other travel guidebooks, we only provide a couple of suggestions for hotels, places to eat and transport arrangements in each city in Pakistan. There are two main reasons for this; firstly, Pakistan's tourism infrastructure is not developed to the same standard as many other countries; some hotels don't even accept foreigners, while others can't be recommended for security considerations. For this reason, we list a couple of places in each location that are reputable.

Secondly, at UrbanDuniya, we believe that an essential part of experiencing a city and a country is to wander and discover for oneself, and Pakistan is a perfect example; interesting diversions and intriguing detours await the keen traveller around every corner. As a result, we have provided guidance for things like eateries and city precincts, but we have not offered prescriptive advice. We do not support the development in Pakistan of a 'banana pancake' tourist scene, where hoardes of travellers frequent the same 'backpacker ghetto' style cafes and restaurants, without really experiencing the country for themselves.

Of course, detailed information is provided for essential aspects of travel, such as emergency services and safety and security advice. We would like our guidebook to be used by travellers who find it a faithful companion where necessary, but who aren't afraid to take their travel "off the page" and, where appropriate, close this book, open their eyes and experience the magic of Pakistan in their own way.

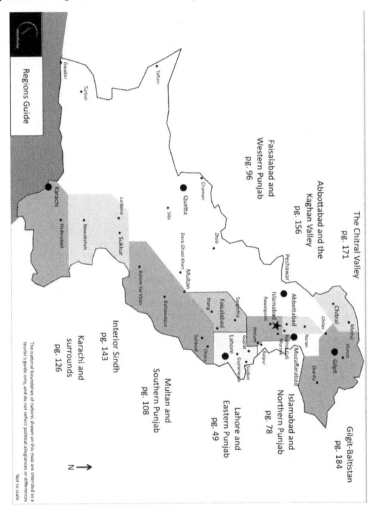

Contents

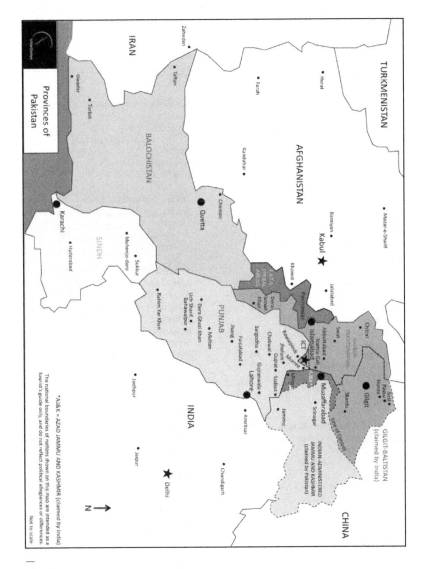

Background Information

Brief History

Pakistan's history as a land is long and dramatic; as a nation state its history spans less than a century, but is no less dramatic. The modern nation of Pakistan was only created in 1947, however the early history of the region is deeply entwined with that of India, Afghanistan, the Middle East and Central Asia.

Pre-Historic Civilisations, Ancient Empires and Early Kingdoms

Some of the earliest evidence of people in the region we now call Pakistan has been found near Islamabad. Crude rock tools have been discovered on the Soan River, with settlement dated to as far back as 500,000 years ago. The next evidence of human civilisation in Pakistan is from 7000 BC, where the city of Mehrgarh existed near modern day Quetta, Baluchistan. It's believed that in the third millennium BC the climate at Mehrgarh became increasingly inhospitable, so the site was abandoned.

It is from the third millennium BC, and encompassing the timeframe of the collapse of Mehrgarh, that the first major documented civilisation emerged in the Indus Valley. The Indus Valley Civilisation was a cosmopolitan network of cities along the Indus River, producing important artifacts from its predominantly Hindu culture, of which some can be viewed at Harappa. However in 1700 BC the Indus Civilisation suddenly declined, leaving important archeological sites in Mohenjodaro in Sindh (page 149) and Harappa in Punjab (page 116) to be rediscovered in the twentieth century.

The last millennium BC saw a return to rural living, with Hindu tribes occupying what is now known as the Vedic period. With the composition of the Rigveda (Hindu sacred text), this period saw a social shift towards the caste-system and, eventually, the development of honoured Hindu kingdoms in the region. During this period, the city of Taxila (near present day Islamabad, page 88) was established, comprising one of the world's earliest universities. Taxila was also an important centre of Buddhism, and is now home to Pakistan's greatest collection of Buddhist relics.

By 500 BC the Achaemenid Empire (also called the First Persian Empire) is known to have ruled over large tracts of what is now Pakistan. Darius the Great ruled from Persepolis in modern-day Iran, and it was during this time that Persian culture, including the ancient Persian religion Zoroastrianism, spread eastwards to the Indus River. Despite the majesty of the Achaemenid Empire, a lack of historical evidence found in the region suggests that the Pakistani region was something of a backwater in the kingdom. Strife within the ruling elite saw the decline of the Persia in the third century BC, setting the stage for one of history's most powerful emperors to sweep through the region.

Alexander the Great snatched the territory of modern-day Pakistan from the Persians, but was unable to motivate his exhausted army any further than the Jhelum River. While occupying the region, the Macedonian Greek leader established settlements and is known to have contributed to the development of local hybrid cultures. Some of these cultures exist today; the non-Muslim Kalasha people who occupy an isolated valley in far northwestern Pakistan are widely speculated to have Greek heritage dating back to this time.

Alexander the Great died in 323 BC, and his successor in Pakistan, Seleucus, established the Seleucid Kingdom and later the Greco-Bactrian Kingdom which never came close to its predecessor's glory. History's next star was to ready shine, in the form of the Hindu emperor Chandragupta Maurya who conquered most of the Greco-Bactrian Kingdom before acquiring the rest through a peace agreement. Maurya showed great interest in Jainism, adding this offshoot of Hinduism to the religious tapestry in Pakistan's early history.

While the Mauryas ruled from the east, the border regions in modern-day Khyber Pukhtoonkhwa came under the influence of Greco-Buddhism, which, as the name suggests, was a nexus between the dying remnants of the late Alexander's empire and the then-burgeoning Buddhist society. The Kushan Empire, a Central Asian Buddhist empire, can be seen as part of this cultural period, and at one stage established a capital at Purushapura (modern day Peshawar). Their influence, along with the Greco-Buddhist Hephthalite Empire, can eventually be seen extending through to Punjab, and as late as the fifth century CE. The Hephthalites are believed to be the ancestors of today's Pathan people.

From 320, the Hindu Gupta Empire ruled over much of modern-day Pakistan before, in the sixth century, fraying at the edges like so many ailing empires do. For decades, small time emperors ruled over their micro-kingdoms, before the most influential event in Pakistan's history took place in 712 CE.

Muslim rule
In the year 610, the Prophet Muhammad (pbuh) began to receive the divine revelations which would form the Qur'an and therefore the basis for Islamic civilisation. In the years after his death, Arab armies conquered much of the Middle East, and under the subsequent Umayyad Caliphate, ruled over much of Pakistan from 712 CE. One army in particular was led by the legendary Muhammad bin Qasim who conquered much of Sindh, and is now lionised in Pakistani history. Hindu kingdoms from the east challenged Muslim rule and indeed ruled parts of Pakistan for some time, but the region had experienced its first contact with Islam and gradually, numbers of locals began to convert to the faith. It was under these late Hindu rulers that the city of Lahore first developed as a metropolis.

The imperial tug-of-war eventually ended when the Muslim Mahmud of Ghazni (from the city of Ghazni in modern day Afghanistan) conquered Peshawar in 1005, quickly followed by northern Punjab, Multan and Kashmir. Ghazni and his successors, known as the Ghaznavid Dynasty, ruled over northwestern India, Afghanistan, and large areas of Pakistan, Iran, Turkmenistan, Uzbekistan, Tajikistan and Kyrgyzstan.

In 1160 the Ghaznavids were defeated in their own city by Mohammad Ghori from Central Asia. Ghori conquered Lahore in 1187, and his successors eventually conquered Delhi, establishing the Delhi Sultanate. The Delhi throne was held by Mamluk, Khalji, Tughlaq, Sayyid and Lodhi dynasties, who ruled over the subcontinent with a loose network of sultanates (kingdoms) until 1526. The Delhi Sultanate saw important developments in the culture of Pakistan, such as bringing relatively consistent Muslim rule for the first time, and the development of Urdu a *lingua franca* for locals as well as Turkish, Persian and Arab traders. Additionally, in 1469, during the Lodhi Delhi Sultanate, Guru Nanak was born in the village of Rai Bhoi di Talwandi in Pakistan, now called Nankana Sahib (page 100) Guru Nanak would go on to found and preach the faith of Sikhism throughout the region, with far reaching implications for early modern and more recent history in the region.

Western Pakistan was lost to Mongol invaders under Timur, but the fatal blow to the Delhi Sultanate was to come in 1526 in the form of the Mughal Empire, lead by Babur. A descendant of Mongol Central Asians, Babur would invade and conquer nearly the whole Indian subcontinent. A brief but ultimately unsuccessful challenge came about from Sher Shah Suri who built the impressive Rohtas Fort near modern day Jhelum (page 94). Mughal rule ushered in a period of cultural development and exchange, opulent royalty, cosmopolitan society and, at several junctures, groundbreaking religious and ethnic tolerance.

Emperor Babur was succeeded by Humayun, Akbar the Great, and then Jehangir, whose tomb still stands just outside of Lahore (page 58). Jehangir's son, Shah Jahan, was overthrown by his son Aurangzeb whose strong but divisive rule would be the last of the great Mughals. Under the Mughal Empire some of the subcontinent's most iconic cities and structures were built, including the Taj Mahal (by Shah Jahan) and Lahore's Badshahi Mosque (under Aurangzeb, page 50).

The Mughal dynasty ruled over parts of Pakistan and India until 1857, but in practice Aurangzeb's death in 1707 would signal the end of Muslim dominance in the region. The empire began to rapidly disintegrate, and in 1739 military commander Nader Shah captured Delhi. After Nader Shah's death, power transferred to Shah's general, who was temporarily defeated by the Hindu Maratha Empire. He wrestled control back, but by then a Sikh empire was growing in power and numbers in Punjab, and the days of Muslim rule were numbered.

After the Mughals; The Sikhs and the British
The Sikh Empire in Punjab only lasted fifty years (1799 - 1849), but its significance was important. It allowed Sikhs and ethnic Punjabis a taste of absolute ruling power as they had never experienced it before; something which would have ramifications for the process of India-Pakistan partition, and for the perceived dominance of Punjabis in the modern Pakistani state.

British rule in the subcontinent had its roots in the British East India Company's expansion across the region. Trading in an array of commodities, the British East India Company was a commercial arm of the British monarchy. It entered India when the Mughal emperor Jahangir allowed it to build a factory in Surat, north of Mumbai, in 1612. The company's big moment came in 1757 when under the command of Major-General Robert Clive ("Clive of India") defeated the Muslim ruler of Bengal in Palashi, in eastern India. The victory allowed the company to extend its duties to the day-to-day rule of the country. The East India Company's expansion across India was typical of a fledgling empire, however it was also aided by the rapid demise of the Mughal Empire after Aurangzeb's death. British forces conquered Sindh in 1843, and defeated the Sikh empire in 1849, thereby gaining Punjab, Kashmir and the North-West Frontier Province (now called Khyber-Pukhtoonkhwa). Balochistan remained under local control after the fall of Nader Shah's empire.

While the East India Company's rule brought about some social changes and institutional reform, Indians were largely relegated to the status of second-class citizens. Widespread discontent was ready to explode into an all-out rebellion when, in 1857, news emerged that British soldiers were using bullets greased with cow and pig fat. This affront to Hindu and Muslim sensibilities sparked the Indian Mutiny; large parts of northern India erupted in violence and British forces cracked down. The British East India Company was dissolved and from 1858 India would come under the direct rule of the British crown. In 1876, a treaty was signed with the local royal families in Balochistan, bringing all of Pakistan's territory under British control.

The British Raj, as it came to be known, would govern India for 99 years, undertaking huge infrastructure projects such as laying the railway network, literally creating the port of Bombay mostly out of reclaimed land, and the founding of New Delhi as a stately new capital city. But while direct rule by Queen Elizabeth and her successors was materially progressive, it destroyed a lot of the social fabric that might have existed previously. Employing the ethos of 'divide and rule', caste and class divisions were exacerbated, religious tension spiked, cultural and social discrimination was rife and the economic welfare of laymen plummeted; it was predicted that a weak nation would be easier to govern.

Despite these measures, the anti-colonial discontent which had flared during the 1857 rebellion began to stir once again. In 1885 the Indian National Congress was formed, and would go on to be a key political player in the road to independence. It was the Bombay chapter of the Indian National Congress that a young British-educated lawyer named Muhammad Ali Jinnah joined in 1904. During his time in the Congress Jinnah increasingly came to represent Muslim interests in the subcontinent, but remained largely loyal to the party's central goal of Indian independence, leading delegations to London in 1913 and 1914. Meanwhile, nationalist leader Mohandas Gandhi returned to India in 1915 to join the Indian National Congress and campaign for independence through non-violent civil resistance.

In 1919 came the event that would galvanise India's independence movement. On 13th April 1919 British soldiers opened fire on a peaceful gathering of protestors at Jallianwala Bagh, a park in Amritsar, Indian Punjab. By the end of the massacre, up to 1,000 Indian men, women and children lay dead, and the call for freedom from the British Empire was louder than ever. Congress' response to the Jallianwala massacre, a renewed commitment to non-violent resistance, proved unacceptable to Jinnah. Already losing confidence in the overall direction of the Congress Party, he quit the organisation in 1920 and moved to London. Gandhi became the Congress leader the following year.

The Creation of Pakistan
From its inception, the Indian National Congress attracted the suspicion of sections of the Muslim community. Largely Hindu in membership, Congress was not perceived to represent the Muslim community, who feared Hindu domination in a future independent India. This led to the formation of the All-India Muslim League in 1906, whose first meeting was held in Dhaka, now the capital of Bangladesh. Initially the All-India Muslim League was established to protect the liberties of Muslims under British colonial rule, and afterwards if independence was ever to eventuate. As it was not initially in conflict with the ethos of Congress, there was no issue with Jinnah becoming a member of the All-India Muslim League as early as 1913 (at the same time as he was a member of Congress).

However after quitting the Congress in 1920, Jinnah had also grown to doubt that party's commitment to Muslim interests. In 1927 he felt vindicated when Congress went back on a promise to provide separate electorates for Muslim-dominated areas. In 1930 influential poet and philosopher Muhammed Iqbal called for a separate Muslim nation on the Indian subcontinent, and in 1933 Muslim nationalist Rahmat Ali published a pamphlet entitled *Now or Never* in which the name 'Pakistan' was coined. 'Pakistan' was originally an acronym for the five northwestern regions in which Muslims constituted a majority; Punjab, Afghania (now known as Khyber Pukhtoonkhwa), Kashmir, Sindh and Balochistan; however 'pak' in Urdu also means 'pure', making Pakistan 'the land of the pure'. The idea of a separate Muslim nation in the Indian subcontinent was taking shape.

In 1937 provincial elections saw the Congress win in most regions of India, including many where Muslims were in a majority. This startled the All-India Muslim League, and Jinnah, into action. Jinnah returned from London to lead the All-India Muslim League at a time when religious tensions were building. In 1940, he headed a meeting of the League in Lahore which was to pass the Lahore Resolution, announcing the League's demand for a separate Muslim state or states in the north of India. The date of the Lahore Resolution, 23rd March, remains an important day in Pakistan's national history, and the ground where the meeting took place is now the site of a national monument (Minar-e-Pakistan, page 54). Meanwhile, right-wing Muslim and Hindu leaders exacerbated the situation with inflammatory speculation about what would happen if the other community held power.

In 1946, the British rulers of India found themselves exhausted by their efforts in World War Two, and slowly losing grip on a country where inter-religious violence was escalating dangerously. It was decided by then-British prime minister Clement Attlee that India would be granted independence, but the task of organising the process was given to the last viceroy of India, Admiral Louis Mountbatten. On 3rd June 1947, Mountbatten and the British government announced that the subcontinent would be partitioned into the separate states of India and Pakistan. Spooked by the rising ethnic violence, the dates of independence were set as the 14th and 15th August 1947, just ten weeks later.

Under the British, a system existed whereby "provinces" were ruled directly by the *raj* (government), and "princely states" would continue to be ruled by their local royal families, who were allowed to stay in power so long as they obeyed the British. The Independence of India Act 1947 stated that provinces with a majority of Muslims (such as western Punjab, Sindh, Balochistan and what is now Khyber-Pukhtoonkhwa) were to join Pakistan. Hindu-domainted areas (such as eastern Punjab) would join India, while princely states (like Kashmir) were required to pick a side.

Jinnah had campaigned for a geographically contiguous state, however Muslims were not only numerous in the northwest of India, but also in the northeastern region of Bengal, which was to be divided into Indian and Pakistani halves. To complicate matters, millions of Muslims lived in the lands of central northern India, but were outnumbered by Hindus, while millions of Hindus lived in areas such as Sindh, Bengal and western Punjab which were to become part of Muslim-ruled Pakistan. Finally, Sikhs, Christians, Zoroastrians and sundry others were given little or no consideration in the process. The process of partitioning India had all the ingredients of a humanitarian catastrophe.

In the summer of 1947, millions of Muslims from Hindu-dominated areas left their cities at short notice and migrated towards the lands which would become Pakistan. Millions of Hindus made a similar move, but in the opposite direction. With nationalistic fervour and ethnic tensions in the subcontinent at their most critical point, the two groups encountered each other and the inevitable violence broke out. Entire trainloads of migrants were burnt alive. Women were raped, children kidnapped and sometimes entire families were butchered by angry mobs. Those who survived the terrible journey arrived in cities such as Delhi, Kolkata, Karachi and Dhaka to ill-prepared refugee camps. Sikhs and anyone else caught in the middle tended to gravitate towards India, although a considerable number also stayed where they were. On 14th August 1947 Britain relinquished control of Pakistan, and on the following day, of India. More than 100,000 lay dead, more than two million people had switched sides, and Pakistan was independent with Karachi as its capital city.

Modern Pakistan

The state which Pakistan's first prime minister Muhammad Ali Jinnah inherited was as troubled as it was aspirational. It was divided into two wings; "West Pakistan" comprising Sindh, Punjab, Balochistan and the North Western Frontier Province (Khyber Pukhtoonkhwa), and "East Pakistan", comprising East Bengal. The two portions of land were separated by 1,000kms of Indian territory. While India inherited much of the institutions of government from the British (such as a relatively modern capital in New Delhi), in Pakistan these all had to be built from scratch. In October 1947 war broke out between Pakistan and India over Kashmir. Additionally, the hundreds of thousands of migrants who had poured into Karachi, Lahore and Dhaka would constitute a refugee crisis that even established, modern states would have difficulty in absorbing. The process of nation-building was compounded by the fact that Jinnah died from complications of tuberculosis on 11th September 1948, just over one year after the birth of Pakistan, and his successor Liaqat Ali Khan was assassinated in Rawalpindi in 1951.

The loss of two figureheads so early in the nation's history left it without a unifying leader, and Pakistan's first constitution was passed only in 1956 after years of turmoil. Disputes over the management of the fragile nation, and increasing civil disorder in Balochistan and Bengal led the military to snatch power in a 1958 coup. General Ayub Khan, commander-in-chief of the Pakistani army, suspended the constitution and in doing so initiated the first of Pakistan's four military regimes. Under Ayub Khan economic development peaked, and Pakistan's capital was relocated to a site near Rawalpindi in the north of the country, to be named Islamabad. In 1965 war erupted again between Pakistan and India, in response to the Pakistani army's infiltration of Indian-held Kashmir; the conflict ended in a stalemate.

Since the beginning, Bengal ("East Pakistan" as it were) had been considered something of a backwater by the majority of Pakistan's rulers who were centred in Karachi, West Pakistan. The issue of East Pakistani political participation was a growing one, aggravated by the centre's refusal to acknowledge Bengali as a national language. Jinnah favoured Urdu, despite this being a foreign tongue for most Bengalis, and despite Bengali being spoken by more people than any other language in West Pakistan. The Urdu-centric bias continued long after Jinnah's death, and by the time Ayub Khan resigned for health reasons in 1969, the call by East Pakistanis to separate from West Pakistan had reached fever pitch.

Replacing Ayub Khan as military leader was general Yahya Khan, who held surprisingly free and fair elections in 1970 in which the East Pakistan-based Awami League took the majority of the vote. Bengali dominance was unacceptable to the powers in Islamabad, so the election results were dismissed. In East Pakistan the successful "Awami Party" leader Sheikh Mujinur Rahman launched a civil disobedience campaign which quickly developed into a guerrilla separatist war. Sensing an opportunity to avenge the events of 1965, India intervened and swiftly routed the Pakistan army in late 1971, and East Pakistan broke away as Bangladesh.

Humiliated by the loss of East Pakistan, General Yahya Khan stepped down and ended military rule, transferring power to Zulfikar Ali Bhutto of the Pakistan People's Party (PPP). The PPP's semi-socialist policies focused on reestablishing the nation after two wars and the traumatic loss of East Pakistan. However Bhutto's reign was increasingly divisive, with land-reforms, nationalisation of many industries, and a small but growing nuclear weapons program. Pakistani society was also increasingly divided along sectarian lines, and in 1974 the parliament passed a motion which legally declared the breakaway Ahmadiyya denomination as "*kufar*" (non-Muslims). A sham election in 1977 was followed by street violence, and General Zia ul-Haq toppled Bhutto to become Pakistan's third military leader. Zia had Bhutto executed in 1979 on trumped-up charges of corruption, and many from Bhutto's PPP party (including his daughter, Benazir) fled the country.

From the outset, Zia ul-Haq revolutionised Pakistan with his policy of 'Islamisation'. In an attempt to legitimise his rule, Zia oversaw the introduction of some *sharia* law concepts such as the punishment of whipping for adultery and amputation of a criminal's hand if convicted of theft. Zia's eleven-year rule was also defined by Pakistan's struggle against the Soviet invasion of Afghanistan, which earned him the support of the USA. Pakistan's economy was at an all-time high, largely aided by war chests in Washington and the massive trade in unlicensed guns and Afghan opium which flooded across the border. However Zia's most dramatic legacy was that under his rule Pakistan was imbibed with an undeniable, conservative and reactionary sense of religious identity. It is difficult to overstate the effect that Zia's social and cultural politics have had on conservative Pakistani society today.

Zia ul-Haq died in a suspicious plane crash near Bahawalpur in 1988, opening the door to the return of democratic rule. The 1990s were characterised by a musical chairs of leaders who presided over an increasingly stagnant economy. In the 1988 elections Benazir Bhutto came to power, but was dismissed two years later when the economy took a nosedive. Fresh elections brought to power Nawaz Sharif, the current leader of the Pakistan Muslim League (N) ("PML-N"), one of the few parties allowed to develop under Zia's iron-fisted rule. Nawaz had only ruled for three years when he was forced out by the military; Benazir would go on to win the 1993 elections. Benazir's second term would last three years when she was dismissed on corruption allegations, and in 1997 elections were held that brought Nawaz Sharif back to power. In 1998 Pakistan tested a nuclear device, bringing it to the brink of war with India, and in May 1999 the Pakistani army infiltrated parts of Indian-held Kashmir, hoping to spark a popular uprising. India responded on a war footing, and Pakistan's forces were comfortably driven back. With the economy in freefall, and Nawaz Sharif's government damaged by its latest Kashmir experience, military leader Pervez Musharraf ousted him in October 1999. Pakistan began its fourth, and most recent period of military rule.

Musharraf began his rule by liberalising the economy and the media and promising to stamp out corruption; the first point was fulfilled to some degree, but the second never really occurred. In September 2001 Musharraf found himself in the unenviable position of leading an unwilling and angry populace into the United States "war on terror", however the money flowed and development began in earnest. Musharraf's policy of "enlightened moderation" riled conservatives in Pakistan, who accused him of being a proxy for America.

Civil unrest spread, particularly in the regions bordering Afghanistan, which had been largely ignored by politicians until that time. Trying to 'enlighten' conservatives and 'moderate' the tribal regions opened a hornet's nest of enemies, who were ready to pounce in 2007 when Musharraf ordered a raid on a hardline mosque in Islamabad. The raid, known as the 'Siege of Lal Masjid', killed at least 154 men, women and children and turned the nation against the military leader. 2007 also saw an increasingly autocratic Musharraf dismiss Pakistan's chief justice and suspend the constitution, triggering a new round of public condemnation. In the face of mounting national outrage, Musharraf set an election date for early 2008.

Late in 2007, Nawaz Sharif and Benazir Bhutto, both of whom had been living in exile since their last tenures, returned to Pakistan to contest the election. On 27th December 2007 Benazir was assassinated by gunmen after a rally in Rawalpindi, and her husband Asif Ali Zadari took over day-to-day running of the PPP. The PPP won a majority in the 2008 polls. During Asif Ali Zadari's reign Pakistan lurched from crisis to crisis; terrorist attacks increasingly targeted densely populated urban areas, the already tattered economy deteriorated even further, power cuts of up to eighteen hours a day became common due to a severe energy deficit, rates of poverty, street crime and corruption rocketed, and floods of biblical proportions affected at least 20% of the country in 2010, destroying infrastructure and leaving millions homeless.

Anti-American sentiment spiked in 2011 when American security contractor Raymond Davis murdered two Pakistani nationals in Lahore. He was then allowed to return to the US a free man - many Pakistanis believed he was a CIA agent, and suspected a cover-up. Rumours of backroom government dealings were fuelled when just five months later Osama bin Laden was alleged to have been found and killed in the military city of Abbottabad, apparently without the consent of the Pakistani agencies. Amid all of this rose Imran Khan, cricketer-turned-politician, who promised to transform the nation if his Pakistan Tehreek-e-Insaf Party (Pakistan's Movement for Justice) are elected.

In 2013 Asif Ali Zardari and the PPP completed their term as a democratically elected government, the first time this has occurred in Pakistan's short life. In new elections Nawaz Sharif and his PML-N party came to power, promising to solve Pakistan's energy crisis, face the challenges of terrorism, and improve the standard of living for millions. After a high profile terrorist attack targeted Karachi's international airport in June 2014, it was the military (with the government's blessing) who came to the rescue, cracking down on militants in the Federally Administered Tribal Areas (FATA) on the border with Afghanistan. However just six months after the counter-terrorism campaign began more than 140 people, mostly children, were massacred in an army-run public school in Peshawar. The "APS attack" as it is known was one of the darkest stains on Pakistan's national psyche, and was the catalyst which united the nation against militancy. Galvinised by the bloody horror, many Pakistanis vowed that the school children's deaths would not be in vain, and became both vocal and socially active against terrorism.

Although the years since the APS attack have indeed witnessed a reduction in terrorism-related deaths, the nation is as divided as ever; unity in the face of violence has regressed into domestic and international finger-pointing, political squabbling continues over trivial issues and terrorism has far from disappeared; bomb attacks in central Lahore in March 2016 and again in February 2017, and one at a shrine in Baluchistan in November 2016 are high-profile reminders of the problems plaguing the nation. The China-Pakistan Economic Corridor (CPEC) is vaunted as a once-in-a-lifetime opportunity to revive Pakistan's standing in Asia; Beijing's $47 billion investment in the country as an access route to the Indian Ocean is indeed the stuff of dreams, but it's yet to be seen whether this will translate into stability and development for regular Pakistanis.

As Pakistan celebrates its 70th birthday in 2017, and ahead of the next general elections in 2018, the national discourse persists on the status of Kashmir, laying the blame for individual terrorist attacks and the threat posed by interfering foreign powers; the much more complex issues of basic development and education, human rights, and the overall direction of the nation receive far from the level of attention they deserve.

Culture and Society

Pakistan occupies a transition zone between India, Afghanistan and Iran. It is a place where these great cultures meet, and that has been one of the major root causes of its instability over its short history. The closer you are to India, the more subcontinental things feel. As you leave the Indian border, you pass through the Pakistani heartland, the 'collision zone' of colourful south Asian family culture and conservative central Asian nomadic traditions. Approaching the western border, the Indian influence dwindles as Pashto language replaces Urdu, green tea replaces milky chai, and Afghan turbans replace simple prayer caps.

Along the way you encounter a melange of regional cultures and languages; Punjabi culture has different customs between Lahore, Faisalabad and Sialkot. South and west of Faisalabad, to Multan and beyond, Punjabi gives way to the desert-based Seraiki culture. Further south, Sindh is known for its distinct culture, while west of Karachi, conservative Baluchi culture is native. North of Lahore, Potohari ("Potwari") and Hindko culture takes over; west of Islamabad is the home of the Pathans and their fiercely independent society, while in the mountainous far north every valley seems to have its own unique language and culture. At first glance these cultures may appear very similar, but scratch the surface and one notices significantly diverse customs and social norms. Some are related, while other regions see themselves as entirely different nations.

To understand "Pakistani culture" is to understand that national borders are merely lines drawn in the sand less than a century ago, and that timeless cultures instead melt into each other gradually over hundreds of kilometres. 'Pakistani culture' is subcontinental at heart, with a Persian/Afghan soul, and a noticeable injection of Arabia.

One thing that is true throughout Pakistan is that family is the bedrock of life, and Islam is integral to the daily functioning of society. For example, the call to prayer is heard periodically through the day, arranged marriages are the norm, and Islamic studies is an important part of the national curriculum. With the exception of some members of the elite classes, most families are large; ten, twenty, even thirty children from several wives is not unheard of - although this is much less common than it once was. Unrelated men and women living together outside of wedlock is not only considered a foreign concept, but is illegal. Pakistan constitutes a largely rural, mostly traditional society, although this is rapidly changing in the posh areas of big cities where some fast food patrons would not look out of place in New York or London.

Until the 1980s, Pakistan resembled something of a Muslim version of India. Since Zia ul-Haq's Islamisation drive in the early 80s, religion has taken on a much more serious and austere role in the nation; music is frowned upon by some sections of society, women and men live a rather (and unofficially) segregated existence and study of the Qur'an takes a much greater priority in the education of children. Questioning of religion is not tolerated by many people, and more women cover their heads than they did in the 1970s. This can be seen partly as a generational shift, but as the notion upon which Pakistan was founded, it is logical that Islam would play a crucial role in building the identity of this 70-year-old nation.

That's not to say that Pakistan is a nation full of puritanical Muslims. Religious parties have never done particularly well in elections, and in 2009 when a video was leaked showing a teenager being extrajudicially flogged for the crime of adultery, almost the entire nation reacted with revulsion. In a nation of about 200 million people, there is much diversity of opinion; much more so than Western tabloid news outlets would have us believe. Because religion and day-to-day life in Pakistan are indivisible, there is also much scope for cultural overlap. Here, Islam sits surprisingly comfortably with many non-Islamic cultural features (such as local traditional festivals).

Romanticism is prominent in Pakistani culture, drawing on the emotional epics of Persian, Afghan and Indian literature and arts. Sufism, an inner, spiritual understanding of Islam, plays an important role in Pakistani culture; the idea of being "drunk with the love of God" is manifested at shrines where devotees dance and sing in faithful elation. This romanticism is also seen in the works of Baba Bulleh Shah, Sultan Bahoo, Waris Shah and Abdul Shah Latif, all of whose writings mixes prose with poetry, spirituality, philosophy and ethereal beauty.

Women hold a particularly important place in Pakistani society, as for many they are seen as the guardians of familial honour. In many families, men do the shopping while women stay inside the home, shielded from potential slights on their integrity. Consequently, women are conspicuously absent from many streets in Pakistan, particularly in poorer and rural areas. This is seen as a matter of respect and loving protection for many families, and not understood as restrictive or repressive as many foreigners might see it. It is worth remembering that despite countless news reports of downtrodden Pakistani women, there are also countless Pakistani women who smash this stereotype.

The other major difference between Pakistan and the west is the degree to which religion pervades public life. Faith is a public affair in Pakistan, and discussions about God are common. Even conversations which are ostensibly non-religious (e.g. - travel plans) are infused with religious themes and terminology (from the common "*in sha Allah*" - "if God wills it" - to the availability of prayer facilities and halal food at the chosen travel destination). Family members, neighbours and even complete strangers are quick to offer advice about their understanding of Islam, boast of the achievements of Islamic civilisation, and often unafraid to highlight the hazards of breaking Islamic code - whether it be to the colleague who offers prayers haphazardly, or the teenager who experiments with illegal alcohol. While this can be very confronting to westerners accustomed to a strictly secular existence, bear in mind that none of it is ill-intentioned, but rather an inseparable part of the fabric of Pakistani life. Remember that not everyone who sports a beard or a headscarf is necessarily extremely religious - there might be any number of reasons for this; personal preference, family or social pressures or even fashion. Likewise, a woman who doesn't cover her head, or a clean shaven man can't be assumed to be non-religious; Islam is still an important part of life for most Pakistanis, regardless of how "modern" they appear.

Major issues facing Pakistan today are headlined by the lagging economy, which has fallen to pieces in the past decade. Rampant corruption in the government and in the private sector is seen as holding the economy back. Unemployment is therefore a major issue, and the brain drain (skilled Pakistanis leaving to find work abroad) is real. Militancy and terrorism are important talking points, gender equality remains an issue and the overall standard of living is often splashed across the newspaper pages. Loadshedding - the routine switching off of electricity to districts - is a trigger issue, with many Pakistanis disgusted that their government can't even provide electricity for more than half the day in some places.

Environmental degradation and the pollution choking large cities are plain for all to see, and between 17% and 60% of the population continue to live in grinding poverty (depending on the exact definition of 'poverty'). That, combined with a flood of unlicensed weapons and an underlying problem of drug use, make for a growing problem of both violent and petty street crime. The status of religious and ethnic minorities is a controversial topic - best avoided if possible. The dispute with India over Kashmir is an open sore for the nation, and one that regularly features on daily news reports. A separatist movement in Balochistan has also gained significant traction in the past decade, but the exact degree to which foreign nations (namely India) support the rebels is not clear. The infiltration of western and specifically American culture is a source of much grief for parents and proud Pakistanis, who see the hegemony of the world's superpower as a threat to their religion, society and values. In many people's eyes the Raymond Davis affair in 2011 confirmed what they already thought; that foreign influence in Pakistan is not limited to the cultural realm.

What to expect as a traveller

As a traveller, you will be treated with remarkable hospitality and certain expectations. Traditional ideas about hospitality mean you will most likely be subject to overwhelming kindness and generosity. Invitations for tea, invitations for dinner, enquiries about your family and offers to exchange email and Facebook IDs are commonplace. Some people are even lucky/unlucky enough to be "kidnapped" by overbearingly nice locals, who urge them to simply abandon their holiday plans and see out the weeks in their family home! Saying "no" in such situations must be done with due sensitivity.

For many Pakistanis the first question is an incredulous "why are you here?!". The sharp decline in tourist numbers and media coverage in recent years has lead many Pakistanis to privately believe that their country is a very undesirable place. Coupled with a widespread perception that life in Western nations is completely rosy (so why would you leave?), your travelling to Pakistan will be met with surprise, excitement and astonishment. Expect to be asked about the immigration process for your country - and don't sugar-coat your answer if you (like most people) are simply unable to help. Many Pakistanis stare at foreigners, although this is rarely a rude gesture, but usually a naive curiosity. As a result, you ought to keep your cool and try to get used to it - to deflect attention some travellers recommend wearing dark sunglasses, dressing to blend in, trying not to look aimless or lost, and memorizing a few useful Urdu phrases.

Toilets are often wet places without toilet paper - if you require it, then you should carry your own rolls. Meals are often eaten sitting on the floor - get used to crossing your legs for long periods of time. Smoking is not as widely accepted as you might think, but the restrictions of western public spaces don't exist in Pakistan either. Time is a fluid concept in Pakistan - things don't happen on time, they happen *in sha Allah* - if (and when) God wills it. It's easier to embrace this rather than try to resist it.

If you've been to India before, Pakistan will be both confronting and comforting. Weapons are much more visible in public than in India, a legacy of the geopolitics of the 1980s. Far fewer women are on the streets, and the level of development is overall lower. However many travellers from India appreciate the significantly lower population and the positives it brings; less crowds, less "herd mentality", less pollution and less filth. Don't expect all your cares to disappear though - this is still very much the subcontinent. If you've never been to the subcontinent, or anywhere else in Asia, get ready to be bowled over by the sights, the sounds and the smells. Terrifying and exhilarating, horrifying and stunning, very little can prepare you for your Pakistan experience. Security is tight and visible, and for some visitors, that is a bit concerning. Some hotels, particularly upmarket hotels, have soldiers stationed out the front with seriously big weapons. Cars are routinely pulled over and searched, and documents inspected, even when driving within a city. Karachi even has military tanks stationed in some suburbs. Try not to let this distract you from the good that Pakistan has to offer, however if such a visible security presence would rattle your nerves too much, you might reconsider whether Pakistan is the right destination for you - it's an important question to ask yourself before booking your trip here.

As you walk around the streets in Pakistan, you'll notice that, within the strong religious and cultural social code, almost anything goes. Men lying around on *charpoys* (string beds) sipping *chai* and watching the world go by, rubbish and human waste littering the ground, people giving to beggars, *hijra* (eunuchs) in colourful clothes dancing along the non-existent pavement, overloaded animals dragging carts through the heat, children of wealthy families taking selfies on their smartphones, palmreaders trying to predict the future, security guards casually toting AK47s, office workers taking *chai* from street vendors, a pair of burka-clad women lugging their groceries with children in tow. Nothing and anything is possible at the same time - the confounding contradictions of Pakistani life makes people-watching a favourite pastime of many. Be prepared for anything and everything - including the downright bizarre.

More than in most countries, be prepared for some very different ideas about the way life works. You will be asked questions about your religion, salary and marital status which would be considered very personal in the west. Food and health raises a whole bunch of new issues; food and drink is considered to be divided into 'hot' and 'cold' categories. Drawing on traditional Persian, Islamic and Ayurvdic principles, the concept states that too much of one type of food can upset a bodily balance - too much mango (considered 'hot') will heat the body and cause digestive problems, while 'cold' yogurt should not be consumed by anyone with a respiratory ailment. Meanwhile, for a country as conservative as Pakistan (or perhaps *because of* social restrictions), sex seems to be thought about and discussed much more than it does in the West - particularly among men. Bureaucracy will drive you crazy - everything seems to have a fee, and don't be surprised if you are asked for a bribe at some point of your trip. Don't be afraid to haggle unless prices are clearly fixed. And be prepared for the electricity to switch off from time to time - it happens with monotonous regularity, especially in the summer (see page 40).

Pakistan is an overall conservative society, and although strict dress laws do not apply, it is sensible to dress appropriately (see page 28). Being a conservative society, public displays of affection between the genders are not acceptable (including holding or shaking hands, or kissing on the cheeks - even as a greeting, and even between married couples). Pakistani men may, in the company of a married couple, speak exclusively to the husband; he is not ignoring the wife, but rather observing a culture in which unnecessary social contact between men and women is avoided. Unmarried couples are not common nor accepted by much of Pakistan - you're better to tell people you're married.

Foreign women are often treated as something of an oddity, especially if they are travelling alone - many people know that the gender dynamics are different in the West, but aren't really sure how to react. Women are rather absent from many Pakistani streets, so a foreign female traveller will inevitably attract some attention. Many women report being given special treatment, some are treated as honorary men and welcomed into the tea shops and restaurants that are usually reserved for Pakistani men only. Some women are completely ignored by men (usually a sign of respect - see above) and have more contact with their Pakistani sisters, while at the negative end of the spectrum, a few women have reported being treated with disdain for travelling alone (in traditional Pakistani society, many "decent" women wouldn't travel alone if they could avoid it). Outright harassment of foreign female travellers is not very common, partly thanks to Islamic social values, while assault is rare but not unheard of. Most foreign women report being repeatedly frustrated by social restrictions, but seldom offended or placed in danger.

Religion is a serious matter, and joking about it is not appreciated and often not tolerated. The preaching of religions other than Islam is also not really acceptable. Atheism and irreligion are not understood by a large percentage of Pakistanis; it might just be easier to say you're a non-practicing Christian. Ramadan is taken seriously in Pakistan, and at this time eating, drinking or smoking in public during daylight hours is poor form and illegal. That said, a long list of people are not expected to take part in the fast, including non-Muslims, travellers, the elderly, the young, the sick and menstruating women. If you do not partake in the fast, your hotel will be able to provide advice on which restaurants will stay open through the day, and where it would be acceptable to puff on a cigarette. However if you do fast - and you might find yourself drawn into it anyway, because many eateries are closed during Ramadan - then the evening feasts and festivities will be a highlight of your holiday!

Urdu and other Languages
The national language of Pakistan is Urdu. It developed on the streets of Delhi and Lucknow as Hindi-speaking traders did business with Afghans, Persians and Arabs. As a result it took on a Muslim flavour, and was increasingly used by Indian Muslims themselves. For example the words for "thank you"; in Hindi it's '*danyavad*', but in Urdu it's '*shukriya*', similar to the Arabic '*shukran*' which means 'thank you'.

As time went on, the language developed further, replacing Hindi words with Persian, Arabic or Turkish words, while maintaining the basic sentence structure. Contrast these sentences; "Welcome to Lahore" is said in Hindi as "*Lahore mein aapka swagath hai*", while an Urdu-speaking Pakistani would say "*Lahore mein aapka khushamdid hai*". The sentence is basically the same, but the Urdu-speaking Pakistani replaces the purely Hindi word '*swagath*' (welcome) with the equivalent word from Persian, '*khushamdid*'.

As a result, Indians and Pakistanis usually converse with only a few minor difficulties, much in the way Americans and British use different English words (lift/elevator, for example). There's debate about whether Urdu and Hindi actually constitute separate languages, or just two dialects of the one language. Pakistani and Indian governments have tried to run with the 'separate language' theory in the past, and some have even tried to 'purify' the languages, with Islamabad preferring the use of Arabic words in place of native Hindi ones, and New Delhi promoting the use of indigenous Sanskrit vocabulary over foreign loan words. This is further complicated by the fact that Indian Muslims still use Urdu in their daily lives, and many Bollywood (Indian) movie scripts are written in the sweeter, more exotic-sounding Urdu (which audiences seem to enjoy).

What sets Urdu and Hindi furthest apart is their alphabets, which are the greatest reflection of their contributing cultural influences. Where Hindi uses the Devnagri script, Urdu uses a modified Arabic script to produce the same sounds and words. The result is that children who learn Urdu are able to read (although not necessarily understand) the original text of the Quran, which is of course in Arabic.

Therefore when Pakistan was carved out of India to be a homeland for Muslims, it made sense for Urdu to be the language of the new nation. The reality on the ground however was quite different, as many Pakistanis refused to give up their local provincial or tribal languages. Although Urdu is spoken across the nation, it remains true to its roots in that it is largely a language of trade, and is only the first language of 8% of Pakistanis.

If you are interested in learning Urdu, there are few institutions in Pakistan which offer regular, quality Urdu classes to foreigners. We recommend an experienced teacher, Mr Naveed Rehman of Lahore, who can offer one-on-one classes at excellent rates. He also tutors online to students overseas. He can be reached at his email address, rehmannaveed72@yahoo.com. A basic Urdu phrase guide is included at the end of this book.

As well as Urdu, a significant number of regional languages exist; from the provincial languages of Punjabi, Sindhi, Baluchi and Pashto, and a wide number of regional languages like Seraiki, Potwari, Hindko, Kashmiri, and countless dialects. These languages are sometimes subjugated in order to promote Urdu as a unifying national language, however this doesn't stop their common use at home and among some sections of society.

Planning

Where to go (routes and destinations)

Pakistan is a medium-sized country with a variety of climates and environs. Where you go in Pakistan will depend on a variety of things, including what sort of holiday you want, what interests you, accessibility and the weather, how much time you have, and safety advice.
If it's culture, history and food that interests you, then you can't go past Lahore and Punjab. It's not that culture isn't available anywhere else, but it is much more accessible here. For natural scenery, the northern mountains of Gilgit-Baltistan and Khyber Pukhtoonkhwa are an obvious choice. Shopping would lead you back to the markets in Lahore or Karachi. And if you want to get off the beaten track, then pretty much the whole country fits the bill, but particularly the south and west of Punjab, and interior Sindh see less visitors than northern Punjab and the mountains.

The places you will visit could also be somewhat dictated by the comfort level you might expect. Needless to say, the largest cities (Karachi, Lahore, Islamabad and Rawalpindi) have the best and most comfortable facilities, and the further you get from them the more you will "rough it". The Karakoram Highway at least sees enough tourists for services to be slightly better than elsewhere, but the lack of travellers to southern Punjab and interior Sindh means that the best hotels aren't as nice you might expect. On the other hand, if saving money is your priority, you will rejoice in the cheap street food and myriad basic (and therefore affordable) accommodation options in the countryside.

Travellers' routes through Pakistan usually incorporate Lahore and either or both of Punjab and Gilgit-Baltistan. Sindh and Khyber Pukhtoonkhwa usually figure less in itineraries because of their less-developed tourism infrastructure, and generally less-stable security environments.

A common trip nowadays is to pop over to Lahore for a couple of days from Amritsar in India - get a Pakistani culture fix (at least enough to say you've been there), and then head back through Wagah to India.

With a week, you could fly into Lahore and spend a couple of days, before heading north along the Grand Trunk Road taking in the sights, before flying out of Islamabad. Alternatively, you could fly into Skardu or Gilgit via Islamabad and spend 5 days or so exploring the northern mountains.

With two weeks, you could base yourself in Lahore and see a bit more of Punjab, or fly to Gilgit or Chitral via Islamabad and do a better exploration of Gilgit-Baltistan and/or the Chitral and Kaghan Valleys.

With a month you could splice the two fortnight itineraries together (in-depth explorations of both Punjab and Gilgit-Baltistan), or alternatively concentrate on a proper four-week exploration of the north, or really get under the skin of Punjab and Sindh. With two or three months to spend in Pakistan, the possibilities are much greater, and you would have the opportunity to see it all, from north to south!

Security is also a consideration when deciding where to go. The security situation around the world is constantly changing, and Pakistan is no different. As a result, we can't give prescriptive safety advice, as things may have changed by the time you read this. It is advisable to keep abreast of international and local Pakistani news events for anything which could alter the security situation in the country. Listen to the advice of your government through their travel advisories, and listen to the advice of locals who would are aware of what is going on inside the country. While Punjab and Gilgit-Baltistan are generally more stable than other parts of the country, they are not immune to the issues which dog other regions. You must still make yourself informed before you plan a trip to Pakistan, and remain informed until and during your journey.

When to go (seasons and holidays)

Pakistan has three broad seasons; winter (October - February), summer (March - June) and the monsoon (July - September). The early or late winter is usually most pleasant for travel in Punjab. In December and January, the middle of winter, temperatures can be very chilly in northern Punjab. On some January days the temperature struggles to reach 12 Celsius in Lahore, and Islamabad even sees snow occasionally. Gilgit-Baltistan and Khyber Pukhtoonkhwa are snowy wonderlands at this time, but travel can be difficult, if not impossible. Southern Punjab, Sindh and Karachi have pleasantly warm winters – but it's never cold.

After a very brief spring, the heat sets in across Pakistan and builds to an oppressively humid crescendo in late June, just before the monsoon hits. The end of summer can be a particularly nice time in Gilgit-Baltistan and Khyber-Pukhtoonkhwa as the snow has melted and the altitude tempers the heat. However the extreme heat (40+ Celsius) across the rest of the country can really spoil the trip there; the deserts of southern Punjab and interior Sindh are even hotter – Multan, Bahawalpur and Sukkur often record temperatures in excess of 50 degrees Celsius. If you travel in Punjab or Sindh in the summer, we recommend accommodation with an air conditioner, or at least an air-cooler. Be aware that 'load shedding' - power outages resulting from a shortfall in power generation - is much more frequent in summer, so if electricity and air conditioning is important to you, enquire with your accommodation if they have a back-up generator.

In late June or early July a moisture-laden wind races north from the Indian Ocean across India and Sindh to form the monsoon. This results in frequent daily downpours across the nation which can really put a dampener on travel plans (pun intended). Some travellers embrace the monsoon as part of the spectacle, and enjoy travelling at this time because it constitutes an "off-season" both in terms of price and crowds. Gilgit-Baltistan is far enough north to avoid the heaviest of the monsoon, but rain sometimes still washes out weak infrastructure, leaving travellers stranded for days. It rarely rains continuously all day long, but does rain very heavily, intermittently throughout every afternoon, and often in the morning. Don't be fooled by the 'end of summer' in June - temperatures remain high during the monsoon, but instead of being hot and humid, it just becomes hot and steamy. By September the rain begins to peter out, and in October a very short and dry 'autumn' sets in before temperatures begin to fall. By late November much of Gilgit-Baltistan and Khyber Pukhtoonkhwa are snowed in (and therefore inaccessible), and Lahore and Islamabad are cool in the day, and quite chilly in the evenings.

Festivals can also be a fun time to be in Pakistan, but you should choose wisely. Pakistan Day is 23rd March and Independence Day is 14th August - both involve lots of flags and banners in the streets, celebratory gunfire in the air, jubilant youths driving around on their motorbikes and families visiting parks and monuments for picnics. The birthday of the Prophet Muhammad (pbuh) (Eid-e-Milad-e-Nabi) attracts similar celebrations. It occurs according to the Islamic calendar. In 2017, it is expected to fall on 2nd December, and it moves back about ten or eleven Gregorian days each year - in 2018 it is predicted for 22nd November, but could change according to the lunar cycle. Muslim saints' *urs* (commemoration of death) occurs at various shrines throughout the country on certain days; see the information about each shrine for details of dates.

Ramadan is a consideration for travellers to Pakistan, due to the restrictions on eating, drinking and smoking in public, and shortened business hours. Most travellers try to avoid this time, but a few are happy to be part of this all-encompassing cultural experience. For more information on travelling during Ramadan, see the boxed text below. Like Eid-e-Milad-e-Nabi, Ramadan is calculated according to the lunar calendar and moves back about ten or eleven days each year. In 2018, Ramadan is expected to begin on the 16th May and last 30 days, but the date could change slightly due to the lunar cycle. The festival at the end of Ramadan, Eid al-Fitr, is a fun affair with special dishes served at seemingly endless feasts, and everyone in a jovial mood.

Similar festivities surround Eid al-Adha, which celebrates Ibrahim's sacrifice for Allah. In 2018 Eid al-Adha is expected to occur on 21st August, but like other Islamic holidays, the date could change slightly due to the lunar cycle, and the date jumps back about ten or eleven days each year. Eid al-Adha is an exciting festival, but culminates in the sacrifice of a live goat, cow or camel, so it might be one to miss if you're squeamish or passionate about animal welfare.

The Mourning of Muharram, a month-long period in which Muslims, particularly Shia Muslims mourn the martyrdom of Imam Hussain, can be a time of high security alert. Sectarian tensions are at an all-time high, especially leading up to and on the Day of Ashura, the tenth day of Muharram. Businesses in Pakistan routinely close for the 9th and 10th days of Muharram, partly out of respect for the day, but partly to guard against any sectarian violence. In 2018 the month of Muharram is expected to begin on 10th September, but as with Islamic holidays, the date could change slightly due to the lunar cycle, and the jumps back about ten or eleven days each Gregorian year. See the boxed text below.

Travelling during Ramadan and Muharram

Travel during Ramadan and Muharram can present unique challenges, but they needn't force you to change your dates as long as you are prepared. Travelling during either period can in fact add to the spectacle – if you're interested in witnessing it.

For more detailed information about travelling during Ramadan, go to www.urbanduniya.com/traveller/travelling-during-ramadan/

For more detailed information about travelling during the mourning of Muharram, go to www.urbanduniya.com/traveller/travelling-during-muharram/

Routes to Pakistan
Air
Most people coming to Pakistan do so by air. Karachi International Airport is the country's biggest hub, but the most useful for travellers are Lahore and Islamabad. Other cities also host international airports, including Multan, Faisalabad, Sialkot, Peshawar and Quetta, however these see less flights and mostly cater to expatriates in the Gulf countries. Pakistani airlines, including the flag carrier Pakistan International Airlines or "PIA" (www.piac.com.pk), Shaheen International (www.shaheenair.com) and Air Blue (www.airblue.com) offer a handful of direct connections.

Middle Eastern airlines including Emirates (www.emirates.com), Qatar Airways (www.qatarairways.com), Etihad (www.etihad.com), Gulf Air (www.gulfair.com) and Turkish Airlines (www.turkishairlines.com) all fly to major cities in Pakistan, and make a logical choice if you are travelling from elsewhere in the Middle East, Europe, the Americas or Africa. Discount carriers like FlyDubai (www.flydubai.com) and Air Arabia (www.airarabia.com) also operate to Pakistan, but their networks don't usually extend to Europe or America.

From Asia-Pacific the choices are more limited; Thai Airways (www.thaiairways.com) flies to the three biggest cities, Air China (www.airchina.com) flies to Karachi from Beijing, and China Southern (www.csair.com) flies to Islamabad from the western Chinese city of Urumqi. From Australia and New Zealand, it might be worth flying via a city in the Gulf, despite the extra hours of travel time.

For Iran, Shaheen International flies from Lahore to the pilgrimage city of Mashhad, and Iran Air (www.iranair.com) flies to Karachi from Tehran. From Afghanistan, Safi Airways (www.safiairways.com) and PIA fly from Kabul to Islamabad, while PIA operates the only flights to India; from Lahore and Karachi to Delhi, and sometimes from Karachi to Mumbai. Be aware that flights between India and Pakistan have a history of being cancelled at short notice, depending on the political climate.

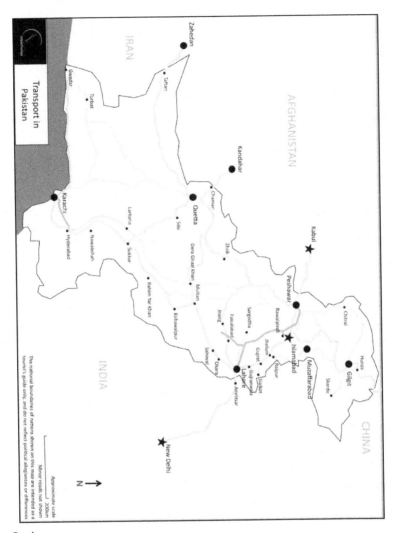

Road

The road link between India and Pakistan is not as tense as you might expect; so long as political tensions aren't being ratcheted up, most travellers report transiting between the two countries fairly easily. Read more about how to travel between Pakistan and India by road on page 65. Be aware that while several roads traverse the India - Pakistan border, there is only one place (Wagah) where you can actually make the crossing legally. At other places (like near Kasur, south of Lahore), the border is marked with a barricade across the road.

The road to China, the Karakoram Highway, is an engineering marvel. It is the world's highest international roadway, and provided your documents are in order, is fairly painless. The same can't be said for the road conditions, which navigates tight twisting gorges and is often blocked by snowfall or landslides. It closes completely every year due to snowfall, officially between October 31 and May 1, but these dates are subject to change according to weather conditions. Read about how to travel from Pakistan to China by road on page 210.

The roads between Pakistan and Afghanistan - through the Khyber Pass or Chaman crossing - and between Pakistan and Iran - through Balochistan – are open but not recommended at this time due to security issues.

Rail

Two trains operate from India to Pakistan; the Thar Express from near Jodhpur to Karachi, and the Samjhauta Express from Amritsar to Lahore. Both trains get cancelled if tensions are running high, and most travellers find road to be an easier option anyway. If however, you are interested in booking yourself on to one of these trains, you can get more information from Pakistan Railways (www.pakrail.gov.pk) or Indian Railways (www.indianrail.gov.in).

The train from Pakistan to Iran via Balochistan operates occasionally, but due to security issues cannot be recommended. There is no train service from Pakistan to Afghanistan or China.

Sea

Pakistan has no passenger ferry services with any countries. Occasionally ferries sail between Karachi or Gwadar (in Balochistan) and ports in southern Iran, but these are chartered for religious pilgrims.

Visas

This is where the real bureaucratic hassle is. As it stands, nationalities of most nations require a visa to enter Pakistan. Some websites contain a list of "visa-free" countries, however you are still advised to check with your local Pakistani mission because requirements change frequently.

Most visitors will need to submit a visa application form with a passport-sized photograph attached, a travel itinerary (flights showing entry and exit dates), and a letter of invitation from a contact or travel service provider in Pakistan. For some nationalities, or for some lengths of visa, a bank statement showing sufficient funds must also be presented. On the visa form, you will be asked for a list of destinations in Pakistan that you wish to visit. This is rarely, if ever checked once *inside* the country, but there's no need to complicate matters by listing any sensitive sites such as the tribal regions, Balochistan, Kashmir, or the border with India besides the legal crossing at Wagah near Lahore. In any case, you would be advised against visiting these areas for your own safety.

Tourist visas cost around US$100. Visas are usually granted in 1 to 2 weeks for the length of time requested, however a maximum timeframe of one month officially applies. For longer visas, further documentation is required - the embassy will advise you. The tourist visa is usually valid for one entry to the country, but multiple entry visas can be applied for. The visa is normally valid for six months from the date of issue, meaning that you have six months to enter Pakistan and begin your stay of designated length.

Officially, visas cannot be applied for outside of your home country. Some people have reported success applying at Pakistani embassies abroad, while others have had to courier their passport back to the Pakistani embassy in their home country. More still have abandoned their Pakistan travel plans altogether. Citizens of the USA often pay more than other nationalities for their visas. Israeli passport holders are not permitted to visit Pakistan, and will not be issued a visa. An Israeli visa in a foreign passport won't necessarily preclude you from visiting Pakistan, but it could prompt questions from officials. Indians, or people of Indian background, are required to compelte extra paperwork, and sometimes visas are only granted for business or pilgrimage purposes. While there are sporadic reports of visas being issued on arrival from China at Sost on the Karakoram Highway, the availability of this yet to be confirmed by the Pakistani foreign ministry, so can't be recommended.

A selection of Pakistani missions in foreign countries are listed below. Information, where incomplete, was not available to us at the time of writing; we apologise for any inconvenience caused.

Afghanistan
Kabul: Pakistan Embassy, Kart-e-Parwan, Kabul; (+93) 20-2202745, 2202746;
www.pakembassykabul.com
Herat: Chaharahy-e-Amreat, Heart; (+93) 40-231291; www.mofa.gov.pk/herat
Jalalabad: Nahiya-e-Suam, Jalalabad; (+93) 60-2001024; www.mofa.gov.pk/jalalabad
Mazar-e-Sharif: Nahia No. 04, Baba Yadgar Road, near Turkish Consulate, Mazar-e-Sharif;
(+93) 50-773065273; www.mofa.gov.pk/mazaresharif

Argentina
Buenos Aires: Olleros 2130, Belgrano, Buenos Aries; (+54) 11-47751294, 47738081,
47722782; www.mofa.gov.pk/argentina

Australia
Canberra: 4 Perth Ave, Yarralumla, ACT; (+61) 02-62731114; www.pakistan.org.au
Sydney: Level 3, 109 Pitt Street, Sydney, NSW; (+61) 02-92205600;
www.pakistan.org.au/high_commision_sydney

Austria
Vienna: Hofzeile 13, A-1190 Vienna; (+43) 1-3687381, 3687382;
www.mofa.gov.pk/austria

Bahrain
Manama: Building No. 35, Road No. 1901, Block No. 319, Hoora, P. O. Box 563, Manama;
(+973) 17244113; www.mofa.gov.pk/bahrain/

Bangladesh
Dhaka: NE(C) 2, Road # 71, Gulshan II, Dhaka-1212; (+88) 02-8825388;
www.mofa.gov.pk/bangladesh

Belgium
Brussels: Avenue Delleur 57, 1170 Watermael-Boitsfort; (+32) 2-6738007;
www.embassyofpakistan.be

Brazil
Brasilia: Shis QL 12 Conj 02 Casa 19, Lago Sul, Brasilia, DF CEP 71630-225; (+55) 61-
33641632, 33641634; www.pakistan.org.br

Canada
Ottawa: 10 Range Rd, Ottawa, ON K1N 8J3; (+1) 613-238 7881; www.pakmission.ca
Montreal: 3421 Rue Peel, Montréal, QC H3A 1W7; (+1) 514-8452297; www.pakmission.ca
Toronto: 7880 Keele Street, Unit 14, Vaghan, ON L4K 4G7; (+1) 905-5320042;
www.pakmission.ca
Vancouver: 1400-510 Hastings St W, Vancouver, BC V6B 1L8; (+1) 604-5691415;
www.pcgv.org

China (People's Replublic of China)
Beijing: 1 Dongzhimenwai Dajie 100600; (+86) 10-65322504; www.pakbj.org.pk
Shanghai: Suite 1111, Tower A, SOHO Zhongshan Plaza, 1055 West Zhongshan Road,
Shanghai 200051; (+86) 21-62377000; www.mofa.gov.pk/shanghai
Guangzhou: Room No. 705-06, Grand Tower , No. 228 Tianhe Road, Guangzhou, 510620;
(+86) 20-85505679; www.mofa.gov.pk/content.php?pageID=Guangzhou
Hong Kong: Rooms 803-804, Tung Wai Commercial Building, 109 – 111 Gloucester Road,
Wan Chai; (+852) 67325455; www.pakconhk.com
Chengdu: No. 2306, One Aerospace Center, No 7 , Xin Guang Hua Street, Jinjiang District,
Chengdu PC 610016; (+86) 28-85268316; www.mofa.gov.pk/chengdu

Czech Republic
Prague: Střešovická 56/854, 162 00 Prague 6 – Střešovice; (+420) 233312868, 233312884;
www.mofa.gov.pk/czechrepublic/

Denmark
Copenhagen: Valeursvej 17, 2900 Hellerup; (+45) 39621188; www.pakistanembassy.dk/contact.html

France
Paris: 18 Rue Lord Byron, 75008 Paris; (+33) 1-45622332; www.pakembparis.com

Germany
Berlin: Schaperstraße 29, 10719 Berlin, Germany; (+49) 30-212440; www.pakemb.de
Frankfurt: Eschenbachstraße 28, 60596 Frankfurt au Main; (+49) 69-69867850; www.pakmissionfrankfurt.de

Greece
Athens: 6, Loukianou Street, 2nd floor, Kolonaki 106 75 Athens; (+30) 251-911511007, 210-7290214; www.mofa.gov.pk/greece/

Hungary
Budapest: 1125 Budapest, Adonis utca 3/A, Budapest; (+36) 1-3558017; www.mofa.gov.pk/hungary

Indonesia
Jakarta: Jalan Mega Kuningan Barat, Block E.3.9, Kav. 5-8, Jakarta Selatan 12950; (62) 21-57851836; www.mofa.gov.pk/indonesia/

India
New Delhi: 2/50-G, Shantipath, Chanakyapuri, New Delhi–110021; (91) 11-26110601, 26110602, 26110605, 24100905; www.pakhcnewdelhi.org.pk

Iran (Islamic Republic of Iran)
Tehran: Block No. 1, Koocha-e-Ahmed Etimadzadeh, Khyaban-e-Dr. Hussain Fatimi, Jamshedabad Shomali, Tehran, 14118; (+98) 21-669413889; www.mofa.gov.pk/tehran
Mashhad: Khyaban-e-Imam Khomeini, Opposite Bagh-e-Milli, Mashhad; (+98) 511-2229845; www.mofa.gov.pk/mashhad

Italy
Rome: Via Della Camilluccia 682, 00135, Rome; (+39) 06-36301775, 3294836; www.mofa.gov.pk/italy
Milan: Via Rosa Massara De Capitani, 11, 20158, Milan; (+39) 02-66703271; www.pakconsulatemilan.com

Japan
Tokyo: 4-6-17, Minami-Azabu Minato-Ku, Tokyo 106-0047; (+81) 03-54217741; www.pakistanembassytokyo.com
Osaka: H-1,4th /F, ITM Building, Asia and Pacific Trade Center, 2-1-10, Nanko Kita Suminoe-ku, Osaka 559-0023; (+81) 06-65693106; www.mofa.gov.pk/osaka

Kuwait
Kuwait City: Villa 46, (Old No.7) Qasima 5, Qitta 11, Street No. 101, Police Station Road, Jabriya, Kuwait, P.O. Box 988, Safat 13010; (+965) 25327649, 25327651; www.mofa.gov.pk/kuwait

Malaysia
Kuala Lumpur: 132 Jalan Ampang, 50450, Kuala Lumpur, Kuala Lumpur, 55000; (+60) 3-2161 8877; www.mofa.gov.pk/kualalumpur

Maldives
Malé: G. Helegeli, Lily Magu, Male; (+960) 3323005; www.mofa.gov.pk/male

Mexico
Mexico City: Hegel 512, Col. Polanco, Del Miguel Hidalgo, 11550 Ciudad de México, Distrito Federal; (+52) 55-52033636; www.mofa.gov.pk/mexico

Nepal
Kathmandu: Pushpanjali, Maharajgunj Chakrapath, Kathmandu, P.O. Box No. 202; (+977) 1-4374024, 4374016; www.mofa.gov.pk/nepal

Netherlands
The Hague: Amaliastraat 8, Den Haag; (+31) 70-3648948; www.embassyofpakistan.com

Norway
Oslo: Eckersbergs Gate 20, 0244 Oslo; (+47) 23-136080; www.pakistanembassy.no

Oman
Muscat: Building No.1702, Plot No.1629/1/4, Road No.10, Way No.2133, Madina Sultan Qaboos Muscat, Oman-P.O. Box 1302PC 112, Ruwi; (+968) 24-603439, 24696511; www.mofa.gov.pk/oman/

Poland
Warsaw: Ul. Wiertnicza 63, 02-952, Wilnaow, Warsaw; (+48) 22-8494808; www.mofa.gov.pk/poland

Qatar
Doha: 30 Diplomatic Area, West Bay, Doha; (+974) 44832525, 44832235 www.mofa.gov.pk/qatar

Romania
Bucharest: Barbu Delavrancea St 22, Dist. 1, 71304, Bucharest; (+40) 21-3187873, 3187876; www.pakemb-romania.ro

Russia
Moscow: 17-Sadovaya Kudrinskaya, Ul, Moscow; (+7) 495-2549791; www.mofa.gov.pk/moscow

Singapore
Singapore: 1 Scotts Rd, #24-02/04, Shaw Ctr, Singapore; (+65) 67376988; www.mofa.gov.pk/singapore

South Africa
Pretoria: 312 Brooks Street, Menlo Park 0081; (+27) 12-3624072, 3624073; www.mofa.gov.pk/southafrica

South Korea (Republic of Korea)
Seoul: 1 - 17 Jangmun-Ro 9GA-GiL Yongsan-gu, Seoul; (+82) 2-7968252; www.pkembassy.or.kr/eng/

Spain
Madrid: C / Pedro de Valdivia 16, Madrid; (+34) 91-3458995, 3458986; www.embajada-pakistan.org
Barcelona: Avinguda Sarria ,27 08029 Barcelona; (+34) 93-4510343; www.pakconsulatebcn.com

Sri Lanka
Colombo: No. 42 & 44, Bullers Ln, Colombo 00700; (+94) 11-2055681; www.pakistanhc.lk

Sweden
Stockholm: Karlavagen 65, 1st Floor, 11449 Stockholm; (+46) 8-203300; www.pakistanembassy.se

Switzerland
Bern: Bernastrasse 47, 3005 Berne; (+41) 31-3501790; www.swisspak.com/web/peb

Thailand
Bangkok: 31 Soi Nana Nua, Sukhumvit-3 Rd, Bangkok; (+66) 2-2530288; www.mofa.gov.pk/bangkok

Turkey
Ankara: Gazi Osman Paşa Mh., Iran Cad. 37 Cankaya, Ankara; (+90) 312-4271410;
pakembassyankara.com
Istanbul: Gullu Sokak 20, 3 Levent, Istanbul; (+90) 212-3245827, 3249154;
www.mofa.gov.pk/istanbul

United Arab Emirates
Abu Dhabi: Plot 2, Sector W59, Diplomatic Enclave, Near Sheikh Zayed Military Hospital,
Abu Dhabi; (+971) 2-4447800; www.pakistanembassyuae.org
Dubai: Umm Hurair One, Khalid Bin Waleed Rd, Bur Dubai; (+971) 4-3973600, 3970412;
www.mofa.gov.pk/dubai

United Kingdom
London: 34-36 Lowndes Square, London; (+44) 20-76649200; www.phclondon.org
Manchester: Pakistan House, 137 Dickenson Rd, Rusholme; (+44) 161-225178;
www.phclondon.org
Birmingham: 10A The Wharf, Bridge Street, Birmingham; (+44) 121-2334123;
www.phclondon.org
Bradford: 12A North Pde, N Parade, Bradford; (+44) 1274-308062;
www.pakistanconsulatebradford.com
Glasgow: 45 Maxwell Dr, Glasgow, Glasgow City; (+44) 141-4275755;
www.phclondon.org

United States of America
Washington: 3517 International Ct NW, Washington; (+1) 202-2436500;
www.embassyofpakistanusa.org
Boston: 1032 Main St, Suite 5. Millis, MA; (+1) 617-2679000;
www.embassyofpakistanusa.org/boston
Chicago: 333 N Michigan Ave 728, Chicago; (+1) 312-7811831; www.cgpkchicago.org
Houston: 11850 Jones Rd, Houston, TX 77070; (+1) 281-8902223;
www.pakistanconsulatehouston.org
Los Angeles: 10700 Santa Monica Blvd 1250, Los Angeles; (+1) 310-4415114;
www.pakconsulatela.org
New York: 12 E 65th St, New York, NY 10065; (+1) 212-8795800;
www.pakistanconsulateny.org

Costs and budget
Pakistan is a very cheap country in which to travel, regardless of your budget. You could
easily get by on $20 a day (or less) by staying in cheap rest houses, eating street food, taking
public transport and walking a lot. You would also need to limit the number of attractions
you pay to enter, and control how much money slips away in *baksheesh* (tips or sometimes
bribes). With this standard of living, you must also take care of your health and security;
most street vendors don't have much time for hygiene, and a pasty (and relatively wealthy)
foreigner staying in a run-down part of town could be a sitting duck for theft or much worse.

For around $40 a day, you could get a nicer lodging - a motel in the country areas, or a nice
hostel or three star hotel in the cities. You could take rickshaws around the city (maybe even
the odd taxi), be less frugal with your entry fees and tips, and eat in nice, mostly clean
restaurants - and quite possibly have a bit of money to spare. For $80 a day, you could look
at taking a domestic flight or two, staying in posher hotels, eat whatever takes your fancy,
and get around town in air-conditioned comfort (where available). $120 puts most five-star
hotels within your reach, or you could probably afford your own personal tour guide (who,
in off-the-beaten-track Pakistan, isn't such a bad idea if you're really not confident, and will
become more like a friend than a guide over the course of your trip). For $180 a day, you
could have it all!

What to pack

There is no definitive list of what to pack and what to leave out, but we hope the following will give you some helpful hints;

- Any required vaccinations. Ask your doctor well in advance; some shots require a month or two to work
- Comprehensive travel insurance
- Informing someone and/or your embassy of your travel plans
- Copies of all your important documents, just in case
- Appropriate clothing (see next section)
- Sandals - they are cool to wear in the heat, and easy to remove at mosques and shrines
- A flashlight/torch - for when the power goes out
- A well stocked medicine and first aid kit, especially if you plan to go out into the countryside
- Any medicines you might require, and a letter from your doctor explaining them
- Sunglasses, a hat and other sun protection
- EU-style plug adaptors
- Electricity shock absorbers
- Pictures of your family back home - they make great conversation subjects, and you *will* be asked about them!
- Water purifying tablets, a small portable water filter, or a plan to stick to bottled water
- Cash in a major currency (US dollars, UK pounds or Euros), but not Indian Rupees unless you change them all at the Wagah border
- A good book - unless you're friends with a local, there's not a whole lot to do at night time, especially out of the cities
- A good camera, especially if you're going north
- For women, sanitary items. They're available in Pakistan, but unless you're in big city department stores, the choice is often limited

- An awareness of the current security situation
- An understanding of the local culture, and what it means to be a responsible traveller
- A sense of adventure - almost the whole country is off the beaten track!

Clothing

Pakistan is 98% Muslim, however it's not governed by Islamic law. As a result, there are no strict rules regarding exactly what you can and can't wear, but you'll fit in much better if you dress modestly.

Men should cover their legs and upper arms; a t-shirt would be acceptable, whereas a singlet top wouldn't be. If you must wear shorts, they should at least extend past the knees (they're not common here, especially out of the big cities).

Women ought to cover their legs, and their arms at least to the elbow, if not the whole arm. Cleavage, the shape of the backside and the split of one's pants should not be discernible; choose loose, baggy and lengthy over short or figure-hugging. A long, covering top (which extends to the mid-thigh) and jeans would be the easiest and most practical solution, but by far the most comfortable option is to buy your own *shalwar kameez* when you arrive; they're cheap, easy to wear, and make a great souvenir. Even a fashionable *kameez* or *kurti* (long, loose top) worn over jeans is popular among some sections of society, and it's refreshingly cool in the hot, humid summers.

You should carry a scarf or light shawl with you to use as a *hijab* (headscarf) when in a conservative area, in a mosque, or just to blend in a bit more.

Pakistani female head coverings come in three broad categories;

- *Dupatta*, which is a long shawl that sits loosely around the shoulders, and can be draped over the head when required

- *Hijab*, a head covering which is fitted in place and stays there for the day. This can be short, falling to just the shoulders and fastened with a few bobby pins, or it can be longer, creating a more tent-like shape which hides the curvature of the body. To this can be attached a *niqab*, or a separate face veil, which allows only the eyes to be seen.

- *Burka*, the shuttlecock-shaped one-piece robe which covers the entire body. Folds of material come together in a more rigid headpiece, while a fabric-mesh window allows the wearer to see out, but no-one to see in. This type of dress has its roots in Afghanistan, but is more visible in Pakistan nowadays with the presence and influence of Afghan refugees.

In Lahore, rough estimations place about 10% of women going about uncovered, about 70% wearing hijab or dupatta, and about 20% of women sporting a *niqab*. *Burka* is not at all common in Lahore, but the closer you get to the border with Afghanistan, the more you see. Karachi is famously more liberal, and more women go around with their heads uncovered, but a sleeveless top would still attract unwatnted attention.

Women and men should take their cues from their surroundings - if you are surrounded by women who are covering their heads (more likely outside the cities), you probably should too. On the other hand, if few other people are covering up - such as in Lahore or Islamabad's upmarket restaurants - there's no need for you to cover up unless you particularly want to.

Know your headgear!
For more information on the terminology of Muslim female coverings, see
http://urbanduniya.com/news-and-opinion/know-your-headgear-different-types-of-muslim-veils/

Practical Information

Transport in Pakistan

Inside Pakistan, your transport options are plane, bus, train and car.

Air

Pakistan's national airline is Pakistan International Airlines (PIA) (www.piac.com.pk), and its reputation is nothing to boast about. On board service is just adequate, its safety record is below average for the region, and its punctuality is underwhelming. That said, they have the most comprehensive network; they fly almost everywhere regularly. Shaheen Air International (www.shaheenair.com) is one of the largest private airlines, and operates a network between the major cities and a couple of international destinations - their on-board service is overall better than PIA's, safety record is marginally better, but they have operated for a much shorter timeframe and don't fly to nearly as many places as PIA. Airblue (www.airblue.com) is a major private airline that offers a limited onboard service on its routes which connect the provincial capitals. Its safety record was ok until a tragic crash near Islamabad in 2010. SereneAir (www.sereneair.com) is a new new airline which started in early 2017, and is yet to prove itself.

Travelling by air in Pakistan is often worth it, as you avoid the hassle of the train and the terror of battling the traffic. It's also the most secure way of travelling long distances, especially if your trip will take you beyond Punjab and Gilgit-Baltistan.

Bus and jeep

Korean company Daewoo (www.daewoo.com.pk), known for vehicle manufacturing in many parts of the world, operates Pakistan's best quality bus line. Their buses also offer the best security for travellers on the highway, with passengers and their luggage passing through security checks before boarding. Passengers book with their identification documents, and are all assigned a seat; as an additional security check just before the bus departs, a digital photograph is taken of every passenger occupying their correct seat. On board an attendant serves water, soft drinks and snacks, but it might also be an idea to bring your own. Daewoo Express buses depart from dedicated terminals, often quite a distance from the main general bus stations in each city. The standard ticket on Daewoo Express buses is called 'Luxury', while on the Lahore to Islamabad/Rawalpindi route larger (and pricier) 'Premium Plus' and 'Gold' seats are also offered. To book, visit the nearest Daewoo Express terminal; online bookings are also possible.

Local buses usually depart from the main bus stand in each city. The bus stations are invariably chaotic, dusty, noisy and confusing for first-timers. Rows of counters belonging to different bus companies sell tickets, and competition is cutthroat. Hawkers run around to drum up business, shouting out the destination of the next bus to depart. If you don't hear these men before you see them, then they'll probably find you before you make it to the counter - don't be surprised if you find yourself surrounded by three or four burly men shouting city names and prices at you. A mere mention of the city you want to go to will see you hustled away by one man who will then sell you ticket and get you on the bus. While it feels like you're being railroaded, some travellers find it an easy way of avoiding the hassle of the bus company counters - the man who takes you away is usually (although not always) the one whose bus is leaving first to your destination, and with an idea of how much you ought to pay, you can decide if the deal he's offering is fair.

Local buses are often crowded and dirty, with luggage (and occasionally passengers) stacked on the roof. Tickets, onboard service and security arrangements are non-existent, vehicle roadworthiness is questionable, and driving skills are variable. Don't expect air conditioning or windows that open (or close). These buses are sometimes coaches, sometimes minibuses; usually something in between - better minibuses are sometimes advertised as a "Coaster" bus. However local buses operate more frequently than Daewoo

Express buses, and to many, many more places. If your destination is some really isolated town and there's no other way to get there, it will still have a local bus service.

To and from Gilgit-Baltistan, you'll need to utilise NATCO, the Northern Areas Transport Corporation (www.natco.gov.pk), or local buses. NATCO tickets can be bought at the departure terminal.

Jeeps and minivans are sometimes the only form of transport in parts of interior Sindh and southern Punjab, Khyber Pukhtoonkhwa and along parts of the Karakoram Highway, especially north of Gilgit.

As a recommendation, and with security in mind, we have provided bus information for Daewoo Express buses where they operate. For smaller cities, information for local buses is provided where applicable.

Train

After years of neglect and mismanagement, Pakistan's Railways are back on track. They are most useful for covering long distances, like from Lahore to Karachi, overnight. A variety of carriages are hauled between major cities, and offer air conditioning and even Wifi in some (rare) instances. Train isn't so helpful for reaching small, out-of-the-way places – that's where buses are useful.

Tickets can be bought at railway stations or railway booking offices – see the individual entries for each city. Timetables can be checked online at Pakistan Railways site www.pakrail.gov.pk, although the e-ticketing facility on the site only allows Pakistanis to book at the present time (a national ID card number is required). Different trains cost different amounts, usually according to their speed and comfort.

Prices given in individual chapters are approximate, and for economy class seats or berths (seats in a shared cabin which fold into individual bunk beds) as indicated. Check at the time of booking if your carriage is air-conditioned – you might need to pay more for that.

Car and Motorcycle

Driving a car in Pakistan is not a terrible idea if you are confident at driving in South Asian conditions. If you are not familiar with the roads in India or Afghanistan, then Pakistan is not the place to test out your competence. Almost anything goes on Pakistan's roads; speeding, cars driving the wrong way down highways, overtaking in the oncoming lane at night without headlights, farmers herding sheep across six-lane motorways, potholes, uneven surfaces, stray animals, a lack of street lights (or electricity), locals walking or sleeping in the lanes, signs and electricity lines dangling down in the path of cars, dust storms in the summer, fog in the winter, floods in the monsoon, military checks, police checks, car searches, bribe-taking… If you decide to drive in Pakistan, it's important to understand the conditions you are facing.

A better option is to hire a car with a driver, to at least alleviate the tension of being responsible. There are some times that having a car is a really good idea when touring; especially for excursions from Lahore, Islamabad, Faisalabad or Multan. Details for suggested prices can be found in the individual city sections of this guide, and are usually best booked through your hotel.

If you choose to rent a car or motorcycle in Pakistan, you can contact the usual car rental companies (such as Avis; 0800-11169; www.avis.com.pk) in the major cities. Buying a car to use while you are in Pakistan is another idea, but could become a bureaucratic nightmare. You will need to contact the National Highway Authority. If you drive your foreign car into Pakistan you will require all the regular documentation - registration papers, insurance papers, international driving permit and a 'carnet de passage' (international motor vehicle document).

Getting around cities

Public transport in Pakistan's big cities is rarely user-friendly. Bus signage is usually written in Urdu and although there are designated stops and fares, buses often stop anywhere people want to get off, and official stops are often only named after the small roads that intersect the route. This means that most travelers will find themselves using a combination of walking and autorickshaws to get around cities.

Qingqi rickshaws (pronounced "ching-chee") are basically motorbikes with a carriage-like trailer tacked on. They seat about five passengers. They are cheaper than autorickshaws, but noisier, slower and less reliable. They sometimes run along set routes, picking up and setting down passengers but not deviating from the main road. In a way they fill the gaps in the bus network, but can also be rented privately (if you do, you'll have to make up the difference in the fare for the four empty seats).

Taxis exist in Karachi and Islamabad, and ride-sharing services like Uber exist in some cities – these are listed where appropriate

Lahore, Islamabad and Rawalpindi and Multan have "Metrobus" routes, a system of dedicated, often raised bus lanes that see buses avoid the traffic delays of the main road below. Lahore's and Islamabad/Rawalpindi's systems are rather useful for travellers while the Multan Metrobus caters primarily for students and workers. Metrobus systems in Karachi and Peshawar are currently under construction, but are not initially expected to serve areas of the average visitor's interest.

Lahore's "Orange Line" Metro train is currently under construction and is slated to open in 2018 or 2019. When it does open it will only be on one line which will be of limited use to the casual tourist, but the grand plan with two more lines to open after 2020 will link popular shopping and commercial areas.

Broke Backpacker Tours
Will Hatton is a professional adventurer and online entrepreneur – he runs his blog at www.thebrokebackpacker.com. He's passionate about Pakistan, and operates Broke Backpacker Adventure Tours (www.thebrokebackpacker.com/broke-backpacker-adventure-tours) – get in touch to find out about his next planned group trip to Pakistan!

Safety
Security is a constantly changing issue, and the advice which we give here can't be relied upon completely. We attempt to aid your visit to Pakistan by providing general safety advice, but cannot be held responsible for decisions made by travellers. It is essential that you make yourself aware of the current security situation by checking government travel advisories, following the news, and heeding advice where available. It is important that you understand that safety is a dynamic and fluid issue, and that things can change quickly. It is also imperative that you understand that safety is often a subjective issue, and that you must make a decision which is right for you, rather than accepting blanket advice about your personal security while travelling.

It's important to keep things in perspective. While several Westerners have been kidnapped in Pakistan in the past, several were working for high-profile (and therefore high-value target) causes such as religious charities or the American government. A few have been travellers, while many other travellers have visited Pakistan incident-free. For most travellers, the danger of violence is much smaller than the danger posed by street crime and reckless driving. For others, the threat of violence is a deal-breaker, and is good reason to cancel their trip. Ultimately, you need to decide what level of risk is appropriate for you - whether a limited tour of the country is advisable, whether a full expedition is suitable, or whether the elevated security concern would ruin an incident-free holiday in any case.

Further reading about safety
For more information on safety in Pakistan, go to http://urbanduniya.com/pakistantraveller-is-pakistan-safe/ - there's a list of considerations and questions to ask yourself before you book your ticket.

Anti-Western sentiment

No place in the world is safe; sadly, each year, people get abducted and/or murdered in most parts of the world. These things happen in Pakistan as well, but you may feel particularly vulnerable because you are not a local. The majority of Pakistanis you meet will want nothing but for you to have an amazing holiday, and a very small proportion would see you as anything but a valued guest.

That said, law and order issues in large parts of the country mean that in some places anything is possible. In these areas if someone hostile to outsiders spots you, the potential for something to go wrong increases significantly. These areas are not easily defined, but at the time of writing it's fair to say that Balochistan, FATA and AJ&K, and particular areas in Sindh and Khyber Pukhtoonkhwa can't be recommended for travel. This leaves Punjab, Gilgit-Baltistan and the Islamabad Capital Territory, as well as most of Sindh and Khyber Pukhtoonkhwa, but these areas are not without their troubles too.

The best advice is to keep a low profile by wearing modest clothing, by frequenting the more liberal areas (where you won't stand out so much), and by travelling with someone, preferably a local. This will not remove all the risk associated with travelling to Pakistan, but it will help somewhat.

Follow the cultural dos and don'ts below, and treat Pakistani culture and Islam with deference. Stay in a decent hotel; one frequented by a variety of travellers, and one which is not unaccustomed to foreign travellers - the ones we recommend should be ok. Five-star hotels have more security than downmarket hotels, but they also make more tempting targets for any would-be attackers. If you are going beyond the major cities it would be advisable to travel with someone - Pakistani if possible, but a foreigner would suffice.

If you are in Pakistan during a time of alert, such as during the first ten days of Muharram, you would be advised to avoid public gatherings or public paces that might be a potential target. Avoid any demonstrations; if you see or hear news of a demonstration, then you are advised to leave the area as quickly as possible provided it is safe to do so.

For more information on safety, go to your government's travel advisory for Pakistan such as the UK's Foreign Office (www.gov.uk/foreign-travel-advice/pakistan) or Australia's Smart Traveller website (smartraveller.gov.au/zw-cgi/view/Advice/Pakistan).

Security officials

Security officials (the police, soldiers, security guards and intelligence officials) in Pakistan are well aware of the local safety situation, and are sometimes overprotective of foreigners travelling through the area. At best this 'protection' will require you to walk around with a guard in tow – this is mandatory for foreigners in the Chitral Valley, Kaghan Valley and is haphazardly enforced in interior Sindh and southern Punjab. The details of how to deal with your guard are listed in each individual chapter. At worst, security officials have questioned foreigners of their intentions, restricted them to their hotel rooms, or even put them on a bus back to a major city "for their safety".

While all of this seems (and for the most part probably is) overzealous and unnecessary, it's incredibly annoying but ultimately harmless. The best advice is to cooperate with any security officials you may come across, because for better or for worse, they're simply doing their job. Pressing them for some flexibility might yield some results, but outright arguing will only make them more determined to do their job.

Guns and street crime

Pakistan is a country with a lot of unlicensed weapons floating around, a lot of poor people, and no shortage of groups with an axe to grind. These three facts make for an uncomfortable nexus in the cities, where street crime has risen in recent years. Lahore recorded a drop in armed hold-up cases recently, but there's no reason to believe that this won't rise again in the future.

Do not walk alone at night, always tell people where you are going and when you expect to arrive, and if you must walk the city streets at night, then only carry as many assets as you would be prepared to lose. Usually armed hold-ups do not result in shooting and the weapon is simply used as a threat, but incidents are numerous where the gunman has followed through on his threat.

Dangerous crime is not at endemic proportions in most parts of Pakistan, but it does happen, so caution is advised. If you are taking a rickshaw or taxi at night, you are advised to travel in a group or book a radio cab (see individual city listings). Try not to wander aimlessly or looking lost; this makes you an easier target for any would-be criminals.

Petty theft is also relatively common - it might be worth investing in a money belt to keep your money and documents concealed and strapped to your body. Be careful of pickpockets in crowded areas, use ATMs with security guards (usually sitting outside), tuck your money away before you exit the ATM booth, and always double check your change from both shopkeepers and moneychangers.

Scams, rip-offs and corruption

Pakistan has a lot of scams, but nowhere near as many aimed at travellers as in neighbouring India. If someone asks you to do a business deal - commonly involving goods being sold on in your country for a profit - then don't indulge.

The same rules apply here as they do at home - if it sounds too good to be true, then it probably is. That also goes for accommodation deals and tours - always find out what you're getting before you pay for it. Negotiate all taxi, autorickshaw and bus fares before you get in. Police will sometimes try to extract money from travellers, occasionally by accusing them of carrying drugs. The best thing to do in this situation is to remain calm and cooperative but firm that you are innocent. Similar situations may occur with traffic stops, document checks or even at passport control.

Traffic

You are much more likely to be a victim of a traffic-related injury in Pakistan than anything else. Try to cross the road with locals, and keep looking both ways for traffic coming the right or wrong direction. Avoid travelling at night time if you can help it - drivers often don't use their headlights even if they have them, and seat belts are non-existent.

Drugs

Drugs, particularly marijuana, are fairly easily available in Pakistan, but by indulging in them you would not only be breaking the law, but opening yourself up to blackmail from any police that may discover your crime. Be aware that some travellers have in the past been set up by drug dealers in cahoots with police.

Health

Please see page 46 for information relating to health in Pakistan.

Cultural dos and don'ts

Your trip to Pakistan will be much more rewarding and safer too if you understand some basic etiquette and try not to offend local sensitivities. To begin with, plan to dress conservatively - see page 28.

Being a conservative place, certain conversation topics are best avoided, and heated conversations are definitely not a good idea. Topics to avoid include the Pakistan Army, their history and their role in the political process, local politics, religious and ethnic minorities, women's rights, the so-called 'war on terrorism', sexuality and human rights. If someone you are with begins to talk about any of these topics, or anything else you think might be sensitive, it's best to appear interested but non-committal. Similarly with the nation's favourite topic, Islam, it is advisable not to be vocal on the matter, but instead treat it with appreciative reverence.

Don't flaunt your wealth (relative or actual) - it's insensitive at best, and at worst downright dangerous. In conversations try to give a balanced perspective of life in the west - many Pakistanis only see the positives of life in developed countries, which can make for uncomfortable comparisons between yours and their lifestyles. Point out the positives of life in Pakistan - there are many. Don't highlight the negative aspects of Pakistan - Pakistanis already hear enough about it in the media, and are understandably sensitive about it.

Take off your shoes when you walk into someone's house, and be sure to wash your hands before and after eating. It's a nice idea to take a gift if you are invited to someone's house, but not expected like it is in some western societies. A small gift from your country is a nice idea, but don't patronise your hosts by giving them a cheap-looking pen! Sweets or flowers are safer territory, or a useful and appropriate gift for their children will make you a winner. Try to take food to your mouth with your right hand - even if you are using cutlery. If you are eating from a communal bowl, or serving yourself, always use your right hand - the left hand is used for washing up in the toilet. If you are drinking from a communal vessel, try to tip the drink into your mouth without touching your lips to the rim. An invitation to join someone for dinner at their home is a serious matter and quite an honour - if you can't go, then you really ought to have a good reason.

Women are best advised not to offer their hand to shake with a man – unless he extends his first. Placing the right hand to the heart (chest) and nodding with a smile is how most Pakistani women greet unrelated men. In business it is considered somewhat rude if you dive straight into work without several minutes of niceties. Expect lots of *chai* and biscuits before anything gets done. If your business appointment arrives late, then don't be too surprised or angry - things work differently here, and people's concept of time isn't the same as in the west. Alternatively, if you are running late, it's still good form to call ahead - blaming your tardiness on the local culture could be seen as taking advantage.

Mosques and other sacred places are the one place where cultural sensitivity is non-negotiable; no shorts, no bare arms, women must cover their heads, and no eating, smoking, joking or inappropriate discussions. Take off your shoes when entering a mosque, and be aware that some sections are designated men- or women-only. Don't walk in front of someone who is praying; you will be standing between them and the sacred *ka'aba* in Mecca.

Eating

Pakistani food is, like the national concept of culture, still in a process of differentiating itself from India. Generally, Pakistani cuisine is similar to that of northern India, but with a lot of Afghan, Persian and even Arabic influences. Expect lots of meat and bread.

Biryani is a layered, spicy and aromatic rice and meat dish. It is possibly the most popular food of the nation, and although having developed in various places in India, it is widely associated with India's Muslim tradition, making it a logical "Pakistani" dish. Another important dish is *karahi*, where meat and a handful of vegetables are braised in a pan - it's really tasty. *Qorma* is a distant relative of the *korma* you may be served in Indian restaurants in the west - but it's still a creamy (if oily) and flavoursome gravy. *Kebabs* are found in many places, and are different from the sandwich wraps that pass as kebabs in many western countries. Instead, these are skewers of spiced meat which are then barbecued over hot coals, but be careful about hygiene, especially if they are made by hand or cooked outside. In the winter months, Punjabis go for *Lahori fish*, a river fish which is fried up and salted - tasty and fattening! Karachiites, being near the sea, have fish all year round. Roasted (or "broasted") chicken is also on the menu in some places. *Dhal* is lentils, cooked in a variety of ways, and *paneer* is a local kind of cottage cheese, usually made from buffalo milk. *Desi ghee* is oily but delicious clarified butter. *Sabzi* means vegetables, *boti* means a piece of chicken, *channa* is chick peas and *kofta* is a fried dumpling of lentils and vegetables or meat.

Be aware that 'curry', as it is called in the west, is not a very well understood concept here - for Pakistanis, local cuisine is just that - "food"! The nearest words to "curry" in Urdu are *shorba* or *salan*, meaning 'gravy'. Other preparations which you'll see frequently include *jalfrezi* (spicy vegetables), *do pyaza* (literally 'double onions'), *makhani* (tomato and butter gravy), *saag* or *palak* are varieties of spinach gravy, and *shahi* ("in the royal style" - usually a rich creamy gravy with nuts). Don't expect *vindaloo*, which is associated with Goa in India, or south Indian specialties - they are a foreign cuisine here. Meat is usually chicken, mutton, lamb, beef or fish. Pork is illegal in Pakistan due to religious sensibilities and prawns and other sealife are not that common. Food is normally eaten with thick **naan** bread cooked in the tandoor, or **roti**, a thinner unleavened bread. Both, but especially *naan*, are heaven when served fresh from the oven. Heavier alternatives are **parathas** (flaky, buttery bread) and **pooris** (deep fried bread) - they're often served for breakfast with **halva**, sweet semolina meal. Rice (*chawal*) may be served too. Side dishes include a multitude of chutneys, spicy pickles and **raita** - soothing mint yogurt.

Snacks are available everywhere in Pakistan where there's a buck to be made. Crisps, biscuits, chocolates and chewy lollies are to be found along side the tetra pack fruit juices and canned and bottled soft drinks at most stalls. Cooked snacks include **samosas**, a fried pastry triangle filled with potato and sometimes meat, **golgoppas** are fried balls of puff pastry filled with (normally unpurified) tamarind water, and **takatak** is offal which is chopped up, fried and salted - named after the sound of the chopping process. Always take care with eating from the street, as hygiene standards are usually well below what your stomach might be accustomed to. Fresh fruit on the street side looks appetising, but it's often pre-cut and splashed with unpurified water to keep it glistening in the sunlight. You're better to buy and cut your own - mangoes in the summer months are rumoured to be the best in the world.

Breakfast is usually an oily vegetable gravy (commonly chickpeas) with naan, but there are also plenty of bakery chains like Gourmet and Cakes & Bakes where you can pick up items like rolls and pastries.

If you're feeling thirsty in Pakistan, you can choose between the standard range of internationally available soft-drinks. Also available are fruit juices, but be careful when you buy the freshly-squeezed variety, as sometimes ice or water is added. *Chai* is milky, usually sweet Pakistani-style tea, and coffee is usually (although not always) the instant variety - often with milk powder and sugar already added. Green tea and Kashmiri green tea (which is actually pink and served with milk) are delicious, and become more available the further north you go. *Kahwa* is a aromatic Pathan beverage said to cure colds and other illnesses. Alcohol is illegal in Pakistan, except for non-Muslims who may purchase it from certain locations like five-star hotels and the Murree Brewery.

Take care with water – regular tap water is not purified, and most travelers drink bottled water. Check that the seal is intact before opening, and try to buy reputed brands, like Nestle, Aquafina or Kinley. Good restaurants and middle class homes and above usually have a water purifier installed.

Freshlime refers to a squeeze of lime juice in a soft drink, while **fresh lime soda** is lime juice with sugar and/or salt and topped up with soda water. Deliciously refreshing in the hot summer months is *lassi*, a whipped yogurt drink served either sweet or salty, but make sure unpurified water hasn't been added in the process. Mango shakes are also a summer quencher. Non-alcoholic beer is reasonably popular in Pakistan.

Sweets in Pakistan include **kheer**, delicious rice pudding, *feerni*, ground rice pudding, **barfi**, cashew nut slice with silver leaf, **gulab jamun**, fried dumplings in syrup, **kulfi**, thick nutty ice cream, and **rasmalai**, spongy dumplings in sweet cream. Ice creams are also available, and at posher establishments you'll find cakes, puddings, mousses and brownies.

If Pakistani food doesn't appeal to you, or if you need a break, then large cities (Lahore, Islamabad and Karachi) boast nearly the full list of western fast food chains, and an ever expanding range of cuisine-specific restaurant, from Italian and Thai to Iranian and Tex-Mex. Chinese is particularly popular, but usually comes with a distinctly Pakistani flavour infusion. Espresso and refreshing western-style cafe drinks can be found in upmarket cafes in the cities.

Catch the biryani express!
Want to try biryani at home? Go to http://urbanduniya.com/lounge-the-city-life/catch-the-biryani-express/ for my easy peasy (if not totally authentic) recipe!

Vegetarians and vegans will have a tough time of it in Pakistan - vegetarianism isn't really understood here as it is in the west, and most 'vegetable' dishes (including *dhal* sometimes) come with meat as an added bonus. If you do find a menu with a substantial vegetarian section and you order a vegetarian-only meal, you may still find the waiter hovering for a moment while you finish ordering - the idea is that no meal is complete without at least a portion of meat. Often you will be limited to lentils and one token vegetable dish on the menu, relegated to 'side dish' status. Apart from the small number of Pakistani Hindus, vegetarian Pakistanis are almost exclusively found in the elite classes, so in upmarket establishments in the big cities you could explain what you want to the waiter. In the countryside you might be better to self-cater; otherwise you can travel with an Urdu-speaker who understands what is required, or try your luck and go it alone with a sense of adventure, an open mind and a very flexible attitude.

Below is a basic food decoder, listing the approximate spellings for the most common dishes, raw ingredients and tastes in Pakistani cuisine, and their approximate spellings. You may use this together with the Urdu guide on page 216 to order in restaurants, or to request particular preparations (eg – not spicy). Spellings may vary from region to region, or restaurant to restaurant. All names listed are in Urdu; occasionally local names may also be used for some items.

Menu decoder
Breads
roti / chappati - flat bread
naan - thick flat bread, usually topped with sesame seeds
paratha - layered flat bread, cooked in butter or clarified butter, sometimes stuffed with meat or vegetables
kulcha - buttery flat bread
poori - deep-fried wheat puff
batura - deep-fried maize puff

Rice dishes
pulao - spiced rice cooked with vegetables and meat
biryani - layered, steamed rice and meat dish
chawal - plain rice, usually parboiled until fluffy
kitchari - lightly spiced soft rice and lentils, usually recommended after stomach ailments

Preparations
samosa - deep fried pastry triangle, filled with meat or vegetables
pakora - deep fried vegetable bites
shwarma - Arabic-style spit-roasted meat wrapped in bread
kebab - spit-roasted meat
tikka - flame-roasted meat
shami kebab - a fried patty of minced lentils or chickpeas with chicken
chappli kebab - a fried beef or mutton mince patty. A Peshawar specialty
keema / qeema - minced meat

jalfrezi - stir-fried semi-gravy with onions, bell peppers, green chilis and other vegetables
do pyaaza - stir-fried semi-gravy with lots of onions and other vegetables
korma / qorma - thick, spiced, oily gravy
nihari - traditionally a spicy beef stew, sometimes made with chicken. A Karachi special.
masala - literally means 'spice mix', can refer to a dry or gravy-based dish with many ingredients
handi - rustic, home-cooked style stew - takes its name from the pot in which it is cooked and served

karahi - braised meat with spices
haleem - slow-cooked shredded chicken and lentil stew
shashlik - Pakistani-Chinese dish with semi-sweet red gravy
manchurian - Pakistani-Chinese dish with semi-sweet brown gravy
chowmein - Thick Chinese noodles cooked with Pakistani spices and vegetables
siri paye - stew made of the brains and foot of a lamb or goat - usually for breakfast, popular in Lahore
takatak - minced goat testicles, shallow-fried on a griddle
yakhni - chicken broth
broast - roasted
sajji - a Balochi specialty, a whole chicken or lamb stuffed with spiced rice then roasted
salan - any thick, creamy gravy
shorba - literally means 'soup', but can refer to broth or any thin gravy

Meat and proteins (*gosht*)
murgh / murghi - chicken
gosht - literally "meat", usually refers to mutton or lamb, sometimes beef
bara gosht - literally "big meat", usually refers to beef
machlee - fish
jheenga - prawns / shrimp
batera - quail
unda - egg
doomba - the fatty rump of a goat or lamb
kaleji / jigar - liver
manz - brains
ojhri - tripe / intestines

Vegetables (*sabzi*)
katchumer salad - finely chopped tomato, onion, tomato and sometimes green chilli
Russian salad – creamy potato-based salad
aloo - potato
gobi - cabbage, sometimes cauliflower
fulgobi - cauliflower (sometimes also called *gobi*)
palak - spinach
saag - wild spinach
dhal - lentils
channa / channa dhal - chickpeas
lobia - kidney beans
gajjar - carrot
kheera - cucumber
mutter - green peas
tamatar - tomato
pyaaz - onion
kaddu - pumpkin
shuljum - turnip
arvi - taro root
bengan / brinjal - eggplant / aubergine
karela - bitter gourd
mirch - chili
shimla mirch - capsicum / bell pepper
zaitoon - olive

Condiments, spices and accompaniments
namak - salt
kali mirch - black pepper
mirch - chilli
nimbu - lemon
pudina - mint

dhaniya - coriander
dahi - plain yogurt
raita - minted yogurt, sometimes with chopped vegetables
ketchup - American-style tomato sauce/ketchup
achchar - spicy picked vegetables
makkan - butter
ghee / desi ghee - clarified butter
tel - oil

Flavours and textures
meetha - sweet
namkeen - salty
mirchi - spicy
karhva - bitter / sour
kachchi - raw / undercooked

Drinks
pani - water
chai - tea, usually served with milk
doodhpati - creamy milk-only tea
kahwah - Pathan-style green tea, served with lemon but without milk
Kashmiri chai - milky tea, pink in colour and served with pistachios
freshlime - semi-sweet/salty lemon and water drink. Sometimes "freshlime soda" - made
with lemonade
lassi - whipped yogurt drink, either sweet or salty

Sweets (*mithai*)
gulab jamun - deep fried milk dumplings in syrup
rasmalai - cheese dumplings in sweet milk
halva - pudding, often made from semolina or nuts, but sometimes carrot, pumpkin or even
lentils
barfi - milk-based slice
kheer - rice pudding
firnee - ground rice pudding
zarda - sweet rice
jalebi - deep fried sugar squiggles

Fruit and nuts (*phul*)
sib - apple
kela - banana
aam - mango
angoor - grape
anar - pomegranate
malta - orange
ananas - pineapple
khubani - apricot
tarbooz - watermelon
kharbooza - melon
khajoor - date
amrood - guava
anjeer - fig
khopra - coconut
arhu - peach
aloo bukhara - plum, literally a "potato of Bukhara" (a city in modern-day Uzbekistan)
falsa - a wild berry, similar to a blueberry
jamun - wild blackberry

moongpali - peanut
khaju - cashew

badam - almond
pista - pistachio
akhrot – walnut

Taste before you travel!
Wanna taste before you travel? Go to www.urbanduniya.com/lounge-the-city-life/book-launch-recipes-for-ramadan and pick up a copy of Recipes for Ramadan – as well as featuring a bunch of Pakistani and north Indian recipes, there is a wide range of recipes from the Middle East, Central Asia, South East Asia and the West!

Business hours
Pakistan's day of rest is officially Sunday, and some lucky workers get Saturday off as well. However outside of major cities, in many villages and towns, Friday is a holiday – the Muslim day of rest. Confused? We are. You can assume that government offices everywhere will be closed on Sunday. Many other businesses are either closed, or keep shorter hours on Sunday. In towns and villages where Friday is a holiday, everything is shut on Friday morning and afternoon, and sometimes evening too. Islamabad, Lahore and Karachi observe a holiday on Sunday, but elsewhere it's wise to check with locals.

Much of the country is eerily quiet for about an hour from about 1pm on Friday, as the faithful flock to mosques to pray. During this time, unless you are planning to attend the mosque, you might find yourself with nothing to do – everything is closed. Conversely, as opposed to the norm in many Western countries, Pakistani shops, eateries and salons stay open until late – in the big cities, you'll nearly always find a place to pick up some groceries, grab a late dinner, or even get your hair cut after midnight.

Electricity
Pakistan mostly uses the European-style two-pin plug socket at 230 V.

Since the early 2000s, the Pakistan's state energy provider WAPDA has struggled to keep up with the increasing demands of a growing population and a widening middle class. The result is 'load-shedding', sometimes referred to in other countries as 'rolling blackouts'. In the hot summer months, when energy demand is at its highest, major cities can experience 12 hours a day without electricity, while some rural areas see 18 or even 20 hours a day without power - usually this takes the form of scheduled 'one hour on / one hour off' outages, but nothing is guaranteed.

Essential services (hospitals) and good businesses (including better hotels and restaurants) will have a generator that automatically starts when the power cuts out - a flickering of the light and the cranking sound of the generator is all you'll notice. Smaller businesses and private homes often have an Uninterrupted Power Supply or UPS, a kind of battery which can power the fans and some lights, but is not strong enough for an air conditioner. The lower middle class and below do without, simply timing their lives around the power outages, and when they do lose power, making use of the cheap hand-held wicker fans that are sold by weavers who work the roadside.

If it is important for you to have air conditioning in the summer (and don't underestimate the heat of a Pakistani summer), then you are advised to check with your accommodation at the time of booking if they have a working generator.

Media
Pakistan's media has undergone a revolution in recent years, with online and television news channels rapidly overtaking newspapers as the nation's preferred source of information. Unfortunately, much of this information is mixed with entertainment to meet commercial goals, and a significant lack of regulation has resulted in a highly sensational media climate. English language news can be found at Dawn (dawn.com.pk), The Nation

---

(nation.com.pk), The Daily Times (dailytimes.com.pk) and The Pakistan Observer (pakobserver.net). Hyperactive local news channels, broadcast in Urdu, sometimes offer their websites in English; you can check out Geo News (geo.tv) and Dunya News (dunyanews.tv). Pakistan Television, or PTV News, is the government's information portal (ptvworldnews.com.pk).

Money

The Pakistani Rupee is the national currency, and is expected everywhere. It is divided into 100 paisa, although the smallest coin you'll see is the near-worthless 50 paisa. A handful of top-end hotels may accept American dollars, or less likely Euros or British Pounds, but you're still better off carrying rupees. The value of the rupee has plummeted in the past decade, and you may find yourself carting around thick bundles of cash. Check all bundles of cash you are given to make sure it is all there, and that all notes are real. It's useful to always keep some small notes with you, because many vendors or autorickshaw drivers baulk at having to change Rs. 1000 or Rs. 5000 notes for a small purchase.

Credit cards are useful at top end hotels; Visa and MasterCards are of some use, American Express less so. Most Pakistanis aren't familiar with Diner's Club card. A cash card is an idea, but only if it's linked to one of the major credit/debit networks. ATMs are found in most large towns and cities, but they can't be relied upon - sometimes they are faulty, while other times they don't recognise international cards. If you plan to go out into the countryside, carry as much cash as you think you'll need, and stash it somewhere safe.

Travellers cheques really aren't worth the hassle.

The golden rule is to rely on cash, but have a back-up option or two. You may carry a major currency to Pakistan and change money there, or you can change it in advance - usually exchange rates are more favourable in Pakistan.

Post

Pakistan's postal service looks archaic like much of the rest of the state-operated infrastructure, but is surprisingly efficient. That's not to say that it works perfectly, but in our experience with Pakistan Post 99% of our letters have reached their destination in a timely (or near-timely) manner. It's comparatively cheap too - sending a postcard abroad will cost you around a dollar, often less (depending on the country). Post offices are mentioned under each major city's listing.

Toilets

Toilets are mostly of the squat kind. Although this method is supposed to be healthier for your insides, it can be awkward for those who aren't accustomed to it. Better ones have a proper porcelain basin built into the floor with textured tiles to prevent your feet from slipping, while in cheaper places you might be faced with a simple hole in a concrete floor. Cleanliness is usually proportionate to the calibre of the establishment. Western-style toilets can be found in higher-end establishments, and some fast food chains.

A water gun is usually attached to a hose beside the toilet, so you can wash your nether regions. Toilet paper is not normally provided in either homes or public toilets, so if you need it, carry your own - it's available from most grocery stores (ask for "toilet roll", "toilet tissue" or "tissue paper roll").

In private homes, the toilet often occupies the same place as the shower area, so the floor is usually wet. A pair of 'bathroom sandals' is usually kept at the bathroom door - you're advised to change into these to avoid traipsing shower water back through the house when you're done.

Telephone and Internet communications

Pakistan's telephone country code is +92, and internet domain suffix is ".pk" .

PTCL, Pakistan's state telephone network, works, but it has largely been superseded by reliable private cellphone companies. Many Pakistanis in the middle class and above use their mobile phones almost exclusively - competition means that services are better and prices are more attractive. Companies include Mobilink/Jazz, Ufone, Warid, Telenor and Zong. If you want to join a local network, you will need to complete a complicated and time-consuming an ID check at a major office of one of these companies – not the smaller offices by the roadside – ask at a shop for the head office. Rates are cheap, and packages are available for SMS, local and international calls. Mobilink/Jazz and Ufone offer 3G data connections, while Zong, Warid and Telenor offer 4G or similar (LTE). Coverage for these companies is bare in Gilgit-Baltistan; there, another company called SCO operates – you'll need to apply for a SIM card in Gilgit.

If you don't want to get a SIM card for your cellphone, you can always use your hotel phone, or if you're counting pennies, go to a PCO (Public Call Office). These retro places still have switchboards and call booths, but can connect you to an international line for cheaper rates. PCOs used to be on the main streets of every major town and city, but are nowadays quite rare.

The popularity of Internet use is spreading across Pakistan, and shows no sign of slowing. We have noted internet cafes under city listings in this book, however given the fast-changing nature of the industry, we can't guarantee that these will exist when you visit - places close down as more and more Pakistanis get internet connections in their homes or on their smartphones, while new places open as less-moneyed neighbourhoods experience an increase in community demand. Speeds are usually slow in internet cafes, but prices seem to rise with the quality of access. An expensive internet cafe with a fast connection might be worth it - paying a cheap rate per minute doesn't achieve much if it takes two hours to check your email.

If you need an (almost) uninterrupted internet connection, go to a PTCL, Zong, Telenor or Mobilink/Jazz office and see the range of portable devices. Evo Wifi Cloud, Evo Wingle and other products in the range are a joint venture between Pakistan's state telecom company and Dubai's Etisalat - while pricey, these will allow you to take the net with you when you travel. Wifi is available in upmarket hotels and eateries, and some mid-range places too - it's usually free, and often surprisingly fast.

Embassies in Pakistan
The below list is for embassies or high commissions in Islamabad. A handful of countries also operate consulates in Karachi, Lahore, Peshawar and Quetta - these are noted under each nation's heading. Information, where incomplete, was not available at the time of writing - we apologise for any inconvenience this may cause. Street addresses sometimes differ from mailing address.

Afghanistan
Islamabad: House 8, Street 90, G-6/3, Islamabad; (+92) 51-2824505;
www.islamabad.mfa.af *(map pg. 82)*
Karachi: Street 26, Block 5 Clifton, Karachi; (+92) 21-821261 *(map pg. 134)*
Peshawar: Gul Mohar Lane, University Town, Peshawar
Quetta: 45 Price Road, Quetta

Argentina
20 Hill Road, Shalimar F-6/ 3, P.O. Box 1015, Islamabad; (+92) 051-2821242/5561 *(map pg. 80)*

Australia
Constitution Ave/Ispahani Rd, Diplomatic Enclave, No. 1, Sector G-5/4, Islamabad, PO Box 1046, Islamabad; (+92) 051-8355500; www.pakistan.embassy.gov.au/islm/home.html *(map pg. 80)*

Austria
House 7A, Street 21, Islamabad; (+92) 051-2818421;
www.bmeia.gv.at/en/embassy/islamabad/the-embassy.html *(map pg. 82)*

Bahrain
Islamabad: House 5, Street 83, Sector G-6/4, Islamabad; (+92) 051-2831117, 2831115, 2831114; www.mofa.gov.bh/islamabad *(map pg. 80)*
Karachi: Bungalow 51, Khayabane Shahbaz, Phase V1, DHA, Karachi; (+92) 021-35171111; www.mofa.gov.bh/karachi/Home.aspx *(map pg. 128)*

Bangladesh
Islamabad: No. 1, Street 5, F-6/3, Islamabad; (+92) 051-2279267; www.bdhcpk.org *(map pg. 80)*
Karachi: 81/1 Street 30, Khayaban-e-Sehar, Phase VI, DHA, Karachi; (+92) 021-35340029, 3534002931; www.bddhc-karachi.org *(map pg. 128)*

Belgium
14 Street 17, F-7/2, Islamabad; (+92) 051-2652636; www.diplomatie.be/islamabad *(map pg. 82)*

Brazil
Number 1, Sreet 72, Sector F-8/3, Islamabad; (+92) 051-2287189; www.islamabade.itamaraty.gov.br *(map pg. 82)*

Canada
Diplomatic Enclave, Sector G-5, Islamabad, PO Box 1042; (+92) 051-2086000; www.canadainternational.gc.ca/pakistan/offices-bureaux/islamabad.aspx?lang=eng *(map pg. 80)*

China (People's Replublic of China)
Islamabad: 1 Zhou-Enlai Ave, Diplomatic Enclave (Extension), Islamabad; (+92) 051-8496178; www.pk.chineseembassy.org *(map pg. 80)*
Karachi: St. 20, Block 4, Clifton; (+92) 021-35874168; www.karachi-china.consulate.org *(map pg. 134)*
Lahore: Canal Bank Rd, near Sheikh Zayed Hospital, New Muslim Town; (+92) 3218647941 *(map pg. 53)*

Czech Republic
House 49, Street 27, Sector F-6/2, Islamabad; (+92) 051-2820679; www.mzv.cz/islamabad/en/index.html *(map pg. 82)*

Denmark
House 16, Street 21, F-6/2, Islamabad, P.O. Box 1118 Islamabad; (+92) 051-2099800; www.pakistan.um.dk *(map pg. 82)*

France
Islamabad: Diplomatic Enclave, G5, Islamabad, PO Box 1068; (+92) 051-2011414; www.ambafrance-pk.org/-France-in-Pakistan *(map pg. 80)*
Karachi: 12 Avenue Mohamed Ali Bogra Road, Bath Island, Karachi; (+92) 021-35873797, 35873798; www.consulfrance-karachi.org.pk *(map pg. 134)*

Germany
Islamabad: Ramna 5, Diplomatic Enclave, Islamabad, PO Box 1027, Islamabad; (+92) 051-2279430; www.islamabad.diplo.de *(map pg. 80)*
Karachi: 92-A/7, Block 5, Clifton, Karachi; (+92) 021-35873782; www.islamabad.diplo.de *(map pg. 134)*

Greece
22 Margalla Rd, F-6-3, F-6, Islamabad; (+92) 051-2825186; www.mfa.gr/islamabad *(map pg. 80)*

Hungary
12 Margalla Rd, F-6/3, 44000; (+92) 051-2077800; iszlamabad.mfa.gov.hu *(map pg. 80)*

Indonesia
Islamabad: Ramna 5/4 Diplomatic Enclave; (+92) 051-2832017;
www.kemlu.go.id/islamabad *(map pg. 80)*
Karachi: E/1-5 Sharah-e-Iran, Clifton, Karachi 75600; (+92) 021-5874619;
www.kemlu.go.id/karachi *(map pg. 134)*

India
Street 3, G-5 Diplomatic Enclave, Islamabad; (+92) 051-2828376; www.india.org.pk *(map pg. 80)*

Iran (Islamic Republic of Iran)
Islamabad: Plots No. 222 - 238, Street No. 2, G-5/1, Islamabad; (+92) 051-8318901;
www.islamabad.mfr.ir *(map pg. 80)*
Karachi: 81 Khayaban-e-Iran Clifton, Karachi; (+92) 021-5874370; www.karachi.mfa.ir *(map pg. 134)*
Lahore: 55/A Shadman II, Lahore; (+92) 042-99263347; www.lahore.mfa.ir *(map pg. 61)*
Peshawar: 18/111-C, Park Avenue, University Town; (+92) 091-5845403;
www.peshawar.mfa.ir
Quetta: 2/33, Hali Road, Quetta; (+92) 081-2843527; www.quetta.mfa.ir

Italy
Islamabad: Plot 196/208, Street 16, Diplomatic Enclave, Islamabad; (+92) 051-2833183;
www.ambislamabad.esteri.it/Ambasciata_Islamabad *(map pg. 80)*
Karachi: 85 Main Clifton; 021-35870031; www.conskarachi.esteri.it/Consolato_Karachi *(map pg. 134)*

Japan
Islamabad: 53 - 70 Ramna 5/4, Diplomatic Enclave 1, Islamabad 44000, PO Box 1119,
Islamabad; (+92) 051-9072500; www.pk.emb-japan.go.jp *(map pg. 80)*
Karachi: 6/2 Civil Lines, Abdullah Haroon Road, Karachi, 75530, Pakistan (G. P. O. Box
No. 3745), Karachi; (+92) 021-35220800; www.kr.pk.emb-japan.go.jp *(map pg. 130)*

Kuwait
Islamabad: 28 Main Margalla Road, F-7 Markaz, Islamabad; (+92) 051-2656663 *(map pg. 82)*
Karachi: Plot No: ST-19/20, E- Street, Block-4, Clifton, Karachi; (+92) 021-5369230,
5369231; www.kuwaitconskhi.wordpress.com *(map pg. 134)*

Malaysia
Islamabad: Plot No. 144 - 150, Street No. 12, Sector G-5, Diplomatic Enclave, 44000,
Islamabad; (+92) 051-2072900; www.kln.gov.my/web/pak_islamabad/home *(map pg. 80)*
Karachi: No. 7-A, Main Khayaban-e-Shamsheer, Phase V, DHA, Karachi 75500; (+92)
021-35295618, 35295619; www.kln.gov.my/web/pak_karachi/home *(map pg. 128)*

Maldives
No. 10, Street No. 04, F-8/3, Islamabad; (+92) 051-2286903; www.maldiveshighcom.pk
(map pg. 82)

Mexico
No. 37, Street 27, Sector F-6/2, Islamabad; (+92) 051-2821740, 2821709, 2821841 *(map pg. 82)*

Nepal
No. 6, Gomal Road, E-7, Islamabad; (+92) 051-2610317; www.nepalembassy.pk *(map pg. 82)*

Netherlands
Number 167, Street 15, Sector G-5, Islamabad; (+92) 051-2004444;
www.pakistan.nlembassy.org *(map pg. 80)*

Norway
House No. 25, Street No. 19, Sector F-6/2, Islamabad, PO Box 1336, Islamabad; (+92) 051-
2077700; www.norway.org.pk *(map pg. 82)*

Oman
Islamabad: House 53, Street 48, Sector F-8/4, Islamabad, PO Box 1194, Islamabad; (+92)
3215533621 *(map pg. 82)*
Karachi: Bungalow no. 19-C, 32nd A Street Off Khayaban-e-Shamsheer, Phase V, Defence
Housing Authority Karachi; (+92) 021-35309795, 35309796 *(map pg. 134)*

Poland
Street 24, G-5/4, Diplomatic Enclave II, Islamabad, PO Box 1032 Islamabad; (+92) 051-
2600844, 2600848, 2600851; www.islamabad.msz.gov.pl/en *(map pg. 80)*

Qatar
Islamabad: 20 University Road, Diplomatic Enclave, G-5/4, Islamabad; (+92) 051-2270833
(map pg. 80)
Karachi: 16 Khayaban-e-Shamsheer, Karachi; (+92) 021-35862171, 3586 2172, 35862173
(map pg. 128)

Romania
House 13, Street 88, Sector G-6/3, Islamabad; (+92) 051-8436601; www.islamabad.mae.ro
(map pg. 80)

Russia
Islamabad: Suhrawardy Rd, Ramna 4, Islamabad; (+92) 051-2600812;
www.pakistan.mid.ru *(map pg. 80)*
Karachi: Plot No. FL-1, Block-4, Scheme-5, Clifton, Karachi; (+92) 021-5830265;
www.rusconsulkarachi.mid.ru *(map pg. 134)*

South Africa
48 Iqbal Rd, F-8/2, Islamabad; (+92) 051-2262354, 2262355, 2262356;
www.dirco.gov.za/foreign/sa_abroad/sap.htm *(map pg. 82)*

South Korea (Republic of Korea)
Islamabad: Block 13, Street 29, Diplomatic Enclave II, G-5/4, Islamabad, P.O. Box 1087,
Islamabad; (+92) 051-2279380; www.pak-islamabad.mofa.gov.kr *(map pg. 80)*
Karachi: No. 101, 29th Street off Khayaban-e-Muhafiz, Block 6 DHA, Karachi; (+92) 021-
35853950, 35853951; www.pak-karachi.mofa.go.kr *(map pg. 128)*

Spain
Street 6, Ramna 5 Diplomatic Enclave, P.O. Box 1144, Islamabad; (+92) 051-2088777;
www.exteriores.gob.es/embajadas.islamabad *(map pg. 80)*

Sri Lanka
Islamabad: 2C, Street 55, F-6/4, Islamabad, (+92) 051-2828723; www.slhcpakistan.org *(map
pg. 82)*
Karachi: 20/1, 18th Street, Kh-e-Shamsheer Phase V, DHA, Karachi; (+92) 021-35346614,
35346615; www.slcgkhi.com *(map pg. 128)*

Sweden
House No. 4, Street No. 5, Sector F-6/3, Islamabad, PO Box 1100, Islamabad; (+92) 051-
2072600; www.swedenabroad.com/en-GB/Embassies/Islamabad/ *(map pg. 80)*

Switzerland
Islamabad: Street 6, Diplomatic Enclave, G-5/4, Islamabad 44000; (+92) 051-2279291,
2279292, 2279293; www.eda.admin.ch/islamabad *(map pg. 82)*
Karachi: 98, Block 5, Clifton, Karachi 75600; (+92) 021-35873987,
35873990; www.eda.admin.ch/eda/en/home/representations/consulate-general-karachi *(map
pg. 134)*

Thailand
Islamabad: Plots No. 1 - 20, Diplomatic Enclave; 1, Sector G-5/4, Islamabad; (+92) 051-8431270; www.thaiembassy.org/islamabad *(map pg. 80)*
Karachi: 151 Main Khayaban-e-Hafiz, Phase VI, Defence Housing Authority, Karachi; (+92) 021-35855405, 35855406; www.thaiembassy.org/karachi/ *(map pg. 128)*

Turkey
Islamabad: Street 1, Diplomatic Enclave, Islamabad; (+92) 051-8319810; www.islamabad.emb.mfa.gov.tr *(map pg. 80)*
Karachi: 29-A Khayaban-e-Hafiz Phase V, Defence Housing Authority, Karachi; (+92) 021-35874334, 35874394; www.karachi.cg.mfa.gov.tr *(map pg. 128)*

United Arab Emirates
Islamabad: Plot 1 - 22, Diplomatic Enclave, Islamabad, PO Box 1111; (+92) 051-2099999; www.uae-embassy.ae/embassies/pk *(map pg. 80)*
Karachi: 17/A, Khayaban-E-Shamsheer, Phase V, Defence House Authority, Karachi; (+92) 21-35810000, 35810004; www.uae-embassy.ae/embassies/pk *(map pg. 128)*

United Kingdom
Islamabad: Ramna 5, Diplomatic Enclave, Islamabad; (+92) 051-2012000; www.gov.uk/government/world/organisations/british-high-commission-islamabad *(map pg. 80)*
Karachi: Shahrah-e-Iran, Clifton, Karachi 75600; (+92) 021-35827000; www.gov.uk/government/world/organisations/british-deputy-high-commission-karachi *(map pg. 134)*

United States of America
Islamabad: Diplomatic Enclave, Islamabad, 44000; (+92) 051-2014000; pk.usembassy.gov *(map pg. 80)*
Karachi: Plot 3, 4, 5, New TPX Area Mai Kolachi Road, Karachi, Mai Kolachi Bypass, Karachi; (+92) 021-35275000; www.pk.usconsulate.gov/embassy-consulates/karachi *(map pg. 128)*
Lahore: 50 Shahrah-e-Abdul Hameed Bin Badees (Old Empress Road), Lahore; (+92) 042-36034000; www.pk.usconsulate.gov/embassy-consulates/lahore *(map pg. 53)*
Peshawar: 11 Hospital Road, Peshawar; (+92) 091-5268800; www.pk.usconsulate.gov/embassy-consulates/peshawar

Visa extensions
Visa extensions can be applied for once you are in Pakistan. Officially this is possible at any offices of the Directorate General of Immigration and Passports across the land, but really, you're better to go to the offices in major cities likes Lahore, Islamabad and Karachi. Usually the process takes a couple of days and generally costs around US$25, but this varies significantly depending on your nationality and length of extension. Visas can be extended for between two weeks and a month, but a handful of travellers have reported receiving an additional three months, or rarely, six.

Health and Medical Services
Information provided in this section is general advice only, and cannot replace consultation with a professional health expert such as a doctor. We strongly advise that you consult a doctor before travelling to Pakistan to receive specialised and personalised health advice.

Before travelling
Before you go to Pakistan, it is essential that you visit a doctor (or even better, a travel doctor) to ask about required and recommended vaccinations, precautions and anything else they may mention. Don't forget to pack sun protection, any required medicines with a letter from your doctor, sanitary items, travel insurance, and if you are going a long way out of the cities, a well-stocked first aid and medicine kit. If you are planning to trek, this requires special planning - you should contact experts before leaving. In Pakistan, you should consult your trekking company or any of the reputable hospitals listed in this guidebook.

In Pakistan

While in Pakistan you will be exposed to a range of bacteria and viruses that you wouldn't normally be. Some of these, for example typhoid, cholera and polio, can be vaccinated against to varying degrees of effectiveness. The biggest threats to your health will come in two forms; food and air. To this, you can add accidents, which occur with frightening regularity on Pakistani roads; few Pakistani families have never been in some way affected by a road accident at some point in their lives.

While 70% of travellers will experience travellers' diarrhoea at some stage, it is often limited to a couple of loose stools and cramping pains, headache, fever, malaise, nausea and/or vomiting. Patients usually only experience a couple of those symptoms at a time, although some suffer all of them at once. Travellers' diarrhoea usually clears up between a couple of hours and a couple of days with the appropriate level of rest, rehydration, careful eating and sometimes medication. Loperamide (sold as Imodium) will stop the loose stools, but will not treat the cause, so there's always the possibility of a relapse. Loperamide is best suited to travellers who are suffering diarrhoea before a long bus ride - it can hold things off until you arrive at your destination. Even mild cases of illness while on holiday in Pakistan are best seen by a doctor anyway, just in case they turn out be something worse. If vomiting or diarrhoea become violent or uncontrolled, or if blood is present in vomit or stools, then prompt medical attention is vital.

To try and avoid getting food poisoning, make sure everything you eat is properly cooked, and has been properly stored before cooking. This is difficult to judge when you are eating out, but it is easier to assume when eating in an upmarket restaurant - although that's by no means guaranteed. Food at buffets should be properly cooked, kept very hot and not reheated. Unpurified water and ice nade from unclean water should be avoided at all costs.

Some travellers find that going vegetarian effectively avoids the worst stomach bugs - undercooked vegetables won't make you sick like undercooked chicken might. A regimen of vegetarianism can be difficult to maintain in Muslim Pakistan though, where meat is considered an integral and honoured part of the culinary and hospitality process. A policy of semi-vegetarianism might be a more realistic compromise - eating meat when it's lovingly homecooked and properly done, and sticking with vegetables when you're eating out and can't be as sure of the restaurant's hygiene standards.

Pollution in the cities can make your throat sore, your eyes itch and your nose run. Sometimes it takes a couple of days to acclimatise, but if you suffer from asthma you should bring all necessary medications. If the pollution really bothers you, try taking a couple of days out in the countryside, or ask about local remedies for the condition; *johar joshanda* is an aniseed-like herbal tea that almost everyone raves about.

If you require medical attention in Pakistan, all medium to large cities have decent private clinics and hospitals which can be recommended - see the individual city chapters for details. The standard of medical facilities can be very good in large cities like Islamabad, and dire in rural areas. While private hospitals cost much more and can vary in quality, they are almost uniformly better than government ("civil") hospitals - with a handful of exceptions. Serious medical cases may be airlifted to countries with better medical infrastructure – travel insurance is an important consideration, as costs are astronomical.

In addition to these issues, travellers in Gilgit-Baltistan should be aware of the potential for Altitude Sickness or Acute Mountain Sickness (AMS). This is caused by a lack of oxygen being supplied to the body from the air at high altitudes. At the least it can cause dizzy spells, headaches and nausea; at worst it can be fatal within hours. Trekkers, and anyone planning to travel above 2500m should speak to their doctor before setting out about the dangers of AMS, and possible management plans.

While travelling

Motion sickness is caused by a conflict between the ears and the eyes in a percentage of people. When the motion detected by the ears' balance, and the movement seen by a person's eyes do not match, the brain reacts as if the body was poisoned and the traveller starts vomiting. Up to 60% of travellers have been shown to be susceptible to motion sickness to varying degrees, although nearly everybody is susceptible if given the right conditions. Sitting near the front or centre of the plane, having a clear view straight ahead while on the road, fresh air, eating lightly and sleeping in transit all help. Smoking, strong odours (like fuel), alcohol, reading a book (especially while in a car or bus), facing sideways or backwards, eating heavily and stress and anxiety are all triggers. Some medicines are useful for preventing motion sickness, but many cause acute drowsiness as well; you should speak with your doctor.

Traveling across timezones can upset your body's sleep cycle, resulting in jet lag. If you are travelling across more than three timezones, you may find yourself feeling sleepy, awake, hungry or even unwell at odd times of the day. The stress of travelling and lack of sleep on flights does not help this. To avoid jet lag, you may start adjusting your meal and sleep times to 'Pakistan time' before you depart, although it's rarely practical. Eating light meals on the flight helps. Try to adapt as quickly as possible by doing things appropriate to the time of day in the new location. If you arrive in the morning, go for a walk and do some gentle exercise, getting natural daylight and eating a light lunch; it might be difficult but you'll feel better for it later! If you arrive in the evening, have a light dinner and get a good night's sleep. And if you arrive in the middle of the night (common in Pakistan), give yourself a bit of a sleep-in, but try to wake up and have breakfast before midday - otherwise you won't be able to sleep the next night!

Lahore *and* Eastern Punjab

Eastern and central Punjab is a heavily populated, pancake-flat land of rice paddies, corn fields and urban conglomerations. Lahore, the provincial capital and Pakistan's second largest city, is the nation's cultural, artistic, educational and culinary hub - simply put, it's the place to be! It's no wonder the locals say "*Lahore Lahore aye*" - "Lahore is Lahore", and there's nothing quite like it.

Wagah, just 30 kilometres from Lahore, is a highlight - you'll never forget the pomp and ceremony of the India - Pakistan border closing ceremony. The people of this region of Punjab are also known for their fun-loving and worldly outlook, tempered with time-honoured tradition.

Sometimes it seems as if you're never truly rid of the big city when travelling in this part of Pakistan, and that's because you're not - large towns, as well as small and large cities are dotted all around the place, and sprawling Lahore threatens to swallow some of them whole in the coming decades.

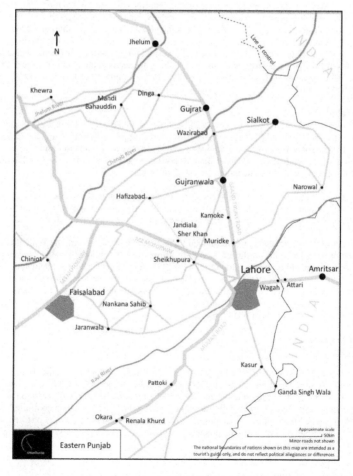

LAHORE

Population: 9.7 million, Elevation: 217m, Telephone code: 042

Pakistan's second largest city and the state capital of Punjab is also its most friendly. Lahore is the cultural hub of Pakistan but is Punjabi to the core; a fun-loving place of music, drama and gastronomic delights. While the roads around the sprawling University of Punjab are leafy boulevards, the frenetic lanes and microstreets of the Walled City are the polar opposite. It's equal parts fun and frenzy, squalor and splendour, refined tradition and exciting exuberance. City streets throb at weekends with young guys on their bikes, heading to the cinema before coffee at 2am - if it's not happening in Lahore, it's probably not happening in Pakistan! No wonder the locals say *"Jine Lahore jai wekhya, o jamya hi nai"* - "whoever hasn't seen Lahore hasn't been born yet".

Lahore's origins are shrouded in history and interwoven with myth. Legend has it that Prince Loh, son of the Hindu Lord Rama set up camp on the banks of the River Ravi and gave his name to the settlement. Documents dating back to seventh century China speak about Lahore, while some historians estimate the city dates back at least 4,000 years. What is certain is that Lahore emerged as the capital of the Punjab region under Hindu rule some time in the first decade of the 11th century, just a couple of years before Mahmud of Ghazni swept in from Afghanistan. Under the Ghaznavid Empire Lahore developed as a literary centre and even served as capital for some time, a tradition continued under the Delhi Sultanate. The Mughals made Lahore an important city, but much of its beautiful architecture came at the end of the Mughal period under Aurangzeb. The short-lived Sikh Empire was centred in Lahore too, but once the British took over the city's prominence began to fade until the Lahore Resolution in 1940 called for a separate Muslim homeland in the subcontinent. Since independence in 1947, Lahore has seen communal disturbances and in the past decade has suffered a spate of bombings, but continues to be Pakistan's most stable and glorious city

Orientation

Lahore is bisected by two main roads; Canal Bank Road and Ferozepur Road. Canal Bank Road (often simply called "Canal") runs from the northeast (towards Wagah and the Indian border) to the southwest, where it continues as a highway towards southern Punjab. Anything to the south or east of Canal Bank Road is generally considered to be new Lahore, while north and west of it is the more congested, older part.

Ferozepur Road runs from near the Walled City in the northwest to the southeastern satellite city of Kasur, and formerly, all the way to the town of Ferozepur which now lies in India. Ferozepur Road is instantly recognisable because it carries the imposing Metrobus line.

For the purposes of travellers, we've divided Lahore into three main areas; the **Walled City** with all of its sights in the northwest, **Central Lahore** with its plethora of staying and eating options, a couple of kilometres north of the Canal/Ferozepur intersection; and upmarket **Gulberg**, a couple of kilometres east of the Canal/Ferozepur intersection. The geographic centre of the city is often considered to be Kalma Chowk, but note that this is not the intersection of Canal and Ferozepur, but two kilometres further south at the intersection of Ferozepur and Main Boulevard Gulberg.

What to see and do in Lahore

Badshahi Masjid (Badshahi Mosque)

Walled City, map pg. 55, Entry free, Open from dawn to dusk

This 'Imperial Mosque', completed in 1671 under the Mughal Emperor Aurangzeb, is Lahore's signature landmark. Between 1799 and 1849 the mosque was used as storage for Sikh Emperor Ranjit Singh's soldiers and horses, a humiliation which is still recalled in today's discourse of South Asian religious politics. After the British wrestled control of Punjab from the Sikh Empire it was returned to Muslim care, and progressively restored. In 1993 the Pakistani government recommended its inclusion on UNESCO's World Heritage List, but it is yet to be nominated.

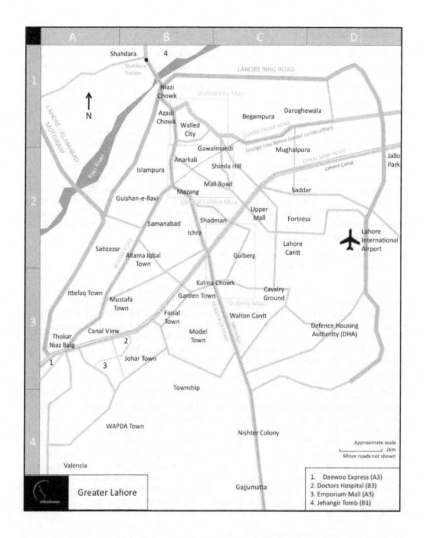

1. Daewoo Express (A3)
2. Doctors Hospital (B3)
3. Emporium Mall (A3)
4. Jehangir Tomb (B1)

Greater Lahore

The beautiful cream marble domes and the carved red sandstone inlaid with marble will stay with you long after you leave. The four minarets guard the courtyard at an impressive 53 metres in height. The entrance steps rise from the tranquil Mughal Gardens - the whole building sits atop a platform, designed to save the mosque in case of flooding. Leave your shoes at the gate, and don't forget to tip the minders when you leave (Rs. 30 is more than enough). Through the grand archway and out into the largest mosque courtyard in the world (with a capacity of 100,000), notice the archways and corridors to either side where ablutions are made. In the centre of the courtyard is a marble fountain, and beyond that is the small flight of steps up to the prayer hall containing ornate marble frescos. If you have been to Jama Masjid in Delhi, India, you will notice the planned similarities in design.

Access to the mosque is through Iqbal Park, near the Azadi Chowk Metrobus stop.

Shahi Qila (Lahore Fort)
Walled City, map pg. 55, Entry Rs. 500, Open 10am - 6pm

The Shahi Qila ("Royal Fort") dates back to the origins of the city and is equally shrouded in myth and mystery, however the existing structure was built under the reign of Mughal emperor Akbar in the second half of the 16th century. Over the years it has been added to by subsequent Mughal, then Sikh and British rulers, before being included on UNESCO's World Heritage List in 1981. There are plenty of treasures, and it's a place that rewards time spent wandering and discovering.

Alamgiri Gate facing the Mughal Gardens, built by Aurangzeb, was the fort's main entrance, but has since been closed. Now the entrance is just north of the gate to the Mughal Gardens, accessed through Iqbal Park, near the Azadi Chowk Metrobus stop. After the ticket gate you climb up the ramp into the structure. At the top of the hill look down to the right; the original entrance from Alamgiri Gate was designed to be wide enough for elephants to walk through, traditionally carrying members of the royal family in their backs. Ahead of you is the white Moti Masjid or 'Pearl Mosque', added to the fort in 1644 by Shah Jahan. Around to the right, and through the grassed area, on the left are the red-and-cream pillars of the Diwan-e-Aam, or the 'Hall of Public Audiences', where Shah Jahan would make speeches and hear his subjects' grievances.

Directly behind the Diwan-e-Aam is Jehangir's Quadrangle, laid out in the style of a traditional Mughal garden, and beyond that is the small room where Jehangir used to sleep. It used to look out across the Ravi River; in three hundred years, the river has changed its course, and now lies several hundred metres to the west, and all you'll see from Jehangir's windows are traffic jams and the Minar-e-Pakistan (page 54). Walking along this 'riverfront' back towards the front of the fort are more rooms and gardens; the first is Shah Jahan's garden with the Diwan-e-Khas (Hall of Private Audiences), then the Ladies Garden with an open courtyard along the 'riverfront' wall. From here you can enter the doorway (if it's open) through to Naulakha and the Sheesh Mahal (Palace of Mirrors), two elaborately decorated restored rooms.

Mughal Gardens
Walled City, map pg. 55, Entry free, Open 24 hours

These lovely gardens, sandwiched between the fort and the mosque, seem to be somewhat quieter than the surrounding city, no matter what time of day. While you're not supposed to walk on the grass, there are some smaller patches of grass around the edge that attract crowds of picnicking Lahoris. Here are a number of important tombs which are worth seeing, the highlight of which is that of visionary Pakistani philosopher Sir Muhammad "Allama" Iqbal. These gardens are surrounded by a high sandstone wall which separates them from the chaos of the walled city, and entry is only by the two gates on the east and west walls. It is one of a couple of important Mughal Gardens still standing in modern Lahore; others include Jehangir Tomb, Chauburji and Shalimar Gardens (pg. 57). Enter the gardens through Iqbal Park, near the Azadi Chowk Metrobus stop.

Samadhi of Emperor Ranjit Singh (Mausoleum)
Walled City, map pg. 55, Unauthorised entry not permitted

This Sikh temple or *gurdwara* dates back to the days of Sikh rule in Punjab, and contains the cremation urns of Sikh ruler Maharaja Ranjit Singh who ruled over Lahore 1801 to his death in 1839. This is a beautifully ornate lotus structure, typical of Sikh architecture. Apart from for organized tour groups, this building has not been open to non-Sikhs for several years due to security concerns; you may be allowed to join a tour group at the gate if your timing is right.

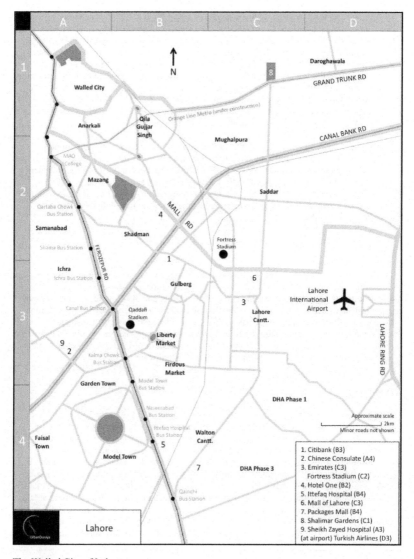

The Walled City of Lahore

map pg. 55

"The Walled City of Lahore", sometimes called "the Old City" or "Old Lahore", refers to a region of the original city which was bound by fortified walls for protection. The city used to be accessed through thirteen gates, only six of which remain, and some of which are quite ornate. In other parts, the walls have been broken through to make way for new roads, however the streets directly adjacent to these historic gates are still known by their traditional names; despite Mori Gate not surviving, many addresses still bear the name "Mori Gate" or "Mori Bazaar".

Taxali Gate and the surrounding area known as Heera Mandi is Lahore's red light district. Here, *mujra* dancing girls work into the night, many (if not all) doubling as prostitutes. Further into the Walled City, near Delhi Gate, is the beautifully-tiled Wazir Khan Mosque, featured in the 2007 Pakistani film Khuda Ke Liye. it dates back to 1635. Nearby is the beautifully restored Wazir Khan Hammam (public baths). Between Taxali Gate and Wazir Khan Mosque is the lovely Sunheri Mosque, replete with carved white marble. It's hidden from the street by a large wall, but its domes are still visible - ask a local to show you the door. Just behind it is Boli Bagh, a secluded park built by the historic Sikh community of Lahore, and welcome respite from the craziness outside. Further north, behind the fort, is the hard-to-find Maryam Zamani Mosque, one of Lahore's oldest.

The Walled City is an exciting, fascinating and unpredictable place to wander around, people watching or shopping from any of the bazaars. Different streets in the city are known for different shopping districts, including Mochi Gate (crockery and fried fish), Shahalam Market (children's wear) Taxali Gate (Peshawari sandals and street food, especially *siri paye*). Streets are crowded and foreigners stand out here, so try to be discreet, and definitely be culturally sensitive in this more conservative area. At times of political or religious tension, this is not the place to go.

Minar-e-Pakistan
Walled City, map pg. 55 Entry free
The Minar-e-Pakistan (Minaret of Pakistan) stands at the exact spot where the Pakistan Declaration was made on 23rd March 1940 (see page 10 for more information). Construction was started in 1960 and completed in 1968, and at 62 metres high it is one of the tallest structures in Lahore. The white marble tower is a modern take on the traditional minaret. The base is shaped in the star of Pakistan, enclosed in two crescent shapes, reminiscent of the national flag. The five platforms at different levels symbolise the struggle for independence from the British Empire for the succession of Pakistan. Nowadays major political rallies are frequently held at this nationally significant location.

Data Darbar
Near the Walled City, map pg. 55, Entry free
Data Darbar is a huge shrine complex paying tribute to the 11th Century Sufi saint Abul Hassan Ali Hajvery (c. 990 - 1077), commonly called Data Ganj Baksh. On celebratory nights, Sufi pilgrims sing and dance at this marvellous shrine, which dates back to the Ghanznavid era. Once you enter through heavy security (no cameras allowed - no exceptions), you cross a large courtyard to the marble tomb. Devotees sway and chant in prayer, while the scent of incense fills the air. Beyond that is a large mosque, fairly modern in design, and not particularly beautiful inside. The security is tight for good reason; many Muslims see the practices of Sufism as being deviant, and a bombing in 2010 killed at least fifty people at the shrine. Note that men and women enter through different doors. The shrine is packed on the the *urs* (death anniversary) of Data Ganj Bakhsh, which in 2018 is expected to fall on around the 1st November, and moves about 10 days earlier each year.

Get more out of Lahore! Go to http://urbanduniya.com/tag/lahore/ for the latest Lahore-related stuff on the website!

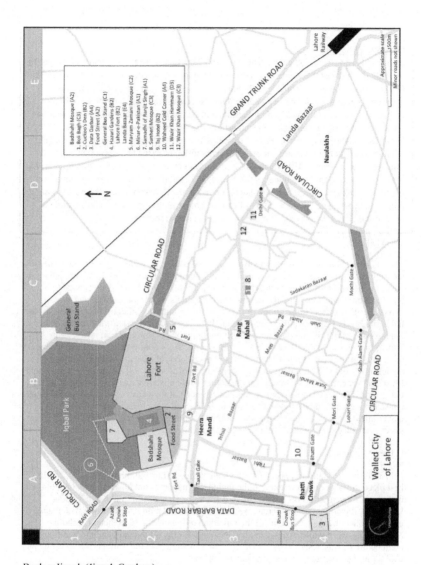

Badshahi Mosque (A2)
1. Bol Bagh (C3)
2. Cuckoo's Den (B2)
3. Data Darbar (A4)
Food Street (A2)
4. General Bus Stand (C1)
5. Hazuri Gardens (B2)
Lahore Fort (B2)
Landa Bazaar (E4)
6. Maryam Zamani Mosque (C2)
7. Minar-e-Pakistan (A1)
8. Samadhi of Ranjit Singh (A1)
9. Sunheri Mosque (C3)
10. Taj Hotel (B2)
11. Waheed Gold Corner (A4)
12. Wazir Khan Hammam (D3)
13. Wazir Khan Mosque (C3)

Bagh-e-Jinnah (Jinnah Gardens)

map pg. 57. Entry free, Open sunrise to sunset

Bagh-e-Jinnah is a pleasant green respite from the hectic city roads outside. A handful of stalls sell cold drinks and chai, but thankfully do not detract from the peace. Within the botanic gardens you can find several important and historic buildings including Quaid-e-Azam Library, also known as Jinnah Library, Masjid Dar-ul-Islam (a mosque), and the cricket ground for the prestigious Lahore Gymkhana (a social and sports club). Next door is the Lahore Zoo. An autorickshaw costs about Rs. 100 from Gulberg, Rs. 200 from Walled City.

Mian Saif ki Haveli
Mian Saif ki Haveli is a 250 year old house with a long family tradition. Mian Asif Riaz, until recently the head of the estate, was a business personality known throughout the Walled City of Lahore. When he 'converted' to Shia Islam, his family and the haveli took on a particularly active role in the city's cultural life. Nowadays the haveli is home to three ceremonial horses known as *zuljinnah*, representing the horse that carried Imam Hussain into battle at Karbala. Every year in Muharram, the horse is decorated with a new headpiece, elaborately encrusted with precious stones and handmade in the haveli. The horse is then paraded through the streets in memorial, sparking the passion of Lahore's Muharram processions. After Mian Asif's untimely demise in 2012, his son Mian Haider Ali took over the day-to-day running of the house, and continues to organise the Muharram procession. Meanwhile on the birthday of Imam Ali, the first Shia Imam, the haveli hosts a huge *jashn* (party) attended by some of Lahore's most prominent personalities, and welcoming all to take part in what has become a family tradition.

The Mall
map pg. 57
The Mall, or "Mall Road" is a long strip of colonial buildings, which segues from gardens and stately freestanding buildings near the intersection with Canal Bank Road through government buildings to shops and then colleges at the intersection at "Lower Mall". Starting from Canal Bank Road, you pass the prestigious Aitcheson College and the Governor of Punjab's House on the right (no photos or entry to either of these), while on the left is the lovely Bagh-e-Jinnah Bagh (Jinnah Park, see entry below). Further along is the Punjab Assembly Hall (no photography) on the right, before you reach an intersection known as Charing Cross. Here begins a strip of attractive colonial structures occupied by modern shops and eateries in varying states of decay and refurbishment. Further along on the left is the old GPO building, still in operation, while further still on the left is the Lahore Museum (see entry below). Finally, at the corner with Ferozepur Road at "Lower Mall" is Government College University Lahore ("GCU"), one of the oldest universities in Pakistan, housed in a grand old building dating back to 1865. Sadly, the high security barriers at Government College University Lahore mean the building can barely be seen from the street, and entry is prohibited without an invitation.

Lahore Museum
map pg. 57, Entry Rs. 250, Open 9am - 4:30pm
Pakistan's biggest museum opened in 1864 but shifted to this building in 1894, and is the best place in Lahore to view some of the region's Hindu and Buddhist heritage. One of the museum's first curators was writer Rudyard Kipling's father John Lockwood Kipling. Despite its illustrious history, foreign visitors might find it a bit disappointing with many exhibits collecting dust and some of them marked only in Urdu. Nonetheless, Lahore's Museum is a worthwhile half day excursion if only for the art displays and the building's architecture (it was designed by Sir Ganga Ram), especially in the warmer months when the cool air in the cavernous halls is a prime attraction.

New Anarkali
map pg. 57
New Anarkali is a shopping district where you can pick up everything from a tailored suit to shoes, a shalwar kameez to a sari, or even just fabric to take home to stitch yourself. On one side street is the humble Mausoleum of Sultan Qutb-ud-Din Aibak, a leader of the early Muslim dynasty in northwestern India. He died in 1210 AD as a result of injuries sustained while playing polo. When you visit the mausoleum, don't forget to look across the road to spot the roof of an old Hindu temple (mandir) - it's the trapezoidal design above the modern shop fronts. Lahore's dwindling Hindu population means the interior has been converted for residential use (so you can't enter), but the exterior structure has been preserved.

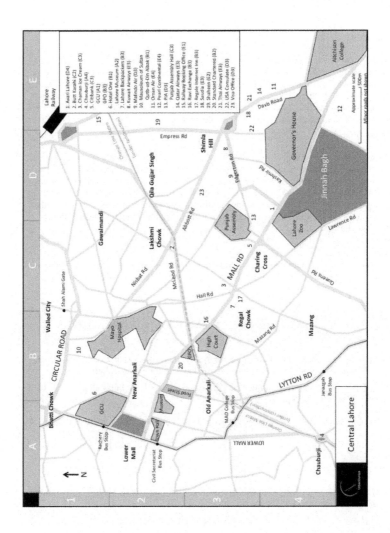

Legend (map key):
1. Asari Lahore (D4)
2. Butt Kabab (C2)
3. Osman Ice Cream (C3)
4. Chaudary (A4)
5. Citibank (C3)
6. GCU (A1)
7. GPO (B3)
8. Hotel One (B1)
9. Lahore Museum (A2)
10. Lahore backpackers (B3)
11. Kuwait Airways (E3)
12. Malindo Air (D3)
13. Mausoleum of Sultan Qutb-ud-Din Aibak (B1)
14. Oman Air (E4)
15. Pearl Continental (E4)
16. Punjab Assembly Hall (C3)
17. PIA (B3)
18. Qatar Airways (E3)
19. Railway Booking Office (E1)
20. Ravi Exchange (B3)
21. Regale Internet Inn (B3)
22. Saudia (E3)
23. Shaheen (C2)
24. Standard Chartered (B2)
25. Thai Airways (E3)
26. USA Consulate (D3)
27. Visa Office (D3)

Shalimar Gardens

map pg. 53, Entry Rs. 200, Open 10am – 5pm

One of three important Mughal gardens in Lahore (the others being the Mughal Gardens near the Lahore Fort, and Chauburji), Shalimar Gardens is often vaunted as the most beautiful. Truth be told, they are something of a faded beauty, but are still UNESCO World Heritage listed. Inside you'll find cascading fountains which for much of the year might be dry; there are 410 fountains spread over three main terraced areas. Other Mughal pavilions include the sleeping chambers, royal baths, grand hall, resting places, public hall, wives quarters, and summer pavilions (by the fountains). The turreted walls and red stone construction, typical of Mughal architecture, dates back to 1641, but are sadly showing signs of neglect. An autorickshaw costs about Rs. 200 from Gulberg, up to Rs. 300 from the Walled City

Chauburji

map pg. 57, Entry free, Open 24 hours

This imposing structure stands in the middle of an intersection on Multan Road. Literally meaning 'four towers', it consists of a central building boasting, unsurprisingly, four towers which look a bit like minarets. Built in 1646 under Mughal rule, it is surrounded by gardens which unfortunately aren't that nice because they're in the middle of a busy intersectionm and at the time of research were covered in dust from the Orange Line Metro construction site nearby. You can walk here from MAO College Metrobus station.

Jahangir Tomb

map pg. 51, Entry Rs. 250, Open 10am - 5pm

The tomb of the fourth Mughal emperor is way out on the western banks of the Ravi River, just to the north of the satellite city of Shahdara. The tomb was completed by Jahangir's son Shah Jahan in 1637. Featuring red stone brought from India's Fatehpur Sikri, visitors to the tomb are greeted by a large Mughal-style garden before approaching the wide but short building. Featuring four tall minarets, the building is significantly smaller than some other Mughal emperors' tombs. The tomb itself is in white marble with inlay featuring floral motifs and Qur'anic verses.

Staying in Lahore

When booking one of Lahore's more mid-to-top end hotels, ask if there are any discounts available off the rack rate - often there are generous savings freely available (sometimes even advertised), but only given to those who ask!

Backpackers

Regale Internet Inn: Surriaya Mansion, 65 The Mall, Lahore; (+92) 042-37311987; www.regale.com.pk

map pg. 57, Dorm Rs. 300, Dbl Rs. 500

Time honoured as Lahore's best budget place to stay, this place has an excellent location, decent (if basic facilities) and a wealth of experience with foreign travellers.

Lahore Backpackers: Amin Building near UBL s.d Vault, 55 The Mall, Lahore; (+92) 0300-8866039; www.lahorebackpackers.com.pk

map pg. 57, Sgl Rs. 900

With a raft of free facilities, Lahore Backpackers is fast building a reputation as the place to stay.

Economy

Hotel One: 105 - A Upper Mall, Lahore; (+92) 0341-220111; www.hotelone.com.pk

map pg. 53, Dbl US$112

A budget-business venture by Pakistan's respected Pearl Continental chain – also branches in Gulberg and near the Walled City.

Sunfort Hotel: 72 - D/1, Liberty Commercial Zone, Gulgerg-III, Lahore; (+92) 042-5763810; www.sunforthotel.com

map pg. 61, Standard Single Rs. 15,000, Standard Double Rs. 17,000, Suite Rs. 18,000

An older building but with good service and in a great location.

Luxury

Avari Lahore: Mall Road, Lahore; (+92) 042-36366366; www.avari.com

map pg. 57, Dbl US$195, Suite US$250

Five restaurants (including an upmarket Japanese restaurant) and broadband wifi internet connection make the Avari among the best hotels in Pakistan.

Pearl Continental: Mall Road, Lahore; (+92) 042-6360210; www.pchl.com

map pg. 57, Dbl US$210, Suite US$650

Six restaurants, two coffee shops, swimming pools, a day spa, tennis courts, mini cinema, golf course and a shopping arcade; the Pearl Continental is the last word in luxury in

Lahore, something reflected by the prices. Some travellers have noted that the Avari is better value, but despite the ageing building, nothing quite matches the Pearl Continental's appointments and service.

Nishat Hotel: Mian Mehmood Ali Kasoori Rd, Gulberg; (+92) 111000777
map pg. 61, Dbl US$277, Suite US$430
A new player in the Lahore hotel game, with everything you would expect from a new hotel of this calibre.

Eating in Lahore
Eating in Lahore can be done at any roadside, but if you are looking for a cluster of sit-down restaurants to choose from, these can be divided into three broad areas which are of use to travellers.

The Walled City, and particularly **Badshahi Food Street** *(map pg. 55)* (running between Badshahi Mosque and the Walled City itself) hosts a cluster of mid-range restaurants that cater to tourists. Among these, **Cuckoo's Den** *(map pg. 55)* is the best known, with the interior of its historic building painted with frescos depicting the dancing girls of Lahore. The rooftop dining area, overlooking the Badshahi Mosque, is a great place to watch the sunset while chowing down on Pakistani cuisine. Note that there is no direct access from Food Street and the Walled City to the mosque; you must enter through Iqbal Park near the Azadi Chowk Metrobus station. Throughout the Walled City you can find cheap eateries dishing up dhal, channa (chick peas), kebabs and samosas. **Taj Hotel** has a particularly good samosa plate with plum chutney and chickpea curry (Rs. 40 single plate) *(map pg. 55)*. **Waheed Cold Corner** has been serving up ice-cold *badam doodh* (almond-infused sweetened milk) and doodh soda (milk and fruit soda squash) since time began. Rs 30 for small, Rs. 80 for large *(map pg. 55)*.

The Mall, between Charing Cross and the Lahore Museum, is home to a glut of fast food restaurants (of both the local and multinational variety) and a handful of local restaurants too, most of them mid-range or below. None that we've tried particularly stand out, but **Chaman Ice Cream** *(map pg. 57)* is the place to head for dessert! They serve up a standard range of flavours with some interesting local varieties thrown in to boot - it's not upmarket, but it's legendary in Pakistan, especially in the hot summers! There's also an Anarkali Food Street just near the museum. Not far from the mall, but definitely worth a try, is **Butt Karahi** *(map pg. 57)* near Lakshmi Chowk - take a rickshaw there. Famed for its Chicken and Lamb Karahi, many other restaurants have tried to imitate their success but none have quite nailed it. Standing with the facia of Lakshmi Chowk behind you, take the street diagonally ahead of you to the right. It's about three doors down on the right, before you hit the lane way. It's got the live (yes, live) chickens clucking out the front and a white and red sign.

Gulberg *(map pg. 61)* is where Lahore's well-to-do go to eat. If you're looking for upmarket Pakistani cuisine, you've come to the right place - go the lip-smacking **Tabaq**. If you're after anything else, you'll probably find it here too; Chinese (**Chinatown**, **Far East**), Thai (**Opium Thai**), Continental (**The Delicatessen, Freddy's Cafe**), Korean (**Udon House**), Italian (**Cosa Nostra**), South Indian (**Bombay Chowpatty**), Lebanese (**Charcoal Grill**), Self-serve Frozen Yogurt (**Tutti Fruitti**), Coffee Bars (**Café Barbera, Coffee and Tea Company**). At Gulberg you'll also find the regular range of international fast food restaurants. A list of Lahore's best restaurants visit www.lahoresnob.com/restaurants_lahore, and of course you can read about the latest hot spots to eat at urbanduniya.com/lahore.

Much of what is in Gulberg also exists at Fortress Stadium and in the Defence Housing Authority ("DHA") as well, but all of this can be a bit of a trek unless you're staying nearby.

Services in Lahore
Airlines
Air Arabia: Office 7, Ground Floor, Big City Plaza, 3-E/11, Gulberg 3; (+92) 042-3577416769 *(map pg. 53)*
Airblue: Ground Floor, Shop 1&2, Asad Center 71-E, Main Blvd, Gulberg 2; 042-35870789 *(map pg. 53)*
Emirates: 1,2 Cantonment Commerical Complex, Abid Majeed Rd, Lahore Cantt; 021-35203377 *(map pg. 53)*
Etihad: 1st Floor, Mall 1, Main Blvd, Gulberg; (+92) 0800-90044017 *(map pg. 61)*
Gulf Air: Lufthansa House, 5-G/2, Block-H, Gulberg II; (+92) 021-35654483 *(map pg. 61)*
Kuwait Airways: Shaheen Complex, Office 8, 7th Floor, Egerton Road; 042-36368206 *(map pg. 57)*
Malindo Air: National Towers, opposite Aiwan-e-Iqbal, Egerton Road; 042-36309671 *(map pg. 57)*
Pakistan International: PIA Bldg, Khalifa Shujauddin Rd; (+92) 042-99036999 *(map pg. 57)*
Oman Air: Al-Malik Plaza, 19 Davis Road *(map pg. 57)*
Qatar Airways: Office 12, 1st Floor Etimad Trade Centre, 17 Davis Road; (+92) 042-36308125 *(map pg. 57)*
Saudia: Carim's Hosue, 6 Davis Road; (+92) 042-36305411 *(map pg. 57)*
Serene Air: Ground Floor, Shop 64A, Fountain Avenue Building, Main Boulevard, Gulberg 2; 042-35817115 *(map pg. 61)*
Shaheen: Carpet Training Institute Bldg, 27 Empress Rd; (+92) 042-99240056 *(map pg. 57)*
Thai Airways: 9-A Davis Road; (+92) 042-630-9791 *(map pg. 57)*
Turkish Airlines: Allama Iqbal Int'l Airport, Level 2 Office 2153; (+92) 042-36660102 *(map pg. 53)*
Uzbekistan Airways: Room 3131, 3rd Floor, Lahore Apt; (+92) 042-6611501 *(map pg. 57)*

Banks
Citibank: EFU House, 6-D, Jail Road *(map pg. 57)*
Standard Chartered: 47 The Mall *(map pg. 57)*
Standard Chartered: 65 Main Boulevard, Gulberg *(map pg. 61)*

Cinemas
Cinemas abound in the area to the north of the Mall, especially along Abbott Road, but for a western-style Cineplex go to Super Cinemas at Vogue Towers, MM Alam Road, Gulberg *(map pg. 61)*

Internet Cafe
Since the rise of wifi, internet cafes have stopped springing up as quickly as they once did - but that's not to say they're all closing down. There are not a lot of internet cafes on The Mall *(map pg. 57)*, so ask your hotel for a recommendation. In the Walled City, there seems to be a cluster of internet cafes in the area known as Urdu Bazaar, just outside of Bhatti Gate, and also just inside the gate. In Gulberg, go to Firdous Market where you'll find a few places to get online *(map pg. 61)*.

Money Exchange
Ravi Exchange has a good reputation, with branches at Mall Road; 5 Mall Mansion, opp. State Bank Building; 042-7230604; www.forex.net.pk *(map pg. 57)*, and Gulberg; 1st Floor, 130 E1, Main Blvd, Nr City Bank, Gulberg III; (+92) 042-5870630 *(map pg. 61)*.

Post Office
Lahore's GPO is on The Mall *(map pg. 57)*, or there is a reliable post office at Liberty Market too *(map pg. 61)*.

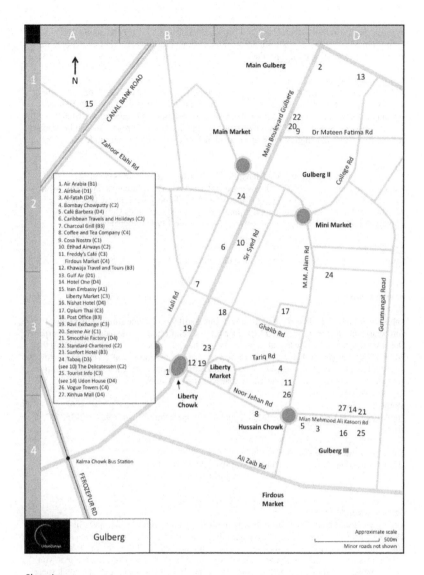

Map legend:

1. Air Arabia (B1)
2. Airblue (D1)
3. Al-Fatah (D4)
4. Bombay Chowpatty (C2)
5. Café Barbera (D4)
6. Caribbean Travels and Holidays (C2)
7. Charcoal Grill (B3)
8. Coffee and Tea Company (C4)
9. Cosa Nostra (C1)
10. Etihad Airways (C2)
11. Freddy's Café (C3)
    Firdous Market (C4)
12. Khawaja Travel and Tours (B3)
13. Gulf Air (D1)
14. Hotel One (D4)
15. Iran Embassy (A1)
    Liberty Market (C3)
16. Nishat Hotel (D4)
17. Opium Thai (C3)
18. Post Office (B3)
19. Ravi Exchange (C3)
20. Serene Air (C1)
21. Smoothie Factory (D4)
22. Standard Chartered (C2)
23. Sunfort Hotel (B3)
24. Tabaq (D3)
    (see 10) The Delicatessen (C2)
25. Tourist Info (C3)
    (see 14) Udon House (D4)
26. Vogue Towers (C4)
27. Xinhua Mall (D4)

Gulberg

Approximate scale
500m
Minor roads not shown

Shopping
For cheap clothes and shoes, go to <u>Landa Bazaar</u> or <u>New Anarkali</u> *(map pg. 57)*, for upmarket brands go to <u>The Mall of Lahore</u>, <u>Xinhua Mall</u> or check out the boutiques on <u>MM Alam Road</u>, all in Gulberg *(map pg. 61)*. <u>Emporium Mall</u> is a new mall in distant Johar Town *(map pg. 51)*, and <u>Packages Mall</u> is another new one near DHA *(map pg. 53)*. For handicrafts and art, try the area around Food Street at Badshahi Mosque *(map pg. 55)*.

Supermarkets
For a wide range of local and imported groceries, the best options are <u>Al-Fatah</u> in Gulberg *(map pg. 61)*, or further afield, <u>Hyperstar</u> is the local brand-name for the French

hypermarket Carrefour – there's one at Fortress Stadium *(map pg. 53)* and another at Emporium Mall *(map pg. 53)*. Zenith Meats have various locations around Lahore, and are known for their hygienic meat products.

Tourist Information
PTDC, 66-D/I, Gulberg III *(map pg. 61)*. Local guide Dilawar "Peter" Masih has a wealth of information to share about Lahore and Pakistan, and is connected with the tourism board. He can be contacted on (+92) 03004973105, or at writetopeterm@yahoo.com. Moazam Ali is a well-connected local and "on the ground" contact for UrbanDuniya – he can be reached at 03217990913 and can give local tips and advice, or even act as a tour guide.

Travel Agency
The Regale Internet Inn; Surriaya Mansion, 65 The Mall, Lahore; 042-37311987; www.regale.com.pk; *(map pg. 57)* has a good travel service if you are near The Mall, while in Gulberg, Khawaja Travel and Tours (Liberty Market, Gulberg III, Lahore; 042-36297358; www.khawajatravel.com) has a good reputation *(map pg. 61)*, as does Caribbean Express Travels & Holidays (UG-41, Eden Tower, 82-E-1, Main Blvd Gulberg) *(map pg. 61)*.

Visa Office
Ground Floor 15-A, Abbott Road, behind the Qila Gujar Singh Police Station *(map pg. 57)*

Help in Lahore
Safety
Lahore is a fairly safe city in which to travel, but it still pays to take some precautions. If you're arriving late at night, call a Metro Radio Cab, don't take a rickshaw from the airport. Don't walk around the city late at night, and dress conservatively if you are heading to the Walled City. Keep your belongings close to you at all times, and be extra vigilant in crowds. The Walled City is not a good place to be at times of political or religious tension. Despite being a generally friendly city, be aware that scams still do exist in Lahore.

Medical Services
Sheikh Zayed Hospital: Campus Road, Block D, New Muslim Town (+92) 042-35865731 *(map pg. 53)*
Ittefaq Hospital: Near H-Block, Model Town (+92) 042-35881981 *(map pg. 53)*
Mayo Hospital: Hospital Road, Lahore (+92) 042-99213666 *(map pg. 57)*
Doctors Hospital: 152-G/1, Canal Bank, Johar Town (+92) 042-35302701 *(map pg. 53)*
24 Hour Pharmacies are available at all major hospitals

Getting around Lahore
Metrobus: Nothing has divided Lahore, both physically and figuratively, quite like the Metrobus project. Pillars of concrete march their way through the city, elevating a fleet of buses high above the traffic and chaos. It's certainly impressive, but is it a miracle solution to Lahore's traffic woes, or a short-sighted vote-grabber? While you're debating that, you can zip between Azadi and Bhatti Chowks (near the Walled City) and Kalma Chowk (near Gulberg) in a matter of minutes, for a flat rate of just Rs. 20 per ride. Buy the tickets from the under- or above-ground ticket booths. Buses are crowded but air conditioned (for what it's worth) and frequent, from 6am - 10pm. Women sit or stand at the front of the bus, men at the back, and photography is not permitted anywhere on the network.

Bus: Buses criss-cross Lahore, but are crowded and not really worth the effort. If you are really pinching the pennies, useful routes include the B-16 (running between Azadi Chowk near Badshahi Mosque, and Liberty Market in Gulberg), the B-28 and B-39 which run from Liberty Market to the airport, and B-54 from Liberty Chowk to the railway station. B-29 crosses The Mall near at the G.P.O. and runs to the railway station.

Autorickshaw and Qinqqi: Autorickshaws ply the roads around Lahore and are probably the easiest way to get around, although the cost adds up if you use them all the time. Expect to pay above the average as a foreigner, even if you haggle; Gulberg to The Mall can cost around Rs. 200, Gulberg to the Walled City would be about Rs. 300, while The Mall to the Walled City would be around Rs. 200. An autorickshaw to or from the airport will most likely cost upwards of Rs. 500, and depending on security arrangements, may not be allowed to approach the terminal building and instead will drop you off in the car park.

Taxi: Taxis don't roam around Lahore like they do in other cities around the world. For the safest and most reliable service, call Metro Radio Cabs on 111-222-787 or go to www.metrocab.com.pk. A cab costs Rs. 400 at a base cost, then Rs. 20 for every subsequent kilometre.

Uber and Careem ride-sharing services have landed in Lahore, with the former also offering female-driver and rickshaw services. Download the applications to your phone and get a quote! Both operate with cash.

Lahore Metro – the "Orange Line"
By the time you read this, it's possible that the Orange Line Metro Train will be operating in Lahore. This huge Chinese - Pakistani project links the western parts of the city with the centre and northeastern area. Travellers may find the link between Chauburji, the existing MetroBus at MAO College station, Lakshmi Chowk, the Railway Station and Shalimar Gardens useful. The Orange Line is marked on the appropriate maps on this book. Fare pricing or station information was not available at the time of printing.

Lahore International Airport
Lahore's International Airport, known as Allama Iqbal International Airport, receives flights all through the day, including many in the dead of the night. The international and domestic terminals are connected to each other. Non-passengers are not allowed to enter the terminal building, and visitors must wait outside in the semi-outdoor concourse. The airport has all the facilities you would expect of a medium-sized airport, including eateries, banks, cellphone outlets, left luggage facilities and a very limited range of duty free shopping.

If you're arriving late at night, call a Metro Radio Cab, don't take a rickshaw from the airport. The cab should cost about Rs. 600 to Gulberg and Rs. 800 to The Mall. Arrival at Lahore is fairly straightforward provided you have all of your documents (i.e. - passport and visa) in order. Keep your luggage receipt sticker which gets attached to your boarding pass before you check in on the flight - a security guard will check this against the sticker on your luggage at baggage reclaim.

Leaving Lahore at the airport is not difficult, although you should be aware that when you check in, you don't always drop your luggage at the counter. Instead, some passengers are directed to the large conveyor at the far right end of the check-in counters and drop your bag there along with everyone else. Also, be prepared for 'helpers' to try and take your bag for you - they expect to be paid for their services, and don't be afraid to tell them no if you don't want help. Similarly, you'll be accosted by people selling passes to the business class lounge for several hundred rupees - this is usually legitimate, but overpriced, and depending on the traveller, unnecessary.

Leaving Lahore
The Daewoo Express bus station used to be in the centre of the city, but has now relocated to the southern fringe at Thokar Niaz Baig *(map pg. 51)*. The local bus station is just north of the Walled City *(map pg. 55)*. The train booking office is across the road from the station and down the street, on a leafy estate *(map pg. 57)*.

Bus
Rawalpindi/Islamabad: Daewoo Express, 4 hours 30 minutes, Rs. 1,200
Abbottabad: Daewoo Express, 6 hours and 10 minutes, Rs. 1100
Mansehra: Semi-frequent buses from Lahore's Lari Adda bus station; 8 hours. Rs. 800
Gujranwala: Daewoo Express, 1 hour 35 minutes, Rs. 320.
Gujrat: Daewoo Express, 2 hours 15 minutes, Rs. 500.
Sialkot: Daewoo Express, 3 hours, Rs. 520.
Jhelum: Daewoo Express, 3 hours 15 minutes, Rs. 580.
Faisalabad: Daewoo Express, 2 hours 15 minutes, Rs. 550.
Chiniot: Daewoo Express, 2 hours, Rs. 540
Sarghoda: Daewoo Express, 2 hours 15 minutes, Rs. 440
Multan: Daewoo Express, 5 hours 15 minutes, Rs. 950.
Bahawalpur: Daewoo Express, 6 hours 40 minutes, Rs. 1,250.
Okara: Daewoo Express, 2 hours 5 minutes, Rs. 500.
Sahiwal: Daewoo Express, 2 hours 30 minutes, Rs. 550.
Karachi: Daewoo Express, 21 hours, Rs. 3,750
Sukkur: Daewoo Express, 13 hours, Rs. 2,400
Hyderabad: Daewoo Express, 19 hours, Rs. 3,380

Train
Rawalpindi/Islamabad: 4 to 5 hours, Rs. 400 (seat)
Faisalabad: 2 hours, Rs. 200 (seat)
Multan: 5 to 6 hours, Rs. 410 (seat)
Bahawalpur: 6 to 7 hours, Rs. 450 (seat)
Rohri/Sukkur: 10 to 12 hours, Rs. 1,400 (berth)
Hyderabad: 15 to 17 hours, Rs. 1,700 (berth)
Karachi: 18 to 20 hours, Rs. 1,250 (berth)

Air
Islamabad: PIA, 55 minutes, from Rs. 6,790 one way
Multan: PIA, 55 minute, from Rs. 6,700 one way
Bahawalpur: PIA, 1 hour, from Rs. 6,500 one way
Karachi: PIA, Shaheen, AirBlue and Serene Air, 1 hour 45 mins, from Rs. 7,400 one way.
Sukkur: PIA, 1 hour 50 minutes, from Rs. 7,900 one way

WAGAH
Wagah *(map pg. 49)* is the name of the village which, in 1947, became the only legal road crossing between a newly demarcated India and Pakistan. People come here for one or both of two reasons; either to cross the border, or to witness the border closing ceremony which takes place nightly.

Border Closing Ceremony
If you're here for the border closing ceremony, you're in for a treat. At about 4:30pm each evening (although times vary according to season and political climate; check locally), specially-constructed grandstands begin to fill with patriotic Lahoris, bored locals and curious tourists. As the excitement grows, volunteers march up and down past the audience, waving Pakistani flags and whipping up nationalist fervour. The same occurs on the Indian side, where the crowd often descends into the street below, dancing and singing; the Pakistani side is usually more subdued, with men and women seated separately according to Islamic social code. As the border closes for the evening, soldiers march out from under the grandstands, kicking their legs, stomping their feet and saluting with almost comedic exaggeration. A Pakistani soldier and an Indian soldier meet at the gate itself to lower their respective flags. Once this is done, they briefly shake hands, and slam the gate closed for the night. The gate gets closed a couple of times during the ceremony, but you'll know when it's officially closed as that's when everyone cheers the loudest. Afterwards, depending on the size of the crowd and the security climate, spectators are sometimes allowed to walk up to the gate and take pictures with the guards, before heading back towards Lahore for the night.

Needless to say, this is not the place to joke around - years of animosity between Pakistan and India mean that soldiers here are armed to the hilt, and while the whole thing might appear quite over-the-top and zany, these guys are serious about their required job which is to defend the border. Apart from while you are in the stands, it pays to be discreet about taking pictures. The razor wire fence marking the border can be seen extending into the distance from either side of the gate, but if you want to take a picture of the line, don't whip your camera out while in the presence of a patriotic and protective guard.

Getting to and from Wagah
Lahore: Taxi drivers and autorickshaw wallahs will no doubt hound you for business - the going rate from Wagah to Central Lahore (22kms away) is Rs. 1,500 for a taxi and Rs. 800 for a rickshaw (including waiting time). There is a bus which plies this route, but it's not frequent enough to consider taking.

Many people coming for the border ceremony travel with a prearranged "tour" from Lahore hotels or agencies. Depending on how much you've paid, the "tour guide" might simply be a driver who drops you off and picks you up from the entrance, or he may follow you right into the stand, expanding on each part of the ceremony. Check what's included when you book.

Going to India

For a border which causes so much anxiety, crossing the border at Wagah is a surprisingly simple if lengthy process - as long as you're not of Pakistani or Indian descent. Make sure all your relevant travel documents are in order, and arrive before 3pm - since the border closing ceremony is an elaborate performance in itself, you can't cross the border immediately before as show preparations are underway.

If you are travelling alone, the easiest thing to do is catch a taxi from Lahore to the border, cross on foot, and then take a taxi from the other side into Amritsar. If you're on a bus, you'll probably end up doing about the same thing, but have to wait in line with your fellow passengers while everyone gets processed. Crossing from India into Pakistan entails a similar process to the one outlined below, but obviously in reverse.

Enter the Pakistani customs room on the left side of the gate, probably where you'll get dropped off. Once you've had your documents inspected and stamped (and possibly your bag inspected), you can change some money (or wait until India), then walk across to the gate under the brick archway. There, your documents will be inspected again, and possibly stamped again by one or two guards. Once you pass this point, you would be well advised not to take photos until you are well and truly in India; the 400 metres of no-man's-land between the two customs posts is a very sensitive area. Begin the short walk across no-man's-land to the border proper. The border is simply a line on the road, rather anticlimactic, but still guarded by soldiers on both sides, standing just a metre or two apart. Check with them if they need to inspect your passport as well - they may well just wave you through. It's just 200 metres now until you reach an Indian security post under the archway bearing a picture of Mahatma Gandhi. Here you'll be herded on to a bus, or given a lift by guards, to Indian passport control. At passport control you will be stamped into India, and then at a customs post you'll almost certainly have you bag searched - you can also change money here too. With this done, you can enter the world's second most populous nation.

Stepping out of the Indian customs post, you step into the tiny village of Attari, where you'll no doubt be assailed by hawkers selling handicrafts and taxi drivers offering a lift into Amritsar (about 32kms away, cost INR 500). After crossing the border, Attari's greatest attraction is undoubtedly the line of refrigerators selling cold drinks.

The journey from India to Pakistan is similar, but the "departure hall" on the Indian side takes longer to navigate – security procedures are lengthy. After clearing passport control you are put on a bus to the border proper, and dropped off on the Indian side before walking across into Pakistan. Once you're in Pakistan you can change money at the NBP (National Bank of Pakistan) building, 400 metres along on the right. Visitors to greet arrivals from India must wait at a holding area about 2 kilometres west of the border. If someone is waiting to greet you at the border, you should make your arrival known to the security guards who will allow your contact to enter the border precinct and meet you.

KASUR
Population: 289,000, Elevation: 218m, Telephone code: 049

Kasur (sometimes spelled Kasoor, or Qasur) is a surprisingly large satellite city of Lahore, near the border with India (map pg. 49). The city features a number of important shrines for anyone interested in the local Punjabi culture. These shrines and their Sufi devotees also mean that Kasur is a great way to sample Pakistan's quasi-religious shrine culture without having to travel further afield.

Because the road is essentially a dead-end - the Indian border can't be crossed here - Kasur is often overlooked as a destination. The road from Lahore used to be an important route towards Delhi, passing Kasur and Ferozepur; the town that gave the road its name. Ferozepur now lies in modern-day India, and Kasur sits in a peculiar cul-de-sac of Pakistan's national highway system.

What to see and do in Kasur
Shrine of Baba Bulleh Shah
Entry free, Always open

Baba Bulleh Shah was a legendary poet and philosopher. Born at Uch Sharif in 1680, he is said to continue to influence poets, writers, singers and even Bollywood directors through his evocative Punjabi, Seraiki and Sindhi musings. Mention his name to any Punjabi and watch their eyes glaze over in a dreamlike trance, and wait for them to start reciting one of his elaborate verses.

When he passed away in 1757 he was buried in Kasur. The shrine now attracts thousands of devotees every day, many of whom believe the auspicious surroundings add something extra to their prayers. Enter through gates to the courtyard; opposite is a mosque, and adjoined to the left is the tomb itself. Inside the tomb expect to see lots of people in solemn thought, and a riot of flower petals adorning the gravesite. Back out in the courtyard you may see incense and candles burning for the departed soul, and you might also see a troupe of musicians and dancers reciting Bulleh Shah's writings as devotional Qawwali (religious songs).

The shrine is in the centre of town, and takes about 10 minutes from the bus station, the shrine of Baba Shah Kamal Chishti or the museum - expect to pay Rs. 100 in an autorickshaw or qingqi.

Shrine of Baba Shah Kamal Chishti
Entry free, Always open

Baba Shah Kamal Chishti was a locally revered saint. He may or may not be related to a much better known saint, Moinuddin Chishti, whose shrine in Ajmer, Rajasthan, India, attracts thousands of visitors each year - more than a few devotees of Kamal Chishti have claimed the link.

The shrine sits atop a hill on the southern outskirts of town, and is populated by dancing and singing Sufi types - although the tomb itself is a small, solemn affair. The hill isn't very high (although it feels high enough while you climb the steps), but it's one of the highest points for miles around, so it affords you a great view over Kasur, and out towards the Indian border.

The shrine is on a hilltop to the south of town, and takes about 10 minutes from the bus station, the shrine of Baba Bulleh Shah - expect to pay Rs. 100 in an autorickshaw or qingqi.

Museum
Entry Rs. 20, Thurs - Tues 10am - 5pm
Not far from the shrine of Baba Shah Kamal Chishti is a small museum recounting the history of Kasur, from the pre-Islamic period to the partition of Pakistan. It takes about 10 minutes to get to the museum - Rs. 100 in an autorickshaw or qingqi.

Ganda Singh Wala Border
15 kilometres southeast of Kasur the Indian border crosses Ferozepur Road. The journey does not end abruptly, but rather with a 2 kilometre series of security checkpoints, roadblocks and watchtowers. The border itself is rather different from that at Wagah - the border here crosses the road diagonally, and the Indian and Pakistani audiences face-off in stands opposite each other.

"Ganda Singh Wala" is actually the name of a locality about a kilometre from the border post. The village's name is in reference to a respected Sikh soldier in the British Indian army in the 19th century. Conversely, and in an apparent act of cross-national/religious friendship, the Indian side of the border and its corresponding settlement "Hussainiwala" is named after a Muslim saint.

The border closing ceremony is for show only, as the border is closed to traffic anyway, and is lower key than the one at Wagah. There's still a fair hare of stomping, saluting and strutting by soldiers, and if you look closely, you'll notice that the design of the border requires Indian and Pakistani soldiers to step into each other's territory for a few minutes while lowering the flags. What are less interesting, however, are the sexist taunts shouted by the men of each audience at the women in the opposing stands - all in the name of patriotism.

The closing ceremony officially starts about 30 minutes before sunset, but this seems to change according to season - usually it's best to be there by about 5pm. Check in Kasur before heading out for the afternoon.

An autorickshaw or qingqi from Kasur (20 minutes) will cost Rs. 300 - 400 for the round trip to the border, including waiting time. The rickshaw will drop you before the checkpoints, from where you walk about 2 kilometres to the border. Note that large bags are not allowed at the border, including camera bags - your rickshaw or qingqi driver may offer to look after them while you are watching the ceremony.

Staying in Kasur
Given the proximity and ease of access from Lahore, few travellers feel the need to stay the night in Kasur.

Eating in Kasur
Kasur's main bazaar, around the shrine of Baba Bulleh Shah, abounds with canteen-style eateries. In the cooler months a local specialty is fried fish, caught from the rivers and canals of the region - ask for *Kasuri machlee* and you'll be pointed in the right direction. In the summer months, ask for "falooda" - an over-the-top dessert drink of jelly, milk, cream, vermicelli noodles, nuts, ice cream and syrupy sherbet. It's served all over Pakistan, but Kasur's is meant to be among the best - just make sure the vendor's shop is clean.

Safety in Kasur
Kasur is a generally safe town - friendly locals are usually surprised to see foreign tourists, and go out of their way to help them out. Don't forget it's still a rural town in Pakistan, and modesty in dress and behaviour goes a long way.

Sufi saints and border bravado
Read about my trip to Kasur! Go to http://urbanduniya.com/traveller/sufi-saints-and-border-bravado-in-kasur/

Getting around Kasur
Autorickshaws and qingqis link the main points around Kasur - nowhere (except Ganda Singh border) costs more than Rs. 150, or takes more than 15 minutes.

Getting to and from Kasur
Kasur's location makes getting here a snap. From any of Lahore's Metrobus stations, head towards Gajjumatta - the last stop to the south (Rs. 20, about 40 minutes from central Lahore). At Gajjumatta you'll see a bunch of minibuses waiting as you exit the Metrobus station - if they don't approach you first, just mention Kasur to one of the drivers and they'll hustle you on to the correct bus to Kasur's dusty bus station (Rs. 40, 45 minutes). From Kasur bus station, autorickshaws and qingqis will be waiting to take you into town for about Rs. 100. The return journey is exactly the same but in reverse - but don't forget that the last bus on the Lahore Metrobus leaves at about 9pm, and Gajjumatta is no place get stranded after dark.

SHEIKHUPURA
Population: 480,000, Elevation: 236m. Telephone code: 056
Sheikhupura *(map pg. 49)* is a medium-sized satellite city of Lahore which hosts a number of factories producing everything from fruit juice bottles to industrial-strength chemicals. It has a long association with the Mughal emperor Jehangir - it was named for one of Jehangir's nicknames "Sheikhu", and stands about 30 kilometres from Jehangir's tomb in Shahdara on the outskirts of Lahore. The most famous sight in town is Hiran Minar.

What to see and do in Sheikhupura
Hiran Minar
Entry Rs. 500, Open sunrise - sunset
If you're looking for inspiration on what to do when your pet deer meets his maker, look no further. Hiran Minar means "Deer Minaret", and indeed, at the base of this 30 metre high stone minaret lies the tomb of Jehangir's beloved pet deer, Mansiraj. The structure was completed in 1606.

Although the minaret is the site's namesake, most visitors come here to admire the large 'tank' (square lake) with an octagonal pavilion in the centre. It is connected to the land near the minaret by a long causeway. Apparently Jehangir's love of animals didn't extend far beyond his own pets, as he used the pavilion as a base while hunting for sport.

The minaret and tank are set among lush gardens which offer welcome respite from the heat in the summer. These gardens were being dug up and replanted when we visited. Early morning is the best time to visit as the pavilion and causeway cast gorgeous reflections on the tank's still water, and the gardens haven't yet filled with day-tripping families. In the afternoon you can take a punt on the tank with one of the pedal-powered boats, or buy snacks from the many vendors which circle the park.

Hiran Minar is about 5 kilometres from the centre of Sheikhupura, and the entrance is via a rural road. Rumours persist that the area is popular with thieves who prey on unsuspecting tourists - it is recommended not to visit alone, or at night time.

Staying in Sheikhupura
Most visitors don't stay in Sheikhupura, preferring to travel from Lahore instead (only 30 kilometres away).

Eating in Sheikhupura
Sheikhupura's main street, around Batti Chowk, abounds with food options - choose from *naan channa* (tandoor bread with chickpea curry) for breakfast, or kebabs with roti for lunch and dinner. There are a few bakeries here too - Gourmet has the usual range of sandwiches, cakes and soft drinks.

Getting around Sheikhupura
Autorickshaws and Qingqis around town or to Hiran Minar should cost Rs. 50 - 100. If you rent the rickshaw to visit Hiran Minar and return, he will ask for about Rs. 800 - 1000 (including waiting time). Bargain hard.

Getting to and from Sheikhupura
Frequent minivans (Hi-Ace) run between Shahdara, the northern terminus of the Lahore Metrobus, and Batti Chowk intersection in central Sheikhupura (Rs. 50, 40 minutes). In Shahdara when you get off the Metrobus, exit the station to the left over the pedestrian bridge, then when you reach the road level ask for transport to Sheikhupura.

When returning simply walk into Sheikhupura's Batti Chowk and mention "Lahore" and you'll be hustled on to a van. Make sure you ask to be dropped off at Shahdara Metrobus Station, as some Lahore-bound vans run all the way to Lari Adda, Lahore's semi-inconvenient local bus stand.

To get to Jandiala Sher Khan, take a van from Batti Chowk (Rs. 50, 30 minutes).

JANDIALA SHER KHAN
Population: 11,000, Elevation: 210m, Telephone code: 056
Jandiala Sher Khan *(map pg. 49)* is a village about 20 kilometres northwest of Sheikhupura where legendary Punjabi poet Waris Shah was born in 1722. He died in 1798 in a village near Pakpattan which now hosts a shrine (pg. 118), but was laid to rest in Jandiala Sher Khan. His mausoleum is something of a pilgrimage site for lovers of the Sufi-influenced writer of which there are many.

What to see and do in Jandiala Sher Khan
Waris Shah Mausoleum
Entry free, Always open
This squat, red brick mausoleum was completed in 1978 after the long-term neglect of the previous tomb at this site. The building and surrounding pretty gardens are in contemporary Mughal style, and are a popular destination for Sufi devotees and poetry aficionados. To reach here ask locals for directions when you get off the van. The tomb is about 200 metres from the main road, about a 5 minute walk.

Staying in Jandiala Sher Khan
Most visitors don't sleep in Jandiala Sher Khan, instead making it a day trip from Lahore, and combining it with Sheikhupura.

Eating in Jandiala Sher Khan
Cheap, basic eateries are on the main street of town.

Getting around Jandiala Sher Khan
Jandiala Sher Khan is small enough to navigate on foot - from the main road to Waris Shah's mausoleum is about 200 metres.

Getting to and from Jandiala Sher Khan
Hi-Ace vans run from Sheikhupura's Batti Chowk (Rs. 50, 30 minutes) and the main street of Jandiala Sher Khan regularly. At Batti Chowk ask for Jandiala Sher Khan and you'll be pointed in the right direction.

From Lahore, some minivans run between Shahdara, the northern terminus of the Lahore Metrobus, and Jandiala Sher Khan (Rs. 100, 1 hour). In Shahdara when you get off the Metrobus, exit the station to the left over the pedestrian bridge, then when you reach the road level ask for transport to Jandiala Sher Khan. If no transport to Jandiala Sher Khan is available, board a van for Sheikhupura (pg. 68) and change there.

To get back from Jandiala Sher Khan, stand on the main road and flag down the minivans as they approach - shout the name "Sheikhupura" or "Lahore", and if they're heading your way, they'll stop. Going to Lahore it might be easier to get a van to Sheikhupura and change. If you are going to Lahore ask to be dropped off at Shahdara Metrobus Station, as some Lahore-bound vans run all the way to Lari Adda, Lahore's semi-inconvenient local bus stand.

GUJRANWALA
Population: 1.9 million, Elevation: 214m, Telephone code: 055
While Gujranwala is an important industrial city on the road between Lahore and Islamabad, we would be lying if we told you there are any outstanding tourist attractions here. Sure, there are a handful of shopping centres, lots of shrines and pretty mosques, and even a temple or two, but none are worth a special trip here, especially if you're coming from culturally-richer Lahore. Gujranwala is sometimes called the 'city of food', but is better known as being home to some of Pakistan's best wrestlers - however neither fact is well represented in tourist-friendly form. Nevertheless many business travellers do find themselves here at some point, so we have provided some basic information about where to stay, eat and how to get around.

Staying in Gujranwala
Economy
Lepari Hotel: Khawaja Plaza, Sheranwala Bagh, GT Road; (+92) 055-4235701; www.lepari.com.pk
map pg. 71, Dbl Rs. 2,000
A just ok option on the main road of the city, with a restaurant.

Luxury
Shelton Hotel: Opposite Gulshan Iqbal Park, GT Road; (+92) 055-3259501; www.sheltonhotel.com
map pg. 71, Dbl Rs. 5,000
The best place to rest your head in Gujranwala - three restaurants including cafe style dining, Pakistani grill and Middle Eastern diner, plus wifi internet access.

Eating in Gujranwala
Gujranwala Food Street and Sialkoti Gate *(map pg. 71)* in the centre of the city are well known for eateries - lots of spicy biryani, kebabs of all sorts (try quail kebab if you're game), and deep fried snacks. There are also the usual international chains littered along GT Road, to the north of the centre.

Services in Gujranwala
Banks
Standard Chartered: Trust Plaza, G.T. Road *(map pg. 71)*

Internet Cafe
There's a dearth of good internet cafes in Gujranwala - ask at your hotel for a nearby recommendation.

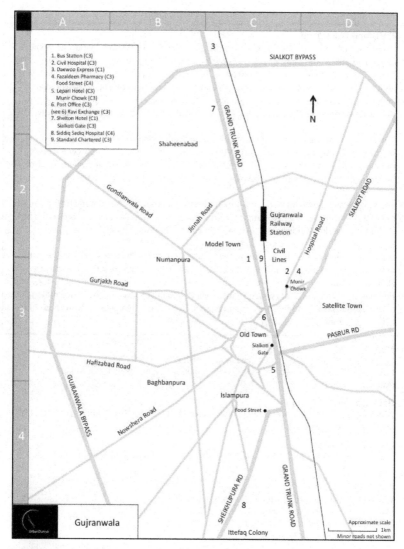

1. Bus Station (C3)
2. Civil Hospital (C3)
3. Daewoo Express (C1)
4. Fazaldeen Pharmacy (C3)
   Food Street (C4)
5. Lepari Hotel (C3)
   Munir Chowk (C3)
6. Post Office (C3)
   (see 6) Ravi Exchange (C3)
7. Shelton Hotel (C1)
   Sialkoti Gate (C3)
8. Siddiq Sadiq Hospital (C4)
9. Standard Chartered (C3)

SIALKOT BYPASS

N

GRAND TRUNK ROAD

Shaheenabad

Gondlanwala Road

Jinnah Road

Gujranwala
Railway
Station

SIALKOT ROAD

Model Town

Numanpura

Civil
Lines

1 9

2 4

Munir
Chowk

Hospital Road

Gurjakh Road

Satellite Town

6

PASRUR RD

Old Town

Sialkoti
Gate

Hafizabad Road

5

Baghbanpura

Islampura

GUJRANWALA BYPASS

Nowshera Road

Food Street

SHEIKHUPURA RD

GRAND TRUNK ROAD

Gujranwala

8

Ittefaq Colony

Approximate scale
1km
Minor roads not shown

Money Exchange
Ravi Exchange: 147 Ali Block, opp. Yasir Cloth Market, Chowk Bank Sq.; (+92) 055-4218268; *(map pg. 71)*

Post Office
G.T. Road, Gujranwala *(map pg. 71)*

Help in Gujranwala
Safety
Gujranwala is a surprisingly conservative city, and foreigners are rare. Be particularly sensitive to the local culture here, and at times of political tension, it might be advisable to base yourself in Lahore and commute here for business trips.

The Grand Trunk Road
Leaving Lahore towards the north or west, you can either take the marvellous motorway, or you can opt for the more direct, but slower Grand Trunk Road (known as G.T. Road). The Grand Trunk Road dates back to early times, but was significantly rebuilt by Sher Shah Suri in the 16th century, and consolidated by the British as a method of linking the colonial Indian capital of Calcutta to Kabul in Afghanistan. Don't expect too much nostalgia if you take this route - while the route still exists in its entirety, it is now a four-lane highway.

Whether you choose the motorway or G.T. Road, you'll probably leave Lahore on the motorway anyway as a method to cross the Ravi River (and to avoid the clogged streets of the Walled City). About 5 kilometres west of the river crossing, the motorway forks, with one spur joining G.T. Road, and the other continuing on towards Islamabad.

The motorway is fairly uninteresting until it nears Islamabad, but G. T. Road offers a couple of points of interest in Central Punjab. From Lahore, the first major centres you'll cross are the unremarkable Muridke and Kamoke, followed by Gujranwala, and then Gujrat.

Gujranwala forms part of what is sometimes called Pakistan's "business triangle", with the enterprising cities of Gujrat and Sialkot (off G.T. Road) making up the other two points. None are major tourist destinations in their own right, but their strong trade links draw in a number of business travellers each year (enough for Sialkot to have its own international airport, for example). Additionally, their distance from Lahore make Gujranwala and Gujrat convenient stops on the road from Lahore to Islamabad.

Medical Services
Siddiq Sadiq Medical Hospital: Sheikhupura Road; (+92) 055-4270002 *(map pg. 71)*
Fazaldeen Pharmacy, as well as other 24-hour pharmacies, are available at Munir Chowk near the civil hospital *(map pg. 71)*

Getting around Gujranwala
A rickshaw around the centre should not cost more than Rs. 100 (probably less), or Rs. 150 out to the Daewoo Stand.

Leaving Gujranwala
The Daewoo Express bus station is on GT Road to the northern edge of town *(map pg. 71)*. The local bus station is located in the centre of town *(map pg. 71)*.

Bus
Lahore: Daewoo Express, 1 hour 35 minutes, Rs. 320
Rawalpindi/Islamabad: Daewoo Express, 3 hours 15 minutes, Rs. 750
Sialkot: Daewoo Express, 1 hours 15 minutes, Rs. 200
Gujrat: Daewoo Express, 50 minutes, Rs. 150
Jhelum: Local buses from Gujranwala's local bus station, 2 hours, Rs. 250
Faisalabad: Local buses from Gujranwala's local bus station, 4 hours, Rs. 350

GUJRAT
Population: 738,558, Elevation: 224m, Telephone code: 053
On the banks of the Chenab River, Gujrat is slightly more attractive than the other major cities between Lahore and Islamabad, but still does not boast lots of attractions to make the trip worthwhile. Gujrat is noted for its pottery and ceramics, but the enterprising businesses that sell them tend to be brick-pit-esque wholesalers, not boutique tourist-oriented business. Business travellers, especially industrial or agricultural engineers, might end up here for meetings, and Gujrat makes a logical halfway-point to break the trip between Lahore and Islamabad - if you must.

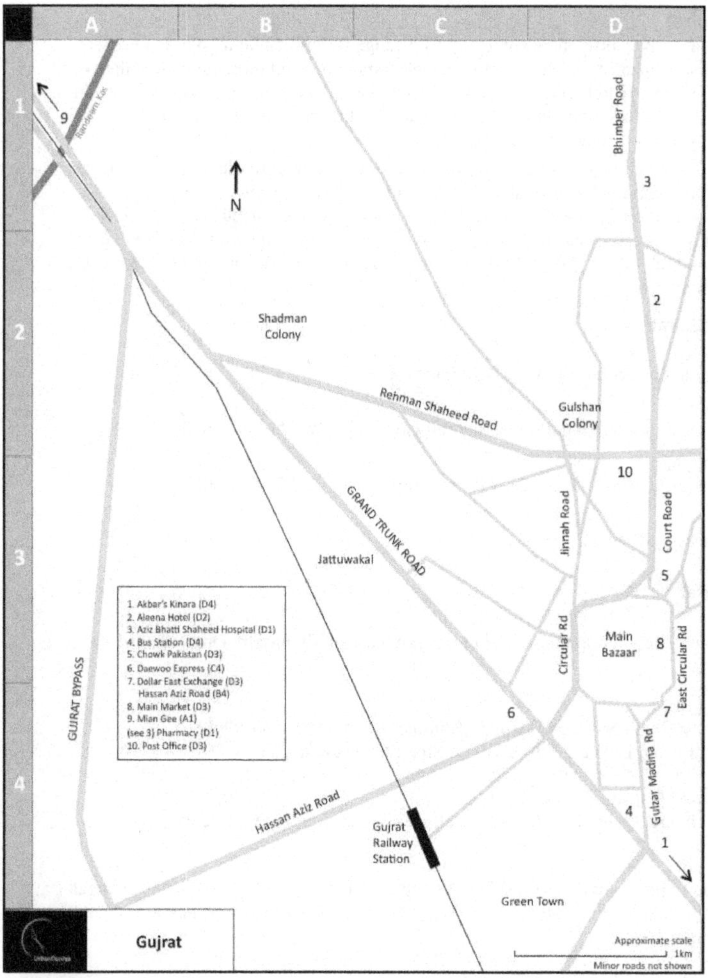
A
B
C
D
1
2
3
4
N
Bhimber Road
Shadman Colony
Rehman Shaheed Road
Gulshan Colony
GRAND TRUNK ROAD
Jattuwakal
Jinnah Road
Court Road
Circular Rd
Main Bazaar
East Circular Rd
Gulzar Madina Rd
GUJRAT BYPASS
Hassan Aziz Road
Gujrat Railway Station
Green Town
1. Akbar's Kinara (D4)
2. Aleena Hotel (D2)
3. Aziz Bhatti Shaheed Hospital (D1)
4. Bus Station (D4)
5. Chowk Pakistan (D3)
6. Daewoo Express (C4)
7. Dollar East Exchange (D3)
Hassan Aziz Road (B4)
8. Main Market (D3)
9. Mian Gee (A1)
(see 3) Pharmacy (D1)
10. Post Office (D3)
Gujrat
Approximate scale
1km
Minor roads not shown

Staying in Gujrat

Economy

Akbar's Kinara: GT Road, Chenab Riverbank, Gujrat; (+92) 053-3589111; www.akbarskinara.com

map pg. 73, Dbl Rs. 6600>, Suite Rs. 8,200>

Three restaurants, a health club and a beauty salon make this a good option, although the location isn't exactly convenient for the city of Gujrat.

Luxury

Hotel One: Mall of Gujrat, GT Road, Gujrat; (+92) 0341-2201111; www.hotelone.com.pk

map pg. 73, Dbl $121>

Pearl Continental's budget business brand.

Eating in Gujrat

If you're in the city centre, there are lots of mid-range and downmarket places to eat at Chowk Pakistan, near Main Market. If you want something a bit more upmarket, then there is **Akbar's Kinara Hotel** with three restaurants serving Pakistani, Continental and Chinese dishes *(map pg. 73)*, ten kilometres to the northwest on the banks of the Chenab River. KFC is also here, if you are longing for foreign fast food.

Mian Gee is a roadside restaurant 20 minutes out of Gujrat towards Jhelum on GT Road *(map pg. 73)*. It's famous for its dhal; travellers on GT Road faithfully stop here to mop up their plates of the scrumptious lentils with fresh tandoor-cooked bread. To get there from Gujrat, you would need your own transport, or negotiate a spot in a mini van from Gujrat's local bus stand (about Rs. 70). Ask to go to the village of Kharian and mention "Mian Gee" - everyone knows it.

Services in Gujrat

Banks

No international banks have representation in Gujrat.

Internet Cafe

There's a bunch of internet cafes near the railway station, on Hassan Aziz Rd *(map pg. 73)*.

Money Exchange

Dollar East: East Circular Rd, Ashraf Plaza, Timbal Chowk; 053-3510487 *(map pg. 73)*.

Post Office

Rehman Shaheed Road, Gujrat *(map pg. 73)*.

Help in Gujrat

Safety

Gujrat sees very few foreign tourists, but it is not particularly unsafe. Dress and behave responsibly.

Medical Services

Hospital: Aziz Bhatti Shaheed Hospital: Bhimber Road, (+92) 053-9260101; *(map pg. 73)*.
24 Hour Pharmacy: is near the Aziz Bhatti Shaheed Hospital

Getting around Gujrat

Rickshaws charge around Rs. 100 for couple of kilometres around the centre.

Leaving Gujrat

The Daewoo Express station is on GT Road in the centre *(map pg. 73)*. The local "general" bus stand is further south down GT Road – it's walking distance, or a rickshaw costs around Rs. 50 *(map pg. 73)*.

Bus

Lahore: Daewoo Express, 2 hours 15 minutes, Rs. 500
Rawalpindi/Islamabad: Daewoo Express, 2 hours, Rs. 550
Sialkot: Daewoo Express, 1 hour 15 minutes, Rs. 400
Gujranwala: Daewoo Express, 50 minutes, Rs. 150
Jhelum: Daewoo Express, 50 minutes, Rs. 150
Faisalabad: Local buses from Gujrat's general bus stand, 2 hours, Rs. 500

SIALKOT

Population: 1.7 million, Elevation: 256m, Telephone code: 052

Sialkot is probably the most pleasant of the cities directly to the north of Lahore, with a lovely old clock tower, ruins of a fort, cathedral, Sikh shrine and a museum devoted to philosopher-poet Sir Muhammad Allama Iqbal, who hailed from this city. While there's not a lot to draw you here specifically, it's not a bad place to end up for a day or two, especially if you're here on business.

What to see in Sialkot

Clock tower
map pg. 76

160 years old, this clock tower is in pure British style but infused with a touch of Mughal elegance. It's a focal point for the city, and makes for pretty photos, especially when it's draped in coloured lights for a festival of some sort.

Iqbal Manzil (Allama Iqbal's birthplace and museum)
Iqbal Manzil Road, map pg. 76, Rs. 200, Open 12pm to 5pm

Iqbal Manzil is the birthplace of visionary philosopher-poet Sir Muhammad "Allama" Iqbal, the man who first floated the idea of Pakistan in the first half of the twentieth century. Bought by his grandfather in the nineteenth century, the house was bought by the government of Pakistan in 1971. After a restoration process, it opened as a museum dedicated to all things Iqbal in 1977. Containing a modest collection of books, scribbled poems, autographs, photos and a couple of curios, foreign visitors could easily overlook the importance of this place to the idea of Pakistani statehood. Important though it may be, Iqbal Manzil might not be your personal highlight of Pakistan unless you have an interest in Pakistani historical identity.

Sialkot Fort
map pg. 76, Open 24 hours

There's hardly anything left of this old fort, which was built in the second century by the Hindu rulers of the region. Dating technology has shown parts of the wall to date back over 5,000 years, suggesting that the site may have existed in another form for much, much longer than the remaining fort. Over the centuries it has been captured, recaptured and captured again by feuding empires, all of which has sadly taken a toll on one of Pakistan's oldest standing structures. With so little left to see, it might only interest historians.

Holy Trinity Cathedral Church (Sialkot Cathedral)
map pg. 76, free, Open 9am - 4pm

This old church, dating back to 1852, was of course built during the British period and is an important piece of colonial architecture in Pakistan. It is frequented by members of Sialkot's significant Christian community, and as a result it is subject to heightened security.

Baba Bari Sahib (Sikh Shrine)
map pg. 76, free, Unauthorised entry prohibited

An old Sikh Shrine on Sankhatra Road, way out past the old city. Don't expect to be let in unless you are Sikh or have a contact who knows someone - security is generally high at Sikh sites in Pakistan.

Staying in Sialkot

Backpacker
Royal Guest House: Paris Rd, Anwar St, opp. P.O. Kutchery; (+92) 052-4261225; www.royalghouse.com
map pg. 76, Rs. 2500

Like staying in someone's home! Comfortable lodging with a restaurant offering Pakistani, continental and Chinese food, and wifi. Breakfast is included in the rates.

Economy
Hotel Taj Palace: Kutchery Road; (+92) 052-4270034; www.taj.com.pk
map pg. 76, Cost Dbl US$70

Large, airy, clean rooms, a coffee shop and a restaurant, and even a swimming pool (although we're not sure how often it gets used).

Hotel Spring Height: 97-A, Aziz Bhatti Shaheed Road, Cantonment; (+92) 052-4261910
map pg. 76, Rs. 4,500

Large clean rooms in this motel-style building. Out of the main centre.

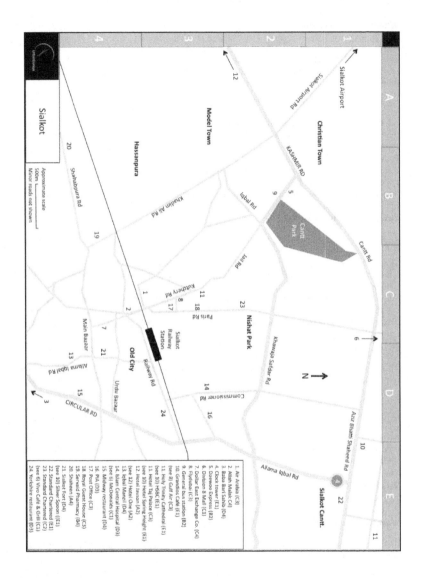

Sialkot

Approximate scale
500m
Minor roads not shown

1. Air Arabia (C3)
2. Allah Malak (C4)
3. Baba Bari Saho (D4)
4. Clock tower (E1)
5. Daewoo Express (B2)
6. Division 8 Mall (C1)
7. Dollar East Exchange Co. (C4)
8. Flydubai (C3)
9. General bus station (B2)
10. Grandos Café (E1)
(see 8) Gulf Air (C3)
11. Holy Trinity Cathedral (E1)
(see 10) HSBC (E1)
11. Hotel Taj Palace (C3)
(see 10) Hotel Spring Height (E1)
12. Hotel Javson (A2)
(see 12) Hotel One (A4)
13. Iqbal Manzi (D4)
14. Islam Central Hospital (D3)
(see 6) McDonalds (C1)
15. Midway restaurant (D4)
16. PIA (D3)
17. Post Office (C3)
18. Royal Guest House (C3)
19. Serwaiz Pharmacy (B4)
20. Shaheen (A4)
21. Sialkot Fort (D4)
(see 10) Silver Spoon (E1)
22. Standard Chartered (E1)
23. Standard Chartered (C2)
(see 6) Vivo Café & Grill (C1)
24. Yorkshire restaurant (D3)

Luxury

Hotel Javson: Defence Road; (+92) 052-324-2971; www.hoteljavson.com
map pg. 76, Rs. 12,000
This is a really nice hotel - large comfy rooms, indoor pool, gym, restaurant, wifi... one of Sialkot's best.

Hotel One: Rauf Towers, Wazirabad Road; (+92) 0341-2201111; www.hotelone.com.pk
map pg. 76, Cost Rs. 12,000
A business hotel by the Pearl Continental chain - all the appointments you would expect.

Eating in Sialkot

Sialkot has no "food street" as such, but rather a series of eating hubs where you can find great bites. Division 8 shopping mall in Cantt has lots of western-style eateries like **Vivo Cafe & Grill** as well as **McDonalds**, while about a kilometre east, near the clock tower, are a bunch of nice restaurants like **Grandiose Cafe** and **Silver Spoon**. Circular Road near the corner with Main Bazaar has a line of eateries like **Midway**. Finally, east and west of the railway station are some good places serving typical Pakistani fare; **Allah Malak** and **Yorkshire** both have good reputations *(all map pg. 76)*.

Services in Sialkot

Airlines
Air Arabia: Sonya Travels, Bashir Plaza, Islamia Clg. Rd; (+92) 0528-0076692 *(map pg. 76)*
Flydubai: 1 Abdullah Trade Center, Kutchery Road; (+92) 0524-273464 *(map pg. 76)*
Gulf Air: Abdullah Trade Ctr, Shop 15-G, Ground Flr, Kutchery Rd; (+92) 052-4268428 *(map pg. 76)*
Pakistan International: Jinnah Islamia College Road,; (+92) 0524-583701 *(map pg. 76)*
Shaheen: 18 Shahab Center, Shahbpura Road, Sialkot; (+92) 0524-3241531 *(map pg. 76)*

Banks
HSBC: Qayyum Trade Center, Aziz Bhatti Shaheed Road, Sialkot Cantt *(map pg. 76)*.
Standard Chartered: Aziz Bhatti Shaheed Road, Sialkot Cantt *(map pg. 76)*.
Standard Chartered: SCCI Road, Paris Road *(map pg. 76)*.

Internet Cafe
Lahore Net Café *(map pg. 76)* is one of a handful of good internet cafes in the neighbourhood directly south of the clock tower.

Money Exchange
Dollar East Exchange: Bano Bazar; (+92) 052-4581561; dollareast.com; *(map pg. 76)*.

Post Office
Paris Road, Sialkot *(map pg. 76)*.

Help in Sialkot

Safety
Sialkot is not especially dangerous, but it doesn't see a lot of casual (i.e. - non business) travellers, so be prepared for lots of curiosity and behave and dress appropriately.

Medical Services
Islam Central Hospital: Commissioner Road, Sialkot (+92) 052-4604948 *(map pg. 76)*.
Servaid Pharmacy: Khadim Ali Road *(map pg. 76)*.

Getting around Sialkot
Expect to pay no more than Rs. 100 for a rickshaw around the centre, or Rs. 150 to Cantt.

Leaving Sialkot
The Daewoo station is on Jail Road in the north *(map pg. 76)*. The local bus station is opposite *(map pg. 76)*.

Bus
Lahore: Daewoo Express, 3 hours, Rs. 520
Rawalpindi/Islamabad: Daewoo Express, 4 hours 45 minutes, Rs. 850
Gujranwala: Daewoo Express, 1 hour 15 minutes, Rs. 200
Gujrat: Daewoo Express, 1 hour 15 minutes, Rs. 400
Faisalabad: Daewoo Express, 4 hours 45 minutes, Rs. 770
Jhelum: Daewoo Express,1 hours 45 minutes, Rs. 320

Islamabad
and Northern Punjab

Northern Punjab is a hilly area, with a population more sparsely distributed than in the central and southern regions. Islamabad and Rawalpindi form an anchor to this region, and make a good base from which to begin a tour. To the south of the cities lies the Potohar Plateau, an undulating tableland which fills the space between Khyber Pukhtoonkhwa and the Jhelum River. It is known for the huge Rohtas Fort, the serene Katas Raj Temples and the Salt Range.

As the Potohar mountains approach the border of Khyber Pukhtoonkhwa, the countryside becomes more barren and the society more cosmopolitan, yet more conservative. You'll see a couple of burka-clad women among the scores of turbaned men outside the Panja Sahib Sikh Gurdwara, and at Taxila lies an ancient Buddhist civilisation. In the hills north of Islamabad, the terrain becomes increasingly rugged and densely forested forming the tranquil foothills of the Himalaya and Karakoram Ranges.

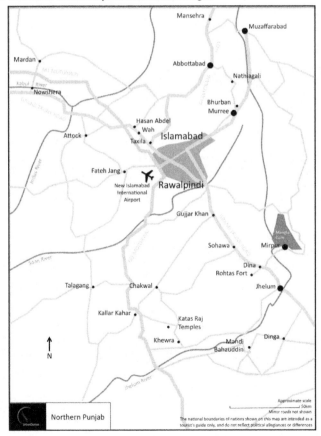

ISLAMABAD and RAWALPINDI

Population: 4.5 million, Elevation: 510m, Telephone code: 051

If you are arriving directly into Islamabad International Airport, you will have a choice of bedding down in either the capital or Rawalpindi, the large military city just 15 kms to the south. The cities are two sides of the one Pakistani coin; Rawalpindi was a garrison city, with chaotic, dusty bazaars filling in the spaces between famous academies and institutes. Islamabad on the other hand is the bureaucratic heart of the nation, imposed by lush hills, bountiful nature reserves, upscale commercial districts and the opulent Shah Faisal Mosque. All of the above considered, Islamabad and Rawalpindi offer a microcosm Pakistan in a neat package.

Rawalpindi has been inhabited for a very very long time, dating back to the days of Taxila, however the city was named Rawalpindi in 1493 and developed under Muslim rule. After the Sikh conquests of the 18th and 19th centuries it developed further, and in 1849 the British marched in and declared it a garrison of the colonial army. It remained a sleepy, if heavily militarised place until 1959 when it was made interim capital of Pakistan while Islamabad was being built to the north. With that, a population boom started, and has hardly stopped since, with the two cities beginning to merge into one large urban agglomeration.

Orientation

The cities of Islamabad and Rawalpindi are like chalk and cheese, not just in character, but in layout too.

The main boulevard of Islamabad is weirdly known as the Blue Area, while the city is bounded on its southern edge by the Kashmir Highway, and on the northern fringe by the Margalla Hills. To the far eastern end is the parliamentary district and the diplomatic enclave; entire swathes of the city which can't be entered without appropriate security checks.

Islamabad is set out on a grid pattern, skewed diagonally along the bases of the hills. Districts are known by their coordinates in the grid; running 5 to 18 east to west, and B to I from north to south. So G-6 is the name of a district, as is E-11. The grid hasn't completely filled out with development yet; anything west of column 11 is interspersed with farmland, while rows north of E are partly obstructed by the Margalla Hills.

Confusing though it may be, Islamabadis have also developed names for these 'suburbs' according to the market at the centre of each. For a tourist, the most important areas are G-7 (Sitara Market) and G-6 (Melody Market), where lots of hotels are; F-7 (Jinnah Super Market) and F-6 (Super Market), where there are lots of shopping and eating options. In addition to this, each sector has 'quarters', so the address "F-6/3" means "Sector F-6, quarter 3". In the middle the Blue Area is a kind of built-up city centre.

In stark contrast to Islamabad, Rawalpindi is a mess of curved roads, thoroughfares and highways with no real focal point except for the military headquarters on the Grand Trunk Road. For tourists, the main areas of interest are Saddar and the Grand Trunk Road, where the museums, military headquarters, and a glut of hotels are located, and the Daewoo Express Terminal way out to the west of town on GT Road.

What to see in Islamabad
Shah Faisal Mosque
map pg. 82, Free, Open sunrise – late

Pakistan's biggest mosque was designed to be the national mosque of this proud country. Built in a modern design inspired by a bedouin tent, and featuring four soaring minarets (90 metres tall), the mosque has a beautiful setting against the backdrop of the green Margalla hills. It was opened in 1986, has come to be a symbol of the capital and the modern Pakistani state. Approaching the mosque from the main street, you walk through parkland and into the mosque grounds - don't forget to remove your shoes. The courtyard has a reported capacity of 200,000, filled during events such as Eid prayers. The cavernous prayer hall, a strikingly modern yet iconically classic design, can hold 74,000 faithful - entrance is

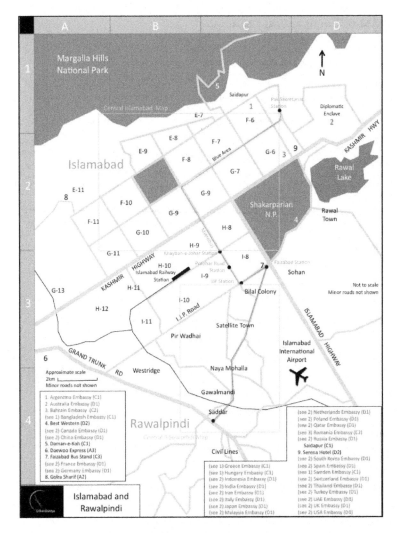

The map contains the following labels:

Margalla Hills National Park

Islamabad

Saidapur
Pak Secretariat Station
Diplomatic Enclave
E-7
F-6
E-8
F-7
E-9
F-8
Blue Area
G-6
KASHMIR HWY
G-7
Rawal Lake
E-11
F-10
G-9
Shakarparian N.P.
Rawal Town
F-11
G-9
G-10
H-8
Rawalpindi
G-11
H-9
I-8
Khayban-e-Johar Station
Peshawar Road Station
Faizabad Station
Sohan
H-10
Islamabad Railway Station
I-9
UP Station
Not to scale
Minor roads not shown
KASHMIR HIGHWAY
H-11
G-13
Bilal Colony
H-12
I-10
I.J.P. Road
Satellite Town
ISLAMABAD HIGHWAY
I-11
Pir Wadhai
Islamabad International Airport
GRAND TRUNK RD
Westridge
Naya Mohalla
Approximate scale
2km
Minor roads not shown
Gawalmandi
Saddar
Rawalpindi
Central Islamabad Map
Civil Lines

1. Argentina Embassy (C1)
2. Australia Embassy (D1)
3. Bahrain Embassy (C2)
(see 1) Bangladesh Embassy (C1)
4. Best Western (D2)
(see 2) Canada Embassy (D1)
(see 2) China Embassy (D1)
5. Daman-e-Koh (C1)
6. Daewoo Express (A3)
7. Faizabad Bus Stand (C3)
(see 2) France Embassy (D1)
(see 2) Germany Embassy (D1)
8. Golra Sharif (A2)

(see 1) Greece Embassy (C1)
(see 1) Hungary Embassy (C1)
(see 2) Indonesia Embassy (D1)
(see 2) Iran Embassy (D1)
(see 2) Italy Embassy (D1)
(see 2) Japan Embassy (D1)
(see 2) Malaysia Embassy (D1)

(see 2) Netherlands Embassy (D1)
(see 2) Poland Embassy (D1)
(see 2) Qatar Embassy (D1)
(see 3) Romania Embassy (E2)
(see 2) Russia Embassy (D1)
Saidapur (C1)
9. Serena Hotel (D2)
(see 2) South Korea Embassy (D1)
(see 2) Spain Embassy (D1)
(see 1) Sweden Embassy (C1)
(see 2) Switzerland Embassy (D1)
(see 2) Thailand Embassy (D1)
(see 2) Turkey Embassy (D1)
(see 2) UAE Embassy (D1)
(see 2) UK Embassy (D1)
(see 2) USA Embassy (D1)

Islamabad and Rawalpindi

via the eastern wall. While everyone is welcome here, it makes sense not to visit during prayer times. A particularly evocative time to visit is in the hour before sunset, when the silhouette of the mosque's clean lines against the milky caramel sky, and the reflection of the sun's light off the shiny tiled floors make for excellent photographs. Back out the front, and towards the east lies the mausoleum of military ruler Zia ul-Haq, who was buried here in 1988.

Daman-e-Koh
map pg. 80, Free
Daman-e-Koh is a mountain lookout just to the north of Islamabad, affording great panoramic views across the city on a clear day. From up here, you can really get a good perspective on how close Shah Faisal Mosque is to the Margalla Hills; it's like looking

down on a toy town. Sometimes monkeys are present in the gardens stretching back from the lookout point, but the area is always full of picnicking families and couples. There are also places to buy souvenirs, and overpriced food and drink. Taxis will probably drop you off in the parking lot. Walk past the line of stalls and up to the lookout for the best views, and don't be afraid to explore along the edge of the mountain; there are lots more vantage points further along. Quite a bit further up the hill is Monal Restaurant - a nice place to sit back, chow down on a meal or unwind with a cup of chai, and watch life in Islamabad unfold in the distance. Pay around Rs. 400 to get here from central Islamabad

Shakarparian Hills and the Pakistan Monument
map pg. 82, free
The Shakarparian Park, sprawled over the Shakarparian Hills in the centre of Islamabad and Rawalpindi, is a pretty and somewhat secluded break from the cities outside, attracting families and couples at the weekend. On a hilltop in the Shakarparian Hills lies the Pakistan Monument, a four-leafed half-flower representing the four provinces of Pakistan, with three smaller petals representing the three territories. Built between 2004 and 2007, and without the auspicious location of, say, Lahore's Minar-e-Pakistan, the monument lacks the gravitas that you might expect. However it has come to be (and continues to become) something of a symbol of the twin cities of Islamabad and Rawalpindi, but still lags behind Shah Faisal Mosque in terms of instant recognition. Pay about Rs. 200 to get here from central Islamabad.

Golra Sharif
map pg. 80, Free, Open sunrise - late
Meher Ali Shah was a respected Sufi scholar who lived from 1859 to 1937. He was born and lived in a small village called Golra approximately 20 kilometres from Rawalpindi. During his life he wrote several important works, and gained prominence for his criticism of breakaway movements within Muslim society. Golra Sharif, as it is now referred to ('sharif' means 'noble', referring to the presence of a shrine), is now almost swallowed up by modern Islamabad's E-11 sector. His shrine is a simple white marble construction that attracts devotees and represents one of Islamabad's few 'historic' sights. Pay Rs. 400 to get here from central Islamabad.

Saidpur Village
map pg. 80, free
This small village in a crevice of the Margalla Hills has been here for longer than anyone really knows, and as a result has an intriguing, if limited historical legacy. What remains in the village are a Hindu temple, Sikh gurdwara, and a Sufi shrine. Since 2006 the site has been the subject of development by the Islamabad local government, encouraging tourism to the otherwise unassuming village. What has resulted are three distinct 'areas' to be explored. The first is on the left as you climb the hill out of Islamabad, and really just resembles an ordinary Pakistani village. Continue further up the hill, and at the end of the main road is the preserved Hindu temple, now surrounded by a glut of slightly fancy restaurants. Look back down the hill and you can see a few tall buildings from Islamabad; this is a nice spot to escape the city for a while and have dinner. Across the stream is the third area of Saidpur which is more of a model Pakistani village, allowing the urbanites to taste rural life for a day, plus a handful of craft shops and art galleries. Pay Rs. 200 to get here in a taxi from central Islamabad, and consider staying for a meal at one of the restaurants.

What to see in Rawalpindi
Army Museum
map pg. 84, US$1, Open 9am - 1pm, 2pm - 4pm
Rawalpindi's Army Museum is one of Pakistan's largest museums. It houses relics from both the colonial and independent eras, paying tribute to one of Pakistan's most important national institutions.

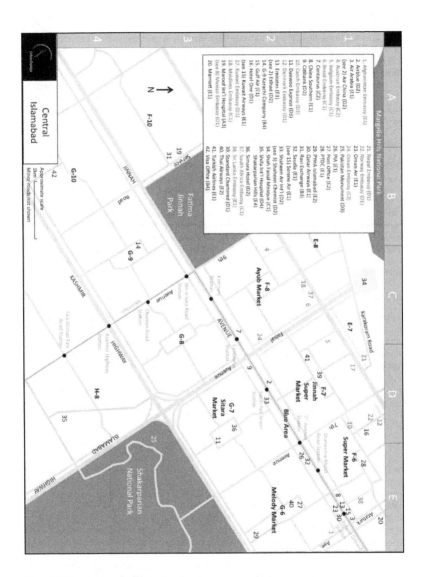

map pg. 84, Entry free, Open 9am – 5pm

Central Islamabad

N →

Approximate scale
1km
Minor roads not shown

Margalla Hills National Park

1. Afghanistan Embassy (E1)
2. Airblue (D2)
3. Air Arabia (E1)
4. (see 2) Air China (D2)
5. Belgium Embassy (C2)
6. Brazil Embassy (C1)
7. Centaurus (C2)
8. China Southern (E1)
9. Citibank (D2)
10. Czech Embassy (D1)
11. Daewoo Express (D3)
12. Denmark Embassy (D1)
13. Emirates (E1)
14. G-9 Karachi Company (B4)
15. Gulf Air (E1)
16. Hotel One (D1)
17. (see 15) Kuwait Airways (E1)
18. Maldives Embassy (D1)
19. Maroof Int'l Hospital (A3)
20. Marriott (E1)
21. Nepal Embassy (D1)
22. Norway Embassy (D1)
23. Oman Air (E1)
24. Oman Embassy (C2)
25. Pakistan Monument (D3)
26. PIA (E1)
27. Post Office (E2)
28. PTDC (E1)
29. PPMA Islamabad (E2)
30. Qatar Airways (E1)
31. Raw Exchange (B3)
32. Saudia (E1)
33. (see 15) Serene Air (E1)
34. Shaheen Air Int'l (D2)
35. (see 3) Shaheen Chemist (D2)
36. Shah Faisal Mosque (C1)
37. Shifa Int'l Hospital (D4)
38. (see 3) Shaheen Hills (E4)
36. Simsara Hotel (D2)
37. South Africa Embassy (C3)
38. Sri Lanka Embassy (E1)
39. Standard Chartered (D1)
40. Thai Airways (A3)
41. Turkish Airlines (E1)
42. Visa Office (B4)

Fatima Jinnah Park

Shakarparian National Park

Murree Brewery

map pg. 84, Entry free, Open 9am – 5pm

If you are not a Muslim and can prove it then you are welcome to come in and visit this surprisingly well-established brewery, and try a bit of Pakistan's only legally home-made beer.

Parks and memorials

Those with a dark sense of humour would say Rawalpindi is known for killing politicians. Three of Pakistan's democratic leaders have met their fate in this city. The first prime minister, Liaqat Ali Khan, was shot in a park after addressing a rally in 1951; the park was subsequently named after him. Socialist leader Zulfiqar Ali Bhutto was hanged in a Rawalpindi prison in 1979 after being overthrown by his own army general two years earlier. And in 2007 Bhutto's daughter Benazir, who held office twice in the 1990s, was killed in terrorist attack after addressing a campaign rally in Liaqat Ali Khan Park. Benazir Bhutto has since been immortalised in the form of several landmarks renamed after her since 2007. Islamabad's international airport is named Benazir Bhutto Shaheed International Airport - '*shaheed*' means 'martyr'.

Needless to say, Liaqat Ali Khan Park *(map pg. 84, Free, Open 24 hours)* has two memorials to its sad history, while Jinnah Park *(map pg. 84, Free, Open 24 hours)* hosts a memorial to Zulfiqar Ali Bhutto. To get here, take a rickshaw from anywhere in the city.

Staying in Islamabad and Rawalpindi
Backpacker
PYHA Islamabad: Shaheed-e-Millat Road, Aabpara, G-6/4, Islamabad; (+92) 051-2824628
Islamabad, map pg. 82, Dorm Rs. 1,500
Islamabad's original traveller's hostel is basic and a bit old, but it's still the only true backpackers in town

Simara Hotel Islamabad: Sitara Market, G-7 Markaz, Islamabad; (+92) 051-2204555
Islamabad, map pg. 82, Sgl Rs. 2,000
Sitara is a basic but functional and quiet hotel bear Islamabad's blue zone.

Economy
Hotel One Islamabad: 18 Street 26, F-6/2, Islamabad; (+92) 0341-2201111; www.hotelone.com.pk
Islamabad, map pg. 82, Sgl US$120
A budget-business venture by Pakistan's respected Pearl Continental chain.

Best Western Islamabad: 6 Islamabad Club Road, Islamabad; (+92) 051-2277460; www.bestwesternisb.com
Islamabad, map pg. 80, Dbl US$60
A secure hotel with liquor license (local beer Rs. 450). Free airport pick up/drop off. Great Pakistani breakfast with western additions if needed. Rooms are average but quiet.

Royalton Hotel Rawalpindi: G-254, Opposite Liaqat Bagh, Liaquat Road, Rawalpindi; (+92) 051-5762300; www.royalton.com.pk
Rawalpindi, map pg. 84, Dbl US$56, Suite US$83
Royalton Hotel gets consistently good reviews from travellers, with comfortable, well appointed air-conditioned rooms

Luxury
Serena Hotel Islamabad: Ramna 5, Khayaban-e-Suhrwardy, Islamabad; (+92) 051-2874000; www.serenahotels.com/serenaislamabad
Islamabad, map pg. 80, Dbl US$329, Suite US$395
Islamabad's top-rated hotel, with seven restaurants and a bakery cafe, swimming pool, day spa, health club, travel desk, wifi and 387 rooms, including a presidential room from US$2,000 per night.

Marriott Islamabad: Aga Khan Road, Shalimar 5, Islamabad; (+92) 051-2826121; www.marriott.com/hotels/travel/isbpk-islamabad-marriott-hotel
Islamabad, map pg. 80, Cost: Dbl US$167, Suite US$441
All the creature comforts that you would expect from this excellent international brand.

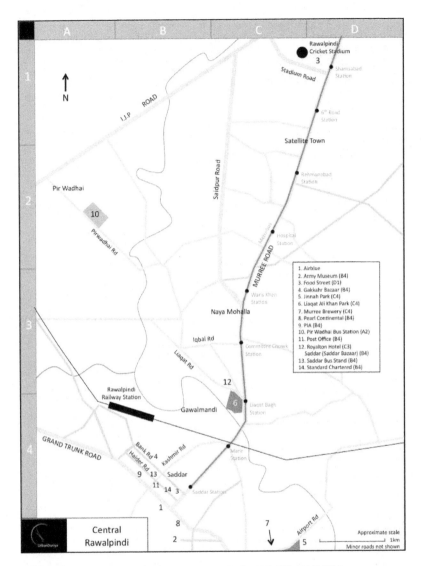

Central Rawalpindi

1. Airblue
2. Army Museum (B4)
3. Food Street (D1)
4. Gakkahr Bazaar (B4)
5. Jinnah Park (C4)
6. Liaqat Ali Khan Park (C4)
7. Murree Brewery (C4)
8. Pearl Continental (B4)
9. PIA (B4)
10. Pir Wadhai Bus Station (A2)
11. Post Office (B4)
12. Royalton Hotel (C3)
    Saddar (Saddar Bazaar) (B4)
13. Saddar Bus Stand (B4)
14. Standard Chartered (B4)

Approximate scale
1km
Minor roads not shown

Pearl Continental Rawalpindi: Mall Road, Rawalpindi; (+92) 051-111505505;
www.pchl.com
Rawalpindi, map pg. 84, Dbl US$160, Suite US$387
Lavishly appointed rooms, four restaurants, a health club and a swimming pool;
Rawalpindi's best.

Eating in Islamabad and Rawalpindi

There is no shortage of street side options in Islamabad and Rawalpindi - in Islamabad head
to the centre of the sector and take a walk around the market to see what's cooking. In

Rawalpindi, reliable places can be found at Food Street, at the northern end of town, and in Islamabad at Melody Market (G-6/2).

If you're looking for something more upmarket, you could start at Islamabad's Jinnah Super Market (F7), Kohsar Market (F6/3) and Centaurus Mall, all home to various western fast food chains plus lots of independent quality restaurants catering to the expat market - dress the part and be prepared for several security checks. For more details of upmarket places to eat in Islamabad, go to www.islamabadsnob.com/restaurants_islamabad.htm

Services in Islamabad and Rawalpindi

Airlines

Air Arabia: 1-E Ali Plaza, Jinnah Ave, Blue Area (+92) 051-2810182 *(map pg. 82)*.

Airblue: Ground Floor, ISE Towers, 55-B Jinnah Avenue, Islamabad *(map pg. 82)*, Office 5 & 6, Pindi Club Building, Mall Rd, Saddar, Rawalpindi (+92) 051-111247258 *(map pg. 84)*.

Air China: G-09 Ground Floor, ISE Towers, 55-B Jinnah Ave, Islamabad; (+92) 051-2894094 *(map pg. 82)*.

China Southern: 15/16 Saeed Plaza, Jinnah Ave. Islamabad; 051-2604378 *(map pg. 82)*.

Emirates: 55-C 1st Floor, Ufone Tower, Jinnah Ave., Blue Area, Islamabad; 0111-225535 *(map pg. 82)*.

Etihad: Islamabad Stock Exchange Tower, Jinnah Ave., Blue Area; 0800-90044017 *(map pg. 82)*.

Gulf Air: Unit 1-A, Shahid Plaza, Jinnah Avenue, F-6/4, Islamabad; (+92) 051-2272210 *(map pg. 82)*.

Kuwait Airways: 1-A Duty Free Shopping Complex, 11 Jinnah Avenue, G6/F6, Islamabad; (+92) 051-2805203 *(map pg. 82)*.

Oman Air: Omar Sharif Plaza, Fazal-e-Haq Rd, Blue Area Islamabad; (+92) 051-2801504 *(map pg. 82)*.

Pakistan International: Alay Plaza, AK Fazal-ul-Haq Rd, Block E, Blue Area, Islamabad (+92) 051-111786785 *(map pg. 82)*; 5 The Mall, Rawalpindi; (+92) 051-9272211 *(map pg. 84)*.

Qatar Airways: Tahir Plaza, Jinnah Ave, Block A, Blue Area Islamabad; (+92) 051-2201981 *(map pg. 82)*.

Saudia: Dodhy Plaza, Jinnah Ave., Block E, Blue Area, Islamabad; 051-2270164 *(map pg. 82)*.

Serene Air: Shop 4, Building 1A, Block R, Shahid Plaza, D-Chowk, Jinnah Ave, Blue Area, Islamabad; (+92) 051-2810180 *(map pg. 82)*.

Shaheen: 62-W, Executive Heights, H Block Fazal-e-Haq Rd, Blue Area (+92) 051-2806143 *(map pg. 82)*.

Thai: 4 and 5, Islamabad Hotel, Civic Ctr, Melody Mkt, Islamabad; (+92) 051-2272140 *(map pg. 82)*.

Turkish Airlines: 13-N, 1st Floor, Bhittai Rd, F-7 Markaz, Islamabad; (+92) 051-8494949 *(map pg. 82)*.

Banks

Citibank: 94-West, Jinnah Avenue, Islamabad *(map pg. 82)*.

Standard Chartered: 6A, F-7 Jinnah Super Mkt, Islamabad (also branches in F-8 and F-6) *(map pg. 82)*.

Standard Chartered: 55 Haider Road, Rawalpindi Cantt., Rawalpindi *(map pg. 84)*.

Cinemas

Centaurus Cineplex: (+92) 111-626384; www.centauruscineplex.com; a big, western-style cinema complex in the landmark Islamabad shopping mall *(map pg. 82)*.

Internet Cafe

In Islamabad, each sector's market has an internet cafe - ask at your hotel, or at local shops. G-7 (Sitara Market) has quite a few. In Rawalpindi, there are several internet cafes in the centre of Saddar Bazaar.

Money Exchange
Ravi Exchange: Shop 18, Hajvery Mansion, 22B, Blue Area, Islamabad; 051-2270763 *(map pg. 82)*.

Post Office
G-6 Markaz, G-6, Islamabad *(map pg. 82)*.
Kashmir Road, Saddar, Rawalpindi *(map pg. 84)*.

Shopping
Centaurus Mall *(map pg. 82)* is a large shopping mall in the heart of Islamabad, with food courts and numerous international brands. For markets, Rawalpindi has Saddar Bazaar and Gakkahr Bazaar *(map pg. 84)* for clothes and tailoring.

Supermarkets
There are lots of supermarkets around Islamabad's Jinnah Super Market; many stock a range of Asian and western groceries. K&N Chicken is a reputable poultry store, with an outlet at F-7's Rana Market.

Tourist Information
Pakistan Tourism Development Corporation (PTDC): Agha Khan Road, Super Market, Islamabad (+92) 051-9202766 *(map pg. 82)*.

Travel Agency
Sonya Travels: 1-E, Ali Plaza, Blue Area, Islamabad; (+92) 051-2810184; www.sonyatravel.net *(map pg. 82)*

Visa Office
13-C Al-Hussain Plaza, G-10 Markaz, Islamabad *(map pg. 82)*.

Help in Islamabad and Rawalpindi
Safety
Owing in part to their proximity to and easy access from the tribal regions, and their high profile as a centre of political power, Islamabad and Rawalpindi have been rocked by bomb attacks in the past. These attacks have usually been aimed at political targets, however a couple of spectacular exceptions remind us that no-one is immune; a truck bomb exploded at Islamabad's Marriott Hotel in 2008 Realistically, the risk of being in the wrong place at the wrong time is low, but it is still a risk. Street crime exists in Islamabad and Rawalpindi - take the usual precautions.

Medical Services
Maroof International Hospital: F-10 Markaz, Islamabad; (+92) 051-2222920 *(map pg. 82)*.
Shifa International Hospital is south of the centre of Islamabad: Pitras Bukhari Road, H-8/4 Islamabad; (+92) 051-8463666 *(map pg. 82)*.
24 Hour Pharmacies are associated with the above mentioned hospitals. Also, Shaheen 24 Hour Chemist is near Citibank, Khyber Plaza, Blue Area, Islamabad *(map pg. 82)*.

Getting around Islamabad and Rawalpindi
Metrobus: The Islamabad/Rawalpindi Metro Bus links the two cities very conveniently, and makes getting from one part of the Blue Area to another simple. Unfortunately it doesn't extend into the actual markets of Islamabad, so few people live or stay near a station. At the Rawalpindi end, a few important points are linked by the regular buses. Each ride, regardless of distance, costs Rs. 20.

Rickshaws and taxis: Rickshaws don't often go to Islamabad - you're more likely to get taxis. A rickshaw around Rawalpindi will cost Rs. 100 to travel between the central sights, or Rs. 150 for longer journeys. In Islamabad, taxis cost about Rs. 200 to travel between two market areas, or more to travel further.

A rickshaw from central Rawalpindi to the Daewoo Terminal is Rs. 300, and from central Islamabad costs Rs. 500. To and from the airport costs Rs. 300 from Rawalpindi and Rs. 700 from Islamabad.

For a taxi, call Metro Radio Cabs on 111-222-787 or go to www.metrocab.com.pk. A cab costs Rs. 400 at a base cost, then Rs. 20 for every subsequent kilometre. Uber and Careem ride-sharing services are in Rawalpindi and Islamabad. Download the applications to your phone - both operate with cash.

Getting between Islamabad and Rawalpindi
To get between the cities, you can either take a taxi (Rs. 400 from central Rawalpindi to Islamabad's Blue Area), or a local bus for Rs. 50 - they depart from Saddar and Pir Wadhai in Rawalpindi and G-9 Karachi Company or in Islamabad. The Metrobus (see above) operates on a route between Islamabad and Rawalpindi.

Islamabad International Airport
Islamabad's Benazir Bhutto International Airport will one day be replaced by a new airport, currently taking shape on Rawalpindi's southwestern outskirts (see below). The current airport is between the two cities, and is fairly unremarkable, however some travellers report being harassed for bribes by security staff before check-in. The tactic is to accuse the traveller of carrying something illegal (such as drugs). Some travellers have paid a bribe to pass, while others have denied any wrongdoing, and after about 15 minutes of stubborn stand-off the guard gives in.

If you arrive late, take a Metro Radio Cab to the city (see above).

New Islamabad International Airport
There's a chance that by the time you visit Islamabad's new airport will have opened. Called by various names, including Gandhara International Airport (a nod to the region's Buddhist heritage), this project has been delayed for years, but at the time of publishing in mid-2017 news was coming in that its inauguration was imminent. If you do arrive at the new airport (check with your airline) then expect to pay much more for a taxi than to the old airport – fares of Rs. 1000 might be reasonable, although this is just an early estimate.

Leaving Islamabad and Rawalpindi
The Daewoo Express bus station closer to Rawalpindi, and on the opposite side of town to Islamabad *(map pg. 80)*. There is a small Daewoo Express office in Islamabad *(map pg. 82)* which operates a shuttle service to the main station for Rs. 50. The two local bus stations are at Pir Wadhai *(map pg. 82)* and Faizabad *(map pg. 80)*, halfway between Islamabad and Rawalpindi. Faizabad is particularly popular with Lahore-bound local buses. NATCO operates from Pir Wadhai.

Bus
Lahore: Daewoo Express, 4 hours 30 minutes, Rs. 1,200.
Gujranwala: Daewoo Express, 3 hour 15 minutes, Rs. 750.
Gujrat: Daewoo Express, 3 hours, Rs. 550.
Sialkot: Daewoo Express, 4 hours 30 minutes, Rs. 850.
Jhelum: Local bus at Rawalpindi's general bus station, 1 hour 30 minutes, Rs. 200
Faisalabad: Daewoo Express, 3 hours 45 minutes, Rs. 900.
Sargodha: Daewoo Express, 3 hours 15 minutes, Rs. 560.
Multan: Daewoo Express, 8 hours, Rs. 1,500.
Bahawalpur: Daewoo Express, 10 hours, Rs. 1,650.

Murree: Daewoo Express, 2 hours, Rs. 270
Abbottabad: Daewoo Express, 2 hours 15 minutes, Rs. 400
Mansehra: Regular local buses from Pir Wadhai, 3 hours, Rs. 300

Peshawar: Daewoo Express, 2 hours, Rs. 420
Gilgit, Chilas and Skardu: NATCO buses operate once a day to Gilgit, from where you can change to Skardu or travel further north. Journey time: 10 hours to Gilgit, Costs: Rs. 1500 – 2200 depending on bus class. The route between Islamabad and Gilgit has occasionally been the target of sectarian attacks, making the option of air travel much more attractive.

Sukkur: Daewoo Express, 16 hours 30 minutes, Rs. 3,070
Hyderabad: Daewoo Express, 18 hours, Rs. 4,030
Karachi: Daewoo Express, 24 hours, Rs. 4,400

Train
Lahore: 4 to 5 hours, Rs. 400 (seat)
Faisalabad: 7 hours, Rs. 370 (seat)
Multan: 10 - 12 hours, Rs. 770 (berth)
Bahawalpur: 11 – 13 hours, Rs. 840 (berth)
Sukkur/Rohri: 18 - 20 hours, Rs. 1,140 (berth)
Hyderabad: 22 - 24 hours, Rs. 1330 (berth)
Karachi: 25 - 27 hours, Rs. 1,440 (berth)

Air
Gilgit and Skardu: PIA, 50 minutes, from Rs. 6,500 one way (see notes below)
Chitral: PIA, 45 minutes, from Rs. 10,500 one way). (see notes below)
Lahore: PIA, 55 minutes, from Rs. 6,786 one way
Multan: PIA, 1 hour 40 minutes, from Rs. 6,600 one way
Sukkur: PIA, 1 hour 20 minutes, from Rs. 7,900 one way
Karachi: PIA, Shaheen, AirBlue and Serene Air, 2 hours, from Rs. 7,400 one way.

Flights to northern Pakistan
Owing to the unforgiving terrain Gilgit and Chitral flights, and to a lesser extent those to Skardu, are often delayed or cancelled due to inclement weather (more common in the monsoon and winter months). In this case, a waiting list is formed. Chaotic scenes at the airport normally ensue on the first clear day after a period of cancellations, with people shouting reasons as to why they need to take the first flight out; if this happens, arrive early and stand your ground.

For this reason, tickets are not normally sold for the Gilgit or Chitral routes more than 45 days in advance, and normally not online. Gilgit and Chitral flights are more susceptible to cancellation as they are operated on 45-seat ATR turboprop aircraft. Skardu flights usually operate on large B737 or A320 aircraft. When booking flights to or from Gilgit, Chitral or Skardu, check with the agent if you need to reconfirm three or one day before the flight.

West of Islamabad

Taxila
Visitors to Taxila *(map pg. 78)* with a keen interest in Buddhism and Buddhist history may leave feeling exhilarated, but many others leave feeling rather underwhelmed. That's not to say that this World Heritage Site isn't worth a trip, but it's important to understand what is here and what is not. Taxila is home to several ruins spread far across a 25 square kilometre area, and as such, car transportation is required. Those limited to public transport usually come away seeing nothing but the small (but undeniably important) museum. As such we recommend hiring a car with a driver to visit this site. What Taxila represents is the ruins of a 6th century BC Achaemenian (ancient Persian) city. It's known that in 326 BC Alexander the Great passed through Taxila on his way through to India. Back under Mauryan rule, one of the world's first universities was built here, before it was recaptured and rebuilt by Greek Buddhist forces, passed on to the Buddhist Kushan Empire, before being lost to history some time in the 5th century AD.

Your best bet is to go to the museum first *(Rs. 200, Open: 08:30am - 12:30pm, 2:30pm - 5:30pm, closed the first Monday of every month)*. From here, keep your entrance ticket, and you can visit the rest of the sites. The first, and most obvious stop, is Bhir Mound, the semi-excavated centre of the original 6th century BC civilisation. It's just to the south of the museum. Directly to the east of the museum is Dharmajika, a large stupa which was built during the Mauryan era. A walking track from here takes you on to Sirkap, the remnants of the 1st century BC Greek city, home to ruins of a Buddhist temple, foundations of homes, a stupa and even a monastery. At the end of the track and across the main road is Jandial, a Greek temple complete with columns. About four kilometres north east of Jandial (and a total of 7kms from the museum) is Jaulian, one of the site's later additions, with a 5th century monastery and stone wall carvings.

Hasan Abdal

Hasan Abdal *(map pg. 78)* is a small town with an important Sikh pilgrimage site. It is believed that this is the place where Guru Nanak was the target of an assassination attempt by a local Sufi preacher. When Baba Wali Kandahari pushed a heavy boulder towards the first guru of Sikhism, Guru Nanak stopped its motion with the palm of his hand and saved his life. The boulder in question now sits in the **Panja Sahib** shrine in the city's centre, complete with holy handprint, attracting thousands of Sikh pilgrims from around the world each year. Unfortunately, due to security measures, entrance to the shrine and associated gurdwara at Hasan Abdal is restricted to Sikh pilgrims and those with government permission. If you are able to visit this site, you will benefit from hiring a car and driver - public transport here is not easily navigable.

Khanpur Dam

This large dam is in Khyber Pukhtoonkhwa, but is quite close to Islamabad – it makes a good day trip for water sports enthusiasts. See page 162.

North of Islamabad

The town of Murree, in the hills above Islamabad, was developed as a 'hill station' for the British colonisers to escape the baking heat of the Punjabi summer. The gentry would roam the forested mountainsides and wait for the first signs of winter before retreating back to the lowlands. Nowadays, Pakistanis flock to the region for the climate, which in summer is still quite hot, but in winter can be snowed in. Come in summer and expect big crowds; come in winter and you'll be well-advised to invest in one of the warm woollen shawls that locals drape themselves in.

Murree is in Punjab, while neighbouring Nathia Gali is in Khyber Pukhtoonkhwa (KPK). Locals speak Hindko, a version of Punjabi closely related to Potohari (the native tongue of Rawalpindi).

Leaving Islamabad, the road climbs steadily, winding its way up into the hills. Signs inform travellers of their altitude, but you'll only need to look out the window on one of the bends to appreciate the rapid ascent. The twisting road climbs 33kms beyond Murree, heading over the border to KPK.

Be aware that some of these roads are snowed over in the winter months, between December and February.

MURREE

Population: 25,000, Elevation: 2,100m, Telephone code: 051

Murree has suffered as a result of its popularity; overdevelopment is rampant, with ugly concrete hotels clinging to the hillsides while the smell of diesel permeates the main street. The real charm of Murree is in the handful of colonial-era buildings which are still standing and browsing the shops in cooler than average temperatures. The Cantonment Area at the other end of the mall is a pleasant respite, offering great views across the valleys and, from

Pindi Point, you can even spy Islamabad and Rawalpindi on a rare clear day. From near here, you can also take a chair lift ride. At the other end of Murree is Kashmir Point, the highest point in the town (2260m) with views to Kashmir.

What to see and do in Murree
Not a lot. Hang out and catch the vibe, take a ride on the chairlift, have a chai while taking in the views.

Staying in Murree
Backpacker
Chinar Hotel: Mall Road, Murree; (+92) 051-3410744
map pg. 91, Dbl Rs. 1,200
Chinnar is nothing inspiring, but with rooms at this price, no-one's complaining.

Economy
Jawa International Hotel: Mall Road, Murree Cantt, Murree; (+92) 051-3412950; www.jawahotels.com
map pg. 91, Dbl Rs. 8,000
A cheap, centrally located 3-star hotel with an eatery

Shangrila Resort Hotel: Ghora Gali Road, Ghora Gali, Murree; (+92) 051-2802138; www.shangrilamurree.com
map pg. 91, Dbl Rs. 11,700, Suite Rs. 23,000
Shangrila Resort is a lovely hilltop cottage-style building with pokey rooms, but great hospitality and a large dining room.

Luxury
Pearl Continental Bhurban: Hotel Road, Bhurban; (+92) 051-3355700; www.pchotels.com/PCHB
map pg. 91, Dbl: $188, Suite $720
Murree's only true 5 star option isn't actually in Murree - it's in Bhurban, about 25 minutes drive further along the mountain range. It comes with all the luxury appointments you would expect at a hotel of its calibre, with several eating options and a stunning mountaintop setting.

Eating in Murree
Thanks to the huge numbers of travellers coming to Murree each year, you won't go hungry here! The centre of town, Mall Road, is lined with eateries, offering local dishes, fast food, Chinese and cafe fare. **Lintotts** *(map pg. 91)* is one very well known restaurant, although it's one of many reliable options.

Services in Murree
Banks
There are ATMs here and a couple of Pakistani bank branches, but no international banks.

Internet Cafe
You can find internet cafes along The Mall, often going by the guise of 'gaming centres'.

Post Office
Upper Jhika Gali Road, Murree *(map pg. 91)*.

Help in Murree
Safety
Murree is a safe destination, however the usual precautions apply here.

Medical Services
CMH Hospital: Jinnah Rd, Murree Cantt. *(map pg. 91)*. Serious cases should go to Islamabad for treatment. There is a dispensary at CMH Hospital *(map pg. 91)*.

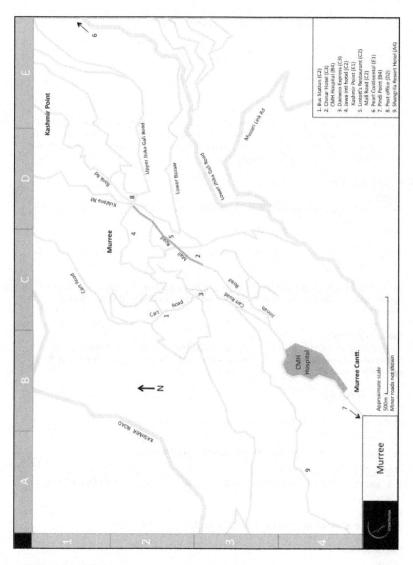

Map legend:
1. Bus Station (C2)
2. Chinar Hotel (C3)
3. CMH Hospital (B4)
4. Daewoo Express (C3)
5. Jawa intl hotel (C2)
6. Kashmir Point (E1)
7. Lintott's Restaurant (C2)
   Mall Road (C2)
8. Pearl Continental (E1)
9. Pindi Point (B4)
   Post office (D2)
   Shangrila Resort Hotel (A4)

Kashmir Point

Murree

Murree Cantt.

CMH Hospital

Murree

Approximate scale
500m
Minor roads not shown

Getting around Murree

A rickshaw or jeep around the centre of town should cost no more than Rs. 50 to Rs. 100, and from the centre of town to the bus stands is around Rs. 100 (due to the winding nature of the roads - you might be better to just walk down the steps).

Leaving Murree

The Daewoo Express bus station is in the centre of town, just down the hill from the main market *(map pg. 91)*. The local bus station is just a bit further down the hill *(map pg. 91)*.

Rawalpindi/Islamabad: Daewoo Express, 2 hours, Rs. 270.
Nathia Gali: Local buses and minivans, 30 minutes, Rs. 70.

JHELUM

Population: 145,000, Elevation: 250m, Telephone code: 054

Jhelum is an important city on the Grand Trunk Road between Lahore and Islamabad. It's home to a large army base, and sits beside the large Jhelum River, but doesn't really have much to attract a tourist. It does, however, serve as a good jumping off point for the Rohtas Fort, Ketas Raj Temples and Salt Range.

Staying in Jhelum
Economy
Faran Hotel and Restaurant: GTS Chowk, Jhelum; (+92) 321-5903593
map pg. 93, Dbl 2,000
Basic rooms make this a cheap Jhelum option.

Tulip Riverside Hotel: GT Road, Jhelum Bridge Sarai Alamgir, District Gujrat; (+92) 0544-652555; www.tulipriversidehotel.com
map pg. 93, Dbl US$58, Suite US$75
In one of the nicest locations of Jhelum, this is a pleasant, somewhat secluded four star option, although the Jhelum River doesn't resemble the Danube by any stretch of the imagination.

Eating in Jhelum
To splash out in Jhelum, go to the **Tulip Riverside Hotel**'s restaurant. Otherwise there is a cluster of cheap options at Shandar Chowk, in the centre of the city, and on Railway Road, just south of the train station.

Services in Jhelum
Banks
Standard Chartered: 1-89/7-B, Kazim Kamal Road, Jhelum Cantt *(map pg. 93)*.

Internet Cafe
MS Internet Café: Mehboob Manzil, Civil Lines, and others nearby *(map pg. 93)*.

Money Exchange
Ravi Exchange: Shop 1, Ground Floor, Saleem Center, Civil Lines; (+92) 054-4621742 *(map pg. 93)*.

Post Office
The GPO is in the centre of town, on GT Road at Cantt Square *(map pg. 93)*.

Help in Jhelum
Safety
Jhelum is fairly safe, but it is small and rather conservative - use common sense when travelling here.

Medical Services
CMH Hospital: Tufail Road, Jhelum Cantt.; (+92) 054-6986100 *(map pg. 93)*.
DHQ Hospital: Hospital Road; (+92) 054-9270262 *(map pg. 93)*.
CMH Pharmacy is associated with the CMH Hospital *(map pg. 93)*. Across the road is Shifa Pharmacy. Shifa Pharmacy also has a branch in the city centre.

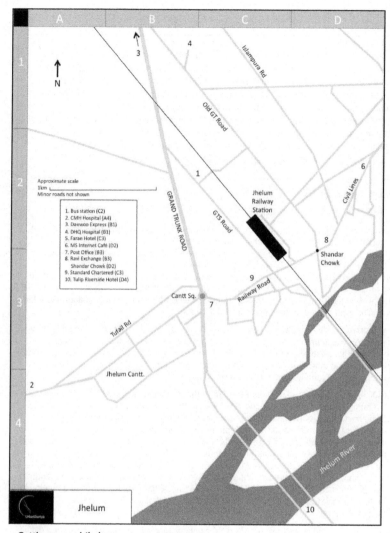

1. Bus station (C2)
2. CMH Hospital (A4)
3. Daewoo Express (B1)
4. DHQ Hospital (B1)
5. Faran Hotel (C3)
6. MS Internet Café (D2)
7. Post Office (B3)
8. Ravi Exchange (B3)
   Shandar Chowk (D2)
9. Standard Chartered (C3)
10. Tulip Riverside Hotel (D4)

Jhelum

Getting around Jhelum
A rickshaw around the centre of town should cost no more than Rs. 50 to Rs. 100. Out to the Daewoo Bus station should cost around Rs. 100 (maybe more, depending on the time of day and where you leave from).

Leaving Jhelum
The Daewoo bus stand is about 2 kilometres north of the centre, on GT Road *(map pg. 93)*. The general bus station is in the centre of town, just off G.T. Road *(map pg. 93)*.

Bus
Rawalpindi/Islamabad: Daewoo Express, 2 hours, Rs. 380
Lahore: Daewoo Express, 3 hours 15 minutes, Rs. 620.
Gujrat and **Gujranwala:** The Lahore-bound Daewoo buses stop in Gujrat and Gujranwala. Other destinations can be reached by local bus from the general bus station.

The Potohar Plateau

The hardy inhabitants of this mountainous area speak Potohari (pronounced 'pot-*waar-ee*'), a dialect of Punjabi related to Hindko Punjabi, which is spoken north of Islamabad. Once upon a time the Pakistan military was dominated by men from this region as they were considered a 'martial race'; that is, more suited to do battle - a semi-racist legacy left behind by the British. The region still churns out a disproportionate number of army generals and military types, however nowadays this has more to do with family and social tradition than with racism. There are some places in this area which are really worth visiting - Rohtas Fort and The Katas Raj Temples are prime examples of just how much Pakistan's tourism industry has to offer if it were given the opportunity to flourish.

Around Jhelum

Rohtas Fort

map pg. 78, Fort: Open to public, Museum: Open 9am - 3pm daily, Entry: Rs. 200

Qila Rohtas, or Rohtas Fort, is an expansive fortress complex on a hilltop to the southwest of Jhelum. About 4 kilometres around, and encompassing the small village of Rohtas, the building was placed on the UNESCO World Heritage List in 1997. It was built in the 16th century by local emperor Sher Shah Suri (also known as Farid Khan), in order to control restive local tribes and as a bulwark against the Mughal empire. The fort wasn't completed until after Sher Shah Suri's death, and quickly fell into the hands of the Mughal empire as it reestablished itself across the north of the subcontinent. Mughal Emperor Jehangir is said to have once spent a night at the fort enroute to Kashmir.

As you drive into the site, head through the first archway (Khawas Khani Gate) and through the park. As you approach the second major archway (Sohali Gate) there is the small but impressive Sher Shah Suri museum on the left - make sure you visit. In the museum you can view swords and other instruments of battle. From the courtyard outside the museum's upstairs door you can view the fort's eastern walls.

Outside again, be sure to view Sohali Gate from the outside the fort walls - walk down the road a bit and turn around. There's no development out here, so it makes for good pictures. Walking back through the park, the are steep steps leading up to the fort walls, and affording great views across the hilly terrain nearby. The whole area is pretty much open for visitors to scramble across and explore - there are no safety boundaries or guard rails, so use common sense and take care. Walking along the fort walls, you can head all the way down to the Haveli of Man Singh, the stout domed structure across the cricket pitch. This was once the home of the governor of Lahore. Looking back towards the museum, and facing the haveli across the cricket pitch is the impressive Shah Chand Wali gate. On the other side of the haveli, back towards the Jhelum Road, lies Rani Mahal. Maps are available from the touts at the carpark.

There's no accommodation at Rohtas Fort. Most people are use Jhelum as a base for a day trip to the site. A couple of small shops sell the usual range of packets of crisps, biscuits, bottled water and soft drinks.

Getting to Rohtas Fort requires a bit of planning. The best way to manage this is to hire a car with a driver from Jhelum - hotels should be able to organise this for less than Rs. 2,000 for the afternoon (it takes about an hour to get there). Alternatively, some people make a longer day trip from Rawalpindi or Islamabad.

If you have a lot of time, very little money, or if you enjoy milling around dusty rural bus stands, you could take public transport. From Jhelum's bus station squeeze on to an overloaded local bus heading for the town of Dina on the Grand Trunk Road (20 minutes, Rs. 50). At Dina's bus stand you'll need to ask around for another local bus to Rohtas (30 minutes, Rs. 50). Coming back from Rohtas requires a similar two-step procedure, although you may be lucky enough to find a bus going all the way through to Jhelum.

14kms west of Dina, at the junction of GT Road and the Sohan Road, are a number of *jalebi* stalls. These twisted sugary sweets are delicious when served hot, and locals say the jalebis from this row of stalls are the best in Pakistan. Coming here is only a really worth it if you have your own transport - and if you're staying in Jhelum, then your driver deserves an extra gratuity for going out of his way.

Katas Raj Temples
map pg. 78, Open dawn – dusk, Entry: Free
Much further south, on the Lahore - Islamabad Motorway corridor, are the Ketas Raj temples and the Salt Range. The Ketas Raj temples (also spelled Katas Raj) are a group of around ten 900-year old Hindu temples built around a beautiful turquoise-coloured pool. Hindu tradition states that the pool was formed when the Lord Shiva shed a tear for his deceased wife. The temples are set amid a park which is frequented by curious Pakistani travellers, keen to engage in a slice of the country's Hindu tradition. Before 1947 the site was were, and to a lesser extent still is, an important Hindu pilgrimage site, and you may well see a visiting pandit bathing in the holy water. There are a couple of shops selling snacks on the road outside Ketas. Beautiful though Ketas is, it's not worth staying the night here, and there aren't any hotels anyway.

Ketas is not a major stopping point for any transport, and nearly all people who come here do so in their own transport. Jhelum makes a good staging post, because you can also visit Rohtas Fort while in the region. That said, Ketas is at least two and a half hours drive from Jhelum, so it is a long day trip. Jhelum hotels should be able to organise a car with driver for the day, for no more than Rs. 4000. Alternatively, you could stay in Chakwal, a town near the Lahore - Islamabad Motorway - but you'd still need to organise a car for the day.

Khewra Salt Range
map pg. 78, Open 9am - 6pm daily, Entry: US$10
To the south of Ketas is the hilly Khewra Salt Range. Inside the hills is Pakistan's largest and the world's second largest salt mines. Up to 600 million tonnes of salt are believed to be stored in the hillsides, which have been turned into a tourist attraction. As you walk through the colourfully-lit mines, you will be able to view model mosques, a model Great Wall of China, and even a statue of poet and philosopher Allama Iqbal made out of salt bricks. Khewra Salt Mines is best combined on a day trip with Ketas Fort.

Faisalabad
and Western Punjab

Dusty and rugged in the northwest; flat, farmed floodplains in the southwest; western Punjab is an often-overlooked frontier region. Pockets of this region see very few, if any foreign travellers, and some are very undeveloped and conservative - Khyber Pukhtoonkhwa, and the Tribal Regions (FATA) are not far away and their proximity is palpable. Tourist attractions are also few and far between, and what does exist is often somewhere between dusty disrepair and historic ruin - the lines are blurred.

The region is also something of a cultural watershed, because apart from in Faisalabad, many of the locals speak a dialect of Seraiki. In this regard, western Punjab is a sort of cultural buffer zone between the Punjabi-speaking districts to the east, and the Pashto-speaking province to further west. The few travellers who do come here are usually visiting for a specific purpose such as work or visiting relatives. On the other hand, western Punjab is well worth exploring for those who want to get even further off the beaten track, and it offers an opportunity to experience traditional life in Punjabi villages which have changed little since 1947 or earlier.

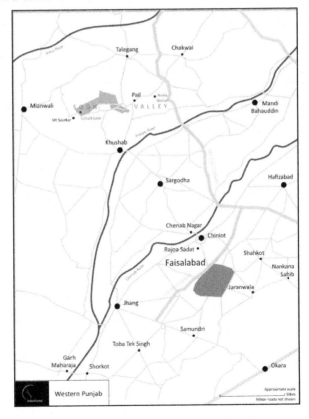

FAISALABAD

Population: 3.5 million, Elevation: 184m, Telephone code: 041

Ask a Pakistani what Faisalabad means to them and they'll probably talk about the city's mighty textile industry ("The Manchester of the East" as it's called). Dig a bit deeper and they might know that it it was named after King Faisal of Saudi Arabia in 1977. Some might also know that it was called Lyallpur when it was first built by the British back in 1892. Trivia buffs might tell you that the streets of the city's main bazaar are laid-out in the design of the Union Jack. It's also the place where famed qawwali master, the late Ustaad Nusrat Fateh Ali Khan (1948 – 1997) was from, and where he was laid to rest. While undoubtedly fascinating, none of these make particularly great reasons to visit Faisalabad for purely tourism purposes. If you do come here however (maybe for work, or if you just *have to* walk around the Union Jack street grid), there are a couple of other things to distract you while you're figuring out where that fat red stripe down the centre of the flag would be.

Orientation

For visitors, Faisalabad consists of three main areas of interest; the Old City, with the clock tower at its centre, Civil Lines, just to the north, and the well-to-do People's Colony a couple of kilometres to the southeast.

What to see in Faisalabad

Ghanta Ghar (Clock tower)
map pg. 98

Faisalabad's clock tower was built by the British in colonial-subcontinental style in 1903 at the heart of what was then called Lyallpur. It remains a focal point for the city, standing at the centre of the Union Jack street layout.

Staying in Faisalabad

Economy

Hotel One: 99C People's Colony, 1 D Ground, Faisalabad; (+92) 341-2201111; www.hotelone.com.pk
map pg. 98, Dbl US$95, Suites US$130

Comfortable, air-conditioned rooms, room service, a coffee shop, Asian restaurant and a gym.

Luxury

Serena Hotel: Club Road, Faisalabad, Pakistan; (+92) 041-2600428; www.serenahotels.com/serenafaisalabad
map pg. 98, Dbl US$170 , Suites US$443

A swimming pool, buffet breakfast, wifi and health club make this Faisalabad's most luxurious option.

Eating in Faisalabad

The old city has lots of cheap places to eat, and around Civil Lines, just to the north of the city, you'll find Pizza Hut and KFC. A great place to go a bit upmarket is on Jaranwala Road in People's Colony, where you'll find a range of restaurants serving Pakistani, Chinese and Continental cuisine, along with a few coffee shops - ask for **Kohinoor City Mall** *(map pg. 98)*.

Services in Faisalabad

Airlines

Air Arabia: Office 15-A Regency Plaza, The Mall (+92) 041-2627120 *(map pg. 98)*.
Flydubai: At Faisalabad International Airport *(map pg. 98)*.
Pakistan International: 26 New Civil Lines, The Mall (+92) 041-9200786 *(map pg. 98)*.
Qatar Airways: Mezzanine Floor, Sitara Tower, Civil Lines, Sitara Chowk, (+92) 041-2609151 *(map pg. 98)*.

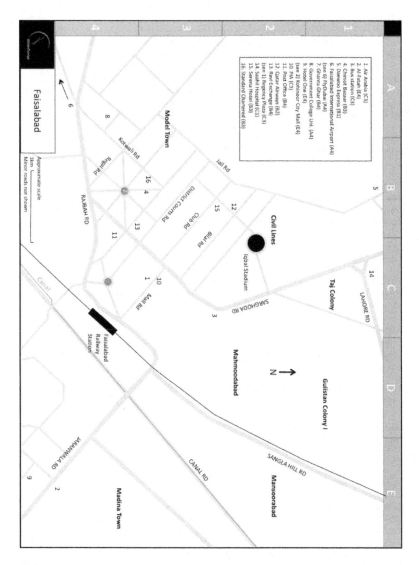

Faisalabad

1 Air Arabia (C3)
2 Al-Fatah (E4)
3 Bus station (C3)
4 Chenot Bazaar (B3)
5 Daewoo Express (B1)
6 Faisalabad International Airport (A4)
7 (see 6) FlyDubai (A4)
8 Ghanta Ghar (B4)
9 Government College Uni. (A4)
10 Hotel One (E4)
(see 2) Kohinoor City Mall (E4)
11 Post Office (C3)
12 PIA (C3)
13 Qatar Airways (B2)
14 Ravi Exchange (B4)
(see 1) Regency Plaza (C3)
15 Saahil Hospital (C1)
15 Serena Hotel (B3)
16 Standard Chartered (B3)

Approximate scale
1km
Minor roads not shown

Banks
Standard Chartered: 69 Kotwali Road *(map pg. 98)*.

Internet Cafe
There are a lot of internet cafes around Government College University *(map pg. 98)*, near the central bazaar area.

Money Exchange
Ravi Exchange: 21 Sadiq Plaza, Main Circular Road, Faisalabad; (+92) 041-261410 *(map pg. 98)*.

Post Office
Railway Road, Faisalabad *(map pg. 98)*.

Shopping
Al-Fatah Supermarket stocks several imported brands and quality local products: Centre Point Plaza, Kohinoor City, Jaranwala Road *(map pg. 98)*.

Travel Agency
Regency Plaza *(map pg. 98)* is home to many reputable travel agencies

Getting around Faisalabad
In a rickshaw, nowhere should cost more than Rs. 200 within the city limits, and expect to pay just Rs. 100 for a one way trip from the centre over to People's Colony or up to Civil Lines. For the airport, you're better to call a Metro Radio Cab on 111-222-787 or go to www.metrocab.com.pk. A cab costs Rs. 400 at a base cost, then Rs. 20 for every subsequent kilometre.

The Careem ride-sharing service is in Faisalabad. Download the application to your phone and get a quote! Careem operates with cash.

Help in Faisalabad
Safety
Faisalabad is not a particularly dangerous city, but nor does it see many foreign tourists, so you'd be wise to be especially aware of local sensibilities and keep your wits about you.

Medical Services
Saahil Hospital: (+92) 041-8782042 *(map pg. 98)*.
24 Hour Pharmacy: Pharmacies abound near the Saahil Hospital. Otherwise Chiniot Bazar *(map pg. 98)* has lots of pharmacies too.

Leaving Faisalabad
The Daewoo Express bus station is at the northern end of town past Civil Lines *(map pg. 98)*. The local bus station is opposite the railway station *(map pg. 93)*.

Bus
Lahore: Daewoo Express, 2 hours 15 minutes, Rs. 550.
Rawalpindi/Islamabad: Daewoo Express, 3 hours 45 minutes, Rs. 900
Sargodha: Daewoo Express, 1 hour 45 minutes, Rs. 300
Chiniot: Minivans from local bus station, 1 hour, Rs. 50
Gujranwala, Gujrat, Sialkot and Jhelum: Local buses from local bus station, 2 hours, Rs. 500
Multan: Daewoo Express, 4 hours 15 minutes, Rs. 700.
Bahawalpur: Daewoo Express, 6 hours 15 minutes, Rs. 1,050.
Okara and Sahiwal: Local buses at Faisalabad's local bus station. 2 hours, Rs. 200 and Rs. 300.
Sukkur: Daewoo Express, 12 hours 20 minutes, Rs. 2,320
Karachi: Daewoo Express, 20 hours 35 minutes, Rs. 3,550.

Train
Lahore: 2 hours, Rs. 200 (seat)
Rawalpindi/Islamabad: 7 hours, Rs. 370 (seat)
Karachi: 17 – 19 hours, Rs. 1,060 (berth)

Air
Karachi: PIA, 1 hour 40 minutes, from Rs. 8,104. Serene Air have also expressed interest in this route, but operations had not begun at the time of research.

Around Faisalabad

A visit to one or two of the villages around Faisalabad, particularly between Faisalabad and Chiniot, is a great way to get a glimpse of traditional Punjabi rural life. Ask at your hotel in Faisalabad, and they should be able to organise something - drivers have connections through family or friends in the farming communities. A day trip from Faisalabad to Chiniot costs about Rs. 4000 (car and driver), or about Rs. 5000 if you stop in a village or two.

NANKANA SAHIB

Population: 60,000, Elevation: 187m, Telephone code: 056

Nankana Sahib *(map pg. 96)* is the town where the first Guru of Sikhism, Guru Nanak Dev Ji, was born in 1469. Back then, the town was called Rai Bhoi Ki Talvandi, but was renamed after the Guru's passing. It remains an important pilgrimage site for Sikhs, many of whom cross the border from India on specially organised tours to visit the shrine in the centre of the town. Unfortunately, unless you are Sikh, you will not be allowed to enter the shrine for security reasons. If you are Sikh, and you are planning to visit, our contact recommends Hafiz Railway Hotel, near the shrine. Getting to Nanhaka Sahib should only cost Rs. 200 on a local bus from either Faisalabad or Lahore's local bus stands. The local bus station is at the opposite end of town to the main shrine.

RAJOA SADAT

Population: 35,000, Elevation: 170m, Telephone code: 0466

One important village near Chiniot is Rajoa Sadat *(map pg. 96)*. Peer Shah Daulat was an important local saint, and a forefather of many spiritual mystics of the region. His much-visited shrine is in the centre of town - ask locals for directions, and take care to act with appropriate reverence. Apart from the shrines of the town, there is the usual stock of farms and their corresponding animals; cattle, horses, goats, donkeys and chickens. Rice paddies dot the landscape. Sugarcane is a major crop in the area, and some stalls extract the juice for drinking by the roadside. Mango trees are also plentiful, and bear fruit in July - August.

Accommodation in Rajoa Sadat, like other villages nearby, would mean getting invited home as a (perhaps paying) guest on a farmhouse. If you are visiting here without a car and driver, an autorickshaw or qingqi from the centre of Chiniot costs approximately Rs. 500, and takes about 20 - 30 minutes. There is no regular public transport directly to Rajoa Sadat from Faisalabad.

CHINIOT

Population: 477,000, Elevation: 179m, Telephone code: 0466

Coming from Faisalabad, Chiniot is one of the first significant non-Punjabi speaking towns - the tongue here is Seraiki. The shift might be subtle, even unnoticeable to the casual traveller, but locals can easily distinguish Chinot's indigenous culture. And to see that culture, you need look no further than the town centre, whose wood furniture market throbs with activity on weekdays (but not Friday).

Just west of Chiniot, the Chenab River lazes its way along the wide plain, interrupted only by bridges and a handful of jagged rocky mounts which stand in stark contrast to the surroundings. Industrial Chiniot is not a pretty place, but if you search hard enough, you might just unearth a gem or two.

What to see and do in Chiniot
Umar Hayat Mahal
map pg. 102, Entry free, Open 9am - 5pm (closes on Friday for 2 hours for prayers)

This is a huge wooden house with a dark history. Umar Hayat, a trader whose family had migrated to Chinot from Calcutta, decided to build a palatial home for his son. As you do. However not long before the house was to be opened in 1935, Umar Hayat passed away. Three years later, finally ready to move in, Umar Hyatt's son Gulzar got married in the house, but was found dead the morning after his nuptials. Consumed with grief at her son's death, Gulzar's mother also passed away soon after. Mother and son were buried together in the inside the house, their other relatives abandoned the building, believing it was cursed.

Nowadays one small section of Umar Hayat Mahal is being used as a library, while the rest of the house is open for viewing. It's dusty, and it's in a romantic (or spooky) state of disrepair. You can walk through all the rooms, around the balconies which once overlooked the main parlour, and even climb up on the rooftop. The steps to the rooftop terrace hang out over the edge of the building, and are quite rickety - the gatekeeper advised us that only one person should use them at a time, so ascend at your own risk. If you choose to climb up, the rooftop affords a great view over Chiniot's bazaar area, and on a clear day some surrounding villages are visible in the distance.

Shahi Masjid (Royal Mosque)
map pg. 102, Entry free, Open sunrise - late
Compared with some of Pakistan's grander mosques, this building doesn't look remarkably royal, but the intrigue is in the detail. The wooden interior walls are intricately carved and decorated in shades of maroon with highlights of vibrant ochre. It was completed in 1655 and is still a functioning mosque, so try not to visit at prayer time unless you plan to partake.

Shah Ismail Shah Bukhari Shrine and Sheesh Mahal
map pg. 102, Entry free, open dawn to dusk
What is commonly known as "Sheesh Mahal" or "palace of mirrors" is actually called Sain Sukh Shrine. A shrine to a local saint Ahmad Mahi Sain Sukh, it is spectacularly decorated with thousands of tiny coloured glass pieces. Next door stands the much taller, better known, but less beautiful shrine to Shah Islamic Shah Bukhari, a local saint.

Bazaar
In the mood for some furniture shopping? You've come to the right place! Pick up some bargains on some seriously heavy, hand-carved wooden bed frames, chairs and dressers, or just wander the streets checking out the handicraft, and watch the masters at work.

Bara Mandir (Big Temple)
map pg. 102, Entry free, Open sunrise - sunset
The Bara Mandir still caters to Chiniot's small Hindu community, and is a testament to the city's relative religious tolerance. The temples main spire can be seen from many points around the inner city. Although visitors are officially welcome here, security restrictions may prevent you from entering the main hall of the building; ask the gatekeeper nicely.

Channa Khaiwa and Chenab River
The rocky outcrop known as Channa Khaiwa, and sometimes referred to as Punj Peer hosts a couple of small shrines for local saints. Some locals also visit to pay tribute to the "Punj Peer", the five important saints of Punjabi literature; Data Ganj Baksh, Sheikh Baba Farid Shakarganj, Baha'ud din Zakariya, Lal Shahbaz Qalandar and Sayyid Jalaluddin Bukhari. Some years ago a handful of Buddhist carvings were discovered in these hills. The hilltop is a steep 15 minute walk from the road, or alternatively you can risk your life with the makeshift cable car which ascends the side of the hill facing the river.

Across the river and on the other side of the road there is a park by the water. Vendors sell cold drinks (both fresh and bottled), and a couple of boats are moored, offering a quick punt on the river (Rs. 50, 10 minutes). Note that swimming in the river is prohibited here, and police enforce this rule.

Visiting the shrines and the park is about a Rs. 200, 10 minute drive in a rickshaw from central Chiniot.

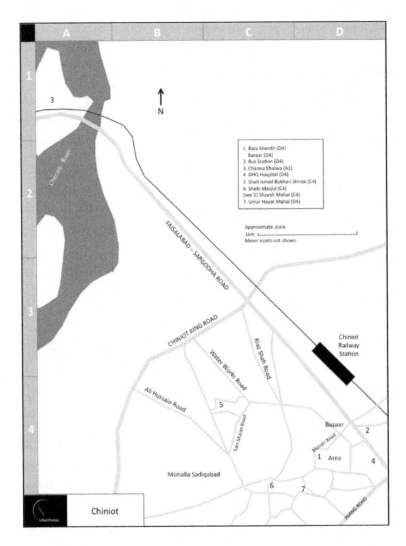

1. Bara Mandir (D4)
   Bazaar (D4)
2. Bus Station (D4)
3. Channa Khaiwa (A1)
4. DHQ Hospital (D4)
5. Shah Ismail Bukhari Shrine (C4)
6. Shahi Masjid (C4)
   (see 5) Sheesh Mahal (C4)
7. Umar Hayat Mahal (D4)

Approximate scale
1km
Minor roads not shown

Chiniot

Staying in Chiniot
Most visitors do not stay in Chinot, instead visiting on a day trip from Faisalabad.

Eating in Chinot
The inner city abounds with cheap eateries serving up daal chawal, chicken korma with naan and biryani.

Help in Chiniot
Safety
Chiniot is a small town, and rather conservative, so you should take care not to offend. Women may feel more comfortable travelling with a male companion.

Medical services
Medical services are available at DHQ Hospital *(map pg. 102)*, but serious cases will be taken to Faisalabad.

Getting around Chiniot
Autorickshaws and qingqis run the streets around Chiniot - you should pay about Rs. 150 from the bus station to the inner city (around Umar Hayat Mahal), or Rs. 50 for short hops around the city. Rickshaws aren't always easily available in the inner city - you might have to walk to the main road to flag one down. Autorickshaws and qingqis also run from the city to the shrines near the Chenab River - that costs about Rs. 200. Chiniot rickshaw drivers also sometimes offer a "city tour" for Rs. 700 – 1,000 for the day - expect to be taken to a furniture showroom at some stage, but if you are paying this much money, insist (politely but firmly) on seeing the things you want to see and getting your money's worth.

Leaving Chiniot
Faisalabad: Minivans from local bus station, 1 hour, Rs. 50
Sarghoda: Local buses from local bus station, 45 minutes, Rs.100

JHANG
Population: 293,000, Elevation: 183m, Telephone code: 0477
The main reason to come to Jhang is to see the tomb/shrine of Heer Ranjha, the couple at the centre of Punjabi literature's most epic love story. The main reason to avoid Jhang is the bitterly sectarian local politics which have brutally divided this semi-desert city. While nowadays Jhang is not a no-go zone, it remains a very conservative community where tensions continue to bubble below the surface.

What to see and do in Jhang
Heer Ranja Shrine
map pg. 104, Entry free, Open sunrise - sunset
Described by Waris Shah in a series of poems in 1766, Heer Ranjha are Punjabi literature's Romeo and Juliet, a love-struck couple doomed by society's strictures. So besotted by them are the Punjabi people that a shrine has been built to pay tribute to Heer who could not live with her lover. The whole story is shrouded in mystery because some state that Heer and Ranjha were in fact real people who lived in the 15th century, although there is no solid evidence to prove this. Additionally, some postulate that Heer Ranjha is in fact not a human love story, but rather a metaphor for man's spiritual longing towards his creator - which may explain the need to build and gravitate towards a shrine.

Safety in Jhang
Jhang is a place where safety should be seriously considered. While most visitors have nothing but praise for Jhangvis (as locals are known), the fact remains that this town teeters on the brink of communal strife. Seek local advice from Faisalabad, Lahore or Multan before setting out for Jhang - if communal tensions are rising, then this is a place to skip.

It is advisable not to "hang around" in Jhang unless you have particular business here. Visiting the shrines and the old city are worthy pursuits, but spending days wandering the streets, conspicuously "soaking up the atmosphere" could attract unwanted attention.

Whatever you do, do not get involved in conversations regarding religion, especially regarding "the Sunni/Shia divide". Also do not get into conversations about local politics, recent local history or terrorism - all of these are trigger issues in Jhang, and the wounds of recent violent episodes are still raw. If someone starts talking with you about any of these, its best to remain non-committal until the topic changes to something lighter.

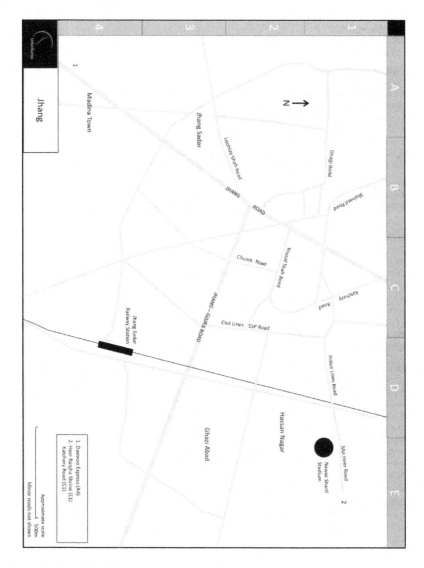

Jhang

N →

Madina Town

Jhang Sadar

Lockary Shah Road

Dhaji Road

JHANG ROAD

Shaheed Road

Church Road

Yousaf Shah Road

Katchery Road

Civil Lines SSP Road

JHANG – GOJRA ROAD

Jhang Sadar Railway Station

Police Lines Road

Ghazi Abad

Hassan Nagar

Nawaz Sharif Stadium

Mai Heer Road

1. Daewoo Express (A4)
2. Heer Ranjha Shrine (E1)
Katchery Road (C1)

Approximate scale
500m
Minor roads not shown

SARGODHA

Population: 1.5 million, Elevation: 190m, Telephone code: 048

Strategically important but culturally uninspiring, Sargodha is a city you will come to on the way to or from the Soon Valley. The city was established about 120 years ago by the British, and since partition has hosted one of Punjab's most important military bases. Due to Lahore's proximity to the Indian border, Sargodha is charged with the defence of central Punjab in the event of war, and proponents of this strategy were vindicated in the 1965 war when Indian forces indeed reached the outskirts of Lahore. Nowadays, Sargodha is growing quickly, but is still a rough-and-ready town on the western edge of Punjab. There are lots of guns in public, a large number of ethnic Pathans mix with the Saraiki and Punjabi-speaking local populace. Sargodha and its nearby farming regions are also known for their production of citrus fruit, giving the town the quixotic moniker of "the California of Pakistan". If you visit in winter, don't forget to sample some of the sweet local oranges.

Staying in Sargodha
Backpacker
Al - Hayat Hotel & Restaurant: Railway Rd, Police Lines Area, Sargodha; (+92) 048-3016737
map pg. 106, Dbl Rs. 1,250
A good enough choice with a restaurant and air conditioned rooms. A short walk to the centre.

Economy
Q's International Hotel: University Road near Khayam Cinema, Sargodha City (+92) 048-3721918
map pg. 106, Dbl Rs. 5,500
It doesn't compare with Lahore or Islamabad's 5-star options, but Q's is a quality Sargodha option with a good restaurant and professional staff.

Eating in Sargodha
There is no "food street" in Sargodha but there are many good restaurants near Queen Chowk; **Queen Restaurant** and **Apna Dera** come recommended. There are dozens of good restaurants near University Rd and some cheap restaurants near Trust Plaza. One recommendation is **Zam Zam** *(all map pg. 106)*.

Services in Sargodha
Internet Cafe
Many internet cafes are nearby and at Al-Rehman Plaza *(map pg. 106)*.

Money Exchange
Ravi Exchange: Shop 1, Ground Floor Club Market, Sheryar Shaheed Bukhari Road *(map pg. 106)*.

Post Office
University Post offfice in University of Sargodha *(map pg. 106)*.

Help in Sargodha
Safety
Sarghoda is a bit of a wild west town – conservative and not used to seeing foreign travelers. It was safe to visit at the time of writing, but stay updated with local news, and behave and dress conservatively.

Medical services
Sadiq Hospital: Main Satellite Town Rd, Sargodha; *(map pg. 106)*.

Getting around Sargodha
Getting around Sargodha will cost no more than Rs.100 in a rickshaw. Some Rickshaw drivers offer a "city tour" for Rs. 250 - they'll drive you around the smattering of attractions like markets, parks and colleges.

Leaving Sargodha
Lahore: Daewoo Express, 2 hours 30 minutes, Rs. 420
Faisalabad: Daewoo Express, 1 hours 45 mins, Rs. 270
Multan: Daewoo Express, 4 hours 30 minutes, Rs. 570
Rawalpindi: Daewoo Express, 3 hours 15 mins, Rs.520
Jhang: Daewoo Express, 2 hours, Rs.410
Chiniot: Local buses from the general bus stand, 45 minutes, Rs.100

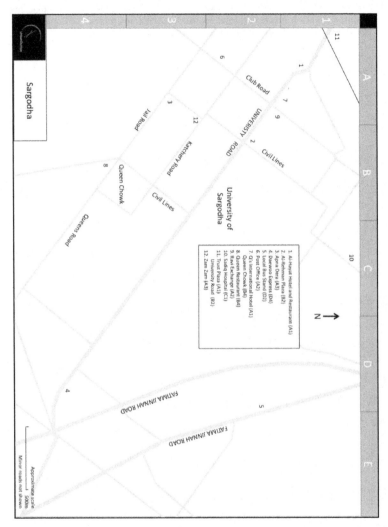

Club Road

UNIVERSITY ROAD

Civil Lines

Jail Road

Katchery Road

Queen Chowk

Civil Lines

Queens Road

University of Sargodha

1. Al-Hayat Hotel and Restaurant (A1)
2. Al-Rehman Plaza (B2)
3. Apna Dera (A3)
4. Daewoo Express (D4)
5. Local Bus Stand (D2)
6. Post Office (A2)
7. Q's International Hotel (A1)
8. Queen Chowk (B4)
9. Queen Restaurant (B4)
10. Sadiq Hospital (C1)
11. Trust Plaza (A1)
12. University Road (B2)
12. Zam Zam (A3)

N →

Approximate scale
500m
Minor roads not shown

FATIMA JINNAH ROAD

FATIMA JINNAH ROAD

Around Sargodha
SOON VALLEY
The part of the Salt Range which extends west from Kallar Kahar towards Mianwali climbs to 1,530 metres at Mt Sakesar, one of the highest points in the otherwise flat province of Punjab. The Soon Valley *(map pg. 96)* below Mt Sakesar is home to a wildlife reserve and some pretty, if not spectacular scenery. The region is home to several Pakistan military installations and much of it is off limits to travellers, but some are open and even the target of a tourism development project to take place in the next few years. At a higher altitude, the valley gets cold in winter and Mt Sakesar even sees snow in December and January, so pack accordingly.

At the eastern end of the valley lies Neela Wahan, a chain of refreshingly clear saltwater lakes which are clean enough to swim in, so bring your togs! The lakes are about an hour's hike from the main road; your driver will direct you. Along the way keep your eyes open for wild peacocks - they're known to frequent the forests in this area. If you visit during the summer months expect to see lots of locals cooling off in the lakes, and if you come during the monsoon you'll also get to see the natural waterfall that cascades off the rocks above. Women are not prohibited from swimming in the lake, but it's still a rare sight and would attract attention - if you want to swim then you should do so fully clothed, and perhaps in one of the smaller lakes away from the hordes of curious young men.

At the other end of the valley lies Uchhali Lake at the base of Mt Sakesar. The salt water lake is almost 4 kilometres long and about one and a half kilometres across, and the surrounding land is mostly flat and brackish. There's not a lot to do here, but you can take a boat out for a punt on the lake (pay around Rs. 100), and during winter the vista of the snow-capped Mr Sakesar is one of the few places to see the white stuff in Punjab. Some visitors hike around the lake, but you probably won't be allowed to climb the mountain for security reasons. As this area is developed in the coming years more options will be opened up for travellers, so ask at your hotel or the PTDC in Sargodha about what there is to see and do.

Due to the presence of military installations, you will probably only be able to visit the Soon Valley on a day trip from Sargodha. Public transport is scarce, and isn't really an option. A car with a driver for the day will cost between Rs. 5,000 and Rs. 7,000, depending on where you want to visit and your bargaining skills - ask at your hotel in Sargodha. The drive from Sargodha to Neela Wahan or Uchhali Lake take about one and a half hours one way. Day trips are also possible from Lahore (three and a half hours one way) and Islamabad or Jhelum (each two hours one way), but cost significantly more - speak to your hotel. Don't bother stopping in Khushab - although it's conveniently located right near the Soon Valley, it is also said to be home to some of Pakistan's nuclear weapons facilities, and foreigners are usually turned away by police or local hotels.

Multan
and Southern Punjab

Southern Punjab is a wide open land of farms, river plains and deserts. The climate is harsh; exposed to the elements, this region is warm in the winter and swelters in the hot dusty summer. Bound by the ruggedly barren Balochistan to the southwest, the lonely, scorching Cholistan/Thar desert to the southeast, and the pancake-flat agricultural plains stretching north to Lahore, Multan has for long been somewhat isolated from the rest of Punjab. Perhaps as a result, this region has traditionally been less prosperous than northern Punjab. However the tyranny of the local environs seem to have bred a unique culture of hospitality, ascetic religious devotees and a culinary tradition which makes use of the ingredients available - nuts, dates, mangos are all associated with this area. Add to this the local tongue of Seraiki (a sort of crossover between Punjabi and rural Sindhi), and this region could be one of Pakistan's most rewarding for the culturally-inclined.

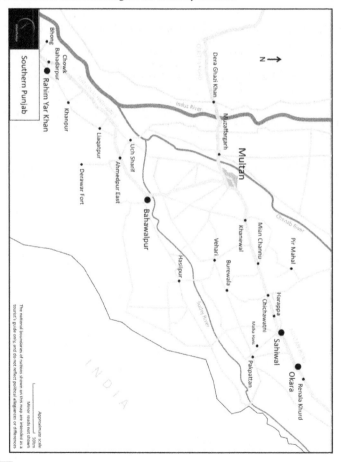

Safety in Southern Punjab

In recent years, some travellers have reported being bailed up by overzealous local police telling them that they are "in danger" and that they "must leave town immediately" for their own safety. This has taken the form of stopping travellers in the street, meeting them as they disembark an incoming bus, or even late night hotel room door knocks. Meanwhile many other travellers have had cordial or no encounters with local authorities. It seems to affect travelers who stay anywhere but the most premium of places. The fact that there doesn't seem to be a consistent official policy suggests that the area isn't especially unsafe, but rather the police are acting arbitrarily. If you are travelling here on your own steam, it is advisable to make yourself aware of the current safety scenario, and if possible, get something in writing with an official signature. That way you will have something to back you up if you are questioned.

If you do have the misfortune of being questioned by a police officer, take solace in the fact that no-one has ever reported mistreatment by them - just a lot of posturing and lecturing about the hazards of independent travel. Be polite but firm, but if they insist then you should cooperate; being put on a bus out of town is a much nicer option than fighting with a country police officer brimming with bravado.

MULTAN

Population: 6 million, Elevation: 120m, Telephone code: 061

Multan is known in Pakistan as the city of saints, and it's easy to see why; the metropolis is studded with scores of shrines paying tribute to *pirs*; masters, adherents and preachers of the mythical Sufi interpretation of Islam. Sufi monuments aside, Multan is home to a delicious saccharine spin on Punjabi and Pakistani cuisine - sweet toothed visitors rejoice - and if you're approaching from the north it is the gateway to the Seraiki belt of southern Punjab. Multan is warm in the winter, and oppressively hot in the summer - temperatures frequently pass 50C between May and July.

Multan is one of the oldest cities in the world, and the region around Multan is believed to have been settled since the Indus Valley Civilisation. After being ruled by successive Hindu rulers, the city was conquered by Alexander the Great in 326BC, before returning to a revolving doors of tribal warlords and local fiefdoms. It came under Muslim rule in 712 but continued to be conquered and reconquered by invading Muslim armies. In 1817 Maharaja Ranjit Singh attacked the city, before the British Raj brought it under their control. The walled city of Multan bears the scars of these successive centuries of warfare. Since partition, Multan has grown to be the administrative centre of southern Punjab.

Orientation

An obvious centre to the city would be the fort and adjacent walled city, along with the clock tower (Ghantar Ghar) at the bottom of the hill. A couple of hotels and eateries in are located in this area, but on the whole it's a grungy, rough part of town which isn't advisable for fragile, much less female, travellers to stay in. The airport is located in the pleasant Cantt area to the west.

What to see in Multan

Mausoleum of Shah Rukn-e-Alam

map pg. 111, Cost: Free, Open to public

This building, a beautiful example of classic Mughal architecture, houses the tomb of one of the subcontinent's most prominent Muslim scholars. Widely considered to be the patron saint of Multan, Rukn-ud-Din Abul Fatah (1251 - 1334) was buried here in 1334. He is often referred to as Rukn-e-Alam, the "Pillar of the World", and was once the head of the Suhrawardiya branch of Sufi Islam. His red brick tomb is adorned with blue glazed tiles and is now very much Multan's most iconic building. The tomb's dark interior has a distinctly otherworldly feel, and is often filled with pilgrims paying their respects to the saint.

Mausoleum of Hazrat Baha-ud-Din Zakaria
map pg. 111, Free, Open to public
Just down the road from the tomb of Shah Rukn-e-Alam, is the tomb for his father, Baha-ud-Din Zakaria (1182 - 1262). Zakaria tomb is much more utilitarian in structure than the lofty ideals of his son's tomb, but is nonetheless an impressive construction. Zakaria is credited with bringing the Suhrawardiya branch of Sufi Islam to the subcontinent, and he also established a centre for religious learning in Multan.

Qasim Bagh Fort and Walled City
map pg. 111, Free, Open to public
Not much is left of Multan's once grand city walls. The best ruins are on the western end, visible as you approach the hill from the clock tower. It's unclear how far back the fort dates, but it's believed to have existed for centuries before the city's capture by Muslim forces in 711 AD. The fort was ruined in 1848 when the British laid siege to Multan, and subsequent neglect by both British and Pakistani rulers have exacerbated the deterioration.

Mausoleum of Hazrat Shamsuddin Sabzwari Multani
map pg. 111, Free, Open to public
This tomb, to the east of the the Mausoleum of Hazrat Baha-ud-Din Zakaria, houses the grave of Shams Tabrez or Shamsuddin Sabzwari Multani, a saint who is said to have lived for 111 years from 1165 to 1276. Local legend has it that Multan's hot climate results from Multani's request to draw the sun closer to himself, thereby scorching Multan. Depending on the weather when you visit, your appreciation of this miracle may vary.

Mausoleum of Hazrat Hafiz Muhammad Jamal Multani
map pg. 111, Free, Open to public
Hazrat Hafiz Muhammad Jamal Multani (1717 - 1811) was a prominent scholar of Sufism, and had memorised the Qur'an at a young age. He was also a poet and a writer. His important (although not huge) tomb is just to the east of the walled city, outside Daulat Gate. It can be a bit difficult to find, so you might need to ask locals to point the way.

Mausoleum of Shah Gardez
map pg. 111, Free, Open to public
About 700m south of Ghantar Ghar is the Mauloseum of Hazrat Muhammad Shah Yusaf Gardezi, a Persian saint who is said to have travelled to Multan in 1088 performing miracles and thus converting people to Islam. What this boxy tomb lacks in size it makes up for in exquisite blue tiling work.

Old City and other shrines
There are literally thousands of shrines in and around Multan, the listing of which is well beyond the scope of this book. If you want to see more, you could walk around the old walled city, stumbling across them as you go, or asking locals for recommendations (but obviously use caution!). Alternatively, you could speak to your hotel about recommendations. Tours are also an option but be sure to explain that you want to see other tombs, not the famous ones you've already seen. Finally, PTDC could help - their details are listed below in 'services'.

Eidgah Mosque
map pg. 111, Free, Open to public
About a kilometre north of the main city is the Eidgah Mosque, the grand mosque of Multan, and the ceremonial mosque for occasions such as Eid. Built in 1735 by Multan's then-governor Nawab Abdul Samad Khan, it is covered in beautiful blue tiles and mosaics.

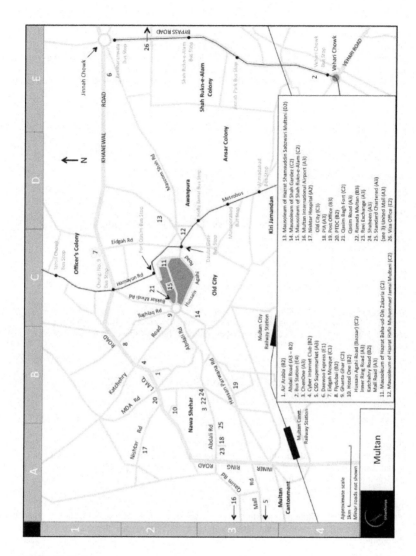

Multan

1. Air Arabia (B2)
2. Abdali Road (A3 – B2)
3. Bus Station (E4)
4. ChenOne (A3)
5. Cyber Internet Club (B2)
6. CSD Supermarket (A3)
7. Daewoo Express (A3)
8. Eidgah Mosque (C1)
9. Flydubai (B2)
10. Ghanta Ghar (C2)
11. Hotel One (B2)
    Hussain Agahi Road (Bazaar) (C2)
    Inner Ring Road (A3)
    Katchehry Road (B2)
    Mall Road (A3)
11. Mausoleum of Hazrat Baha-ud-Din Zakaria (C2)
12. Mausoleum of Hazrat Hafiz Muhammed Jamal Multani (C2)

13. Mausoleum of Hazrat Shamsuddin Sabzwari Multani (D2)
14. Mausoleum of Shah Gardei (C2)
15. Mausoleum of Shah Rukne-Alam (C2)
16. Multan International Airport (A3)
17. Nishtar Hospital (A2)
    Old City (C3)
18. PIA (A3)
19. Post Office (B3)
20. PTDC (B2)
21. Qasim Bagh Fort (C2)
    Qasim Road (A3)
22. Ramada Multan (B3)
23. Ravi Exchange (A3)
24. Shaheen (A3)
25. Standard Chartered (A3)
    [see 3] United Mall (A3)
26. Visa Office (E2)

Staying in Multan

Economy

Hotel One: 9 Lalazaar Colony, Multan; (+92) 341-2201111; www.hotelone.com.pk
map pg. 111, Dbl US$140
A budget-business venture by Pakistan's respected Pearl Continental chain.

Luxury

Ramada Multan: 76 Abdali Road, Multan; (+92) 061-4540877
map pg. 111, Dbl: US$215, Suite: US$235
Previously known as the Holiday Inn, it has been taken over by Ramada Hotels. Rooms offer mod-cons, and rates include buffet breakfast. Three restaurants, wifi, room service, a gym, pool and conference room.

Eating in Multan

There are countless places to eat in the centre of Multan, but hygiene standards are questionable. For a more reliable selection of sit-down restaurants, including the popular nationwide Bundu Khan chain and international options like Subway and Chinese restaurants, go to the area around Mall Road, Inner Ring Road and Abdali Road near Multan Cantt.

Services in Multan

Airlines

Air Arabia: 15 Faisal Arcade, opp. Divisional Sports Ground; (+92) 061458689899 *(map pg. 111)*.

Flydubai: Chungi 7, Kutchery Rd; (+92) 061-111225539 *(map pg. 111)*.

Pakistan International: 65 Abdali Road; (+92) 061-9200071 *(map pg. 111)*.

Qatar Airways: 1st Floor, S.S Mall, opp. Mission Hospital, Main Nusrat Rd, Multan Cantt; (+92) 061-4510151 *(map pg. 111)*.

Saudia: GSA Southern Travels, 1 Faisal Arcade, LMQ Road, opp. Divisional Sports Ground; (+92) 4541411 *(map pg. 111)*.

Shaheen: 64/4 Abdali Road; (+92) 061-9201445 *(map pg. 111)*.

Banks

Standard Chartered: Jalil Centre, Abdali Road, Multan *(map pg. 111)*.

Internet Cafe

There isn't a profusion of good internet cafes in Multan. If your accommodation can't recommend a good one, you can try the Cyber Internet Club (LMQ Rd, Katcherhry Chowk, Qadirabad) *(map pg. 111)*.

Money Exchange

Ravi Exchange: 28 Lower Ground Fl., Main Mrkt, Khan Ctr, Abdalli Rd; *(map pg. 111)*

Post Office

Hassan Parwana Road, Multan *(map pg. 111)*.

Shopping

ChenOne and United Mall are the main shopping malls in Multan *(map pg. 111)*. They're on Abdali Road, about halfway from Ghanta Ghar to Cantt. Hussain Agahi Road Bazaar *(map pg. 111)*, just near Ghanta Ghar (south of the big shrines) is the main traditional market area.

Supermarkets

It doesn't resemble Lahore's Hyperstar by any stretch of the imagination, but CSD Supermarket *(map pg. 111)* in Multan Cantt is the city's best bet for one-stop grocery shopping.

Tourist Information

Pakistan Tourism Development Corporation (PTDC) is at the Hotel Sindbad, Nishtar Chowk, Bahawalpur Road (+92) 061-512640 *(map pg. 111)*.

Travel Agency

There are lots of travel agencies along Katchehry Road *(map pg. 111)*, about a kilometre east of Ghantar Ghar.

Visa Office

Alfalah Market, U-Block, Near Madni Chowk, New Multan *(map pg. 111)*.

Help in Multan
Safety
Multan is a conservative city and you should dress and behave appropriately. It is advisable to be extra cautious in dealings and while travelling here; most people leave with no complaints other than the dust and the heat, but a kidnapping incident in 2012 (involving two aid workers) means no-one should be complacent about security. Note the issue of overzealous police officers described on page 109.

Medical Services
Nishtar Hospital: Nishtar Road, Multan; (+92) 061-9200231 *(map pg. 111)*.
Pharmacy: Nishtar Road, opposite Nishtar Hospital (see above) *(map pg. 111)*.
Also, a couple of pharmacies which are open late, but not 24 hours, on Qasim Road, along Abdali Road past the Inner Ring Road *(map pg. 111)*.

Getting around Multan
Rickshaws around the major sights of Multan should cost about Rs. 100 a ride in the city centre. To get out into the suburbs, expect to pay anywhere from Rs. 150 to Rs. 250. A rickshaw from the airport to the city will cost about Rs. 250, but you may well want to take a Metro Radio Cab; call 111-222-787 or go to www.metrocab.com.pk. A cab costs Rs. 400 at a base cost, then Rs. 20 for every subsequent kilometre.

The Multan Metrobus links a handful of important local sites for just Rs. 20 per ride, but apart from perhaps the transport junction at Vehari Chowk, the MetroBus doesn't link anywhere of great interest for travellers.

Travel agencies can organise day trips to Uch Sharif *(map pg. 108)*. Speak to your hotel about a recommended agency, or otherwise there are plenty along Katchehry Road.

Multan International Airport
Multan International Airport has been expanded in recent years. The low volume of tourist traffic it sees means it's a fairly easy place to pass through, although if you're arriving late at night, you'd be better advised to take a Metro Radio Cab (see above).

Leaving Multan
The Daewoo Express bus station is in the east of the city *(map pg. 111)*. The local bus station is southeast of the city, near Vehari Chowk *(map pg. 111)*.

Bus
Lahore: Daewoo Express, 5 hours 15 minutes, Rs. 950.
Rawalpindi/Islamabad: Daewoo Express, 8 hours, Rs. 1,500.
Faisalabad: Daewoo Express, 4 hours 15 minutes, Rs. 700.
Okara: Daewoo Express, 2 hours 55 minutes, Rs. 650.
Sahiwal: Daewoo Express, 2 hours 30 minutes, Rs. 530.
Bahawalpur: Daewoo Express, 1 hour 45 minutes, Rs. 300.
Rahim Yar Khan: Daewoo Express, 5 hours, Rs. 950.
Sukkur: Daewoo Express, 8 hours 20 minutes, Rs. 1,570.
Karachi: Daewoo Express, 14 hours, Rs. 2,850.

Train
Lahore: 5 to 6 hours, Rs. 410 (seat)
Rawalpindi/Islamabad: 10 - 12 hours, Rs. 770 (berth)
Karachi: 13 – 15 hours, Rs. 910 (berth)
Rohri/Sukkur: 6 – 7 hours, Rs. 430 (seat)
Hyderabad: 10 – 12 hours, Rs. 800 (berth)

Air
Islamabad: PIA, 1 hour 40 minutes, from Rs. 6,600.
Karachi: PIA and Shaheen, 1 hour 30 minute, from Rs. 6,500.
Lahore: PIA, 55 minute, from Rs. 6,700.

OKARA and RENALA KHURD

Population: 1.8 million, Elevation: 105m, Telephone code: 044

Okara is an important agricultural city on the road between Lahore and Multan, but boasts little in the way of tourist attractions. Nearby, the town of Renala Khurd is home to the Mitchells Fruit Farms Factory, which produce a popular range of jams in Pakistan. The two towns are about 16 kilometres apart, but Renala Khurd is much smaller - travellers would be better to stay in Okara because of the better facilities. Most people who visit do so enroute from Lahore to Multan - few hang around for much longer than a couple of hours.

What to see in Okara and Renala Khurd

Mitchells Fruit Jam Factory
map pg. 115

Mitchells is Pakistan's oldest food company, established in 1933 as Indian Mildura Fruit Farms Ltd. and changing its name to Mitchells after partition in honour of its founder Francis J. Mitchell. The company is among Pakistan's most successful, producing jams, cordials, sauces, pickles, confectionary and chocolates. Our favourite is the Golden Apple Jam!

You can visit the Mitchells factory to shop at the Fair Price Shop (five minutes walk from Kalma Chowk in the centre of town - ask for directions), or if you ask nicely enough, you might be given a free tour of the factory.

Staying in Okara

Economy
Sheish Mahal: Okara Lahore Road, Okara; (+92) 0315-6010970
map pg. 115, Dbl Rs. 2,000
One of Okara's only half-decent options; not suitable for solo women.

Eating in Okara and Renala Khurd

Delhi Hotel *(map pg. 115)* in Okara has a good reputation, with Pakistani staples and a range of desserts. If you're looking for relatively upmarket (and we use the term loosely), head to Okara Cantt (Rs. 50 in a rickshaw one way, 20 minutes *(map pg. 115)* - here you'll find nicer eateries serving Pakistani and Chinese dishes.

Churi Bazaar *(map pg. 115)* is the place to go for food in Renala Khurd. **Al Hammad Hotel** is supposed to be the pick of the lot, with lots of Pakistani dishes on the menu.

Services in Okara

Banks
No major international banks have representation in Okara or Renala Khurd.

Internet Cafe
Heading along Church Road in Okara *(map pg. 115)*, away from the railway line, there are several internet cafes on the left.

Post Office
In Okara, near the corner of Church Road and Bainazeer Road; follow the railway line along, and it's one block west form Church Rd, then one block to the right *(map pg. 115)*.

Help in Okara and Renala Khurd

Safety
Small and conservative, Okara and Renala Khurd are not good places to come unstuck. Remember where you are, and behave and dress conservatively.

Medical Services
Government (DHQ) Hospital: is in the north of town, past Company Bagh (044-2511193)
(map pg. 115)
Pharmacy is to be found at the hospital.

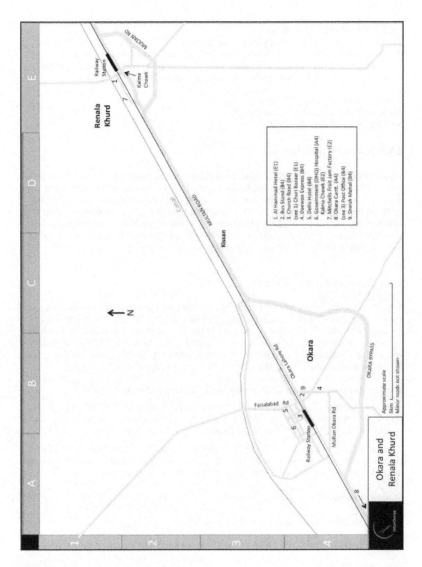

Map legend:

1. Al Hammad Hotel (E1)
2. Bus Stand (B4)
3. Church Road (B4)
(see 1) Churi Bazaar (E1)
4. Daewoo Express (B4)
5. Delhi Hotel (B4)
6. Government (DHQ) Hospital (A4)
Kalma Chowk (E2)
7. Mitchells Fruit Jam Factory (E2)
8. Okara Cantt. (A4)
(see 3) Post Office (B4)
9. Sheikh Mahal (B4)

Okara and Renala Khurd

OKARA BYPASS

Approximate scale
5km
Minor roads not shown

Getting around Okara and Renala Khurd

A rickshaw around Okara costs no more than Rs. 70, including to the Okara Daewoo Terminal. Renala Khurd is smaller than Okara, and you wouldn't pay more than Rs. 30 to get anywhere around the town; Mitchells is within walking distance of the centre.

From Renala Khurd to Okara, expect to pay Rs. 50 to be squashed into a local van - you can catch this from Okara's general bus stand *(map pg. 115)*. A rickshaw between the Okara and Renala Khurd would cost around Rs. 150, but some rickshaw wallahs might baulk at being asked to leave the city limits.

Leaving Okara and Renala Khurd
The Okara Daewoo Express bus station is on the main Lahore to Multan Road *(map pg. 115)*, but many services also arrive and leave from Okara Cantt Daewoo Express station *(map pg. 115)*, kilometres away - be sure to confirm. Okara's general bus station is just east of the centre *(map pg. 115)*. Buses stop in Renala Khurd at Kalma Chowk in the centre *(map pg. 115)*.

Lahore: Daewoo Express, 2 hours, Rs. 400
Multan: Daewoo Express, 3 hours, Rs. 650
Sahiwal: Local buses; 1 hour, Rs. 300

SAHIWAL and HARAPPA
Population: 2 million, Elevation: 152m, Telephone code: 040
Harappa is one of the sites where visitors can observe the remains of the up to 5000 year-old Indus Valley Civilisation. Although the discovery of what is now an archaeological site was no doubt show-stopping for archaeologists, it's debatable whether Harappa warrants a trip by the average tourist; it's still very much an archaeological dig in parts, the sights aren't breathtaking, and it's predictably hot and dusty. The city of Sahiwal, 24 kilometres to the east, is the usual jumping-off point to get to Harappa, and although there's not much to see there, it could conceivably serve as a place to break the journey between Lahore and Multan.

What to see in Sahiwal and Harappa
Harappa Historic Site
Spread over a huge site west of the main town of Harappa, the historic site is where the Indus Valley's civilisation's second largest settlement was (the largest was Moenjodaro, in present day Sindh, pg. 149). Not much is left of this site; most of it has been looted over the centuries. For serious history buffs, a 1 - 2 kilometre trail takes in the highlights of what is left; a mound which was once a fortress, an ancient cemetery, and the grave-like footprint of a long-since ruined barn. More interesting is the Harappa Archaeological Museum *(map pg. 117, Rs. 200, Open: 8:30am - 12:30pm, 2:30pm - 5:30pm in summer, 9am - 4pm in winter)*, showing artefacts that have turned up at the site such as tools, toys, and even shell ware.

To get to Harappa, you can hire a Toyota Hiace or similar van from Sahiwal's main bus station, or more conveniently, you can organise it through your hotel. The van plus driver should cost Rs. 1,200 - Rs. 1,500 for the round trip, including waiting time.

Alternatively, you can catch a local bus for about Rs. 40 one way, but these will usually drop you in Harappa village, leaving you with a hot dusty walk through fields to the site. An autorickshaw will cost around Rs. 800 for the round trip, including waiting time.

Staying in Sahiwal
Economy
Iris Hotel: Railway Road, Sahiwal; (+92) 040-4226727
map pg. 117, Dbl Rs. 5,000
The best hotel in Sahiwal is not a luxurious affair, but the rooms have TVs and air con.

Eating in Sahiwal
There are no main food precincts in Sahiwal and Harappa, however Karbala Road, leading through the bazaar in Sahiwal, has several basic Pakistani eateries. The Iris Hotel serves Pakistani food, along with a smattering of Chinese and continental dishes, and there's a decent **Italian Pizza Hut** just west of the bazaar *(all map pg. 117)*. Don't forget to taste some of the sweet treats that this area is known for; walnut halwa, sohan halwa and gajar halwa.

Services in Sahiwal
Banks
No major international banks have representation in Sahiwal

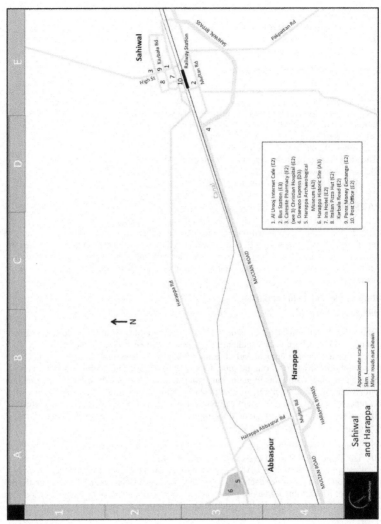

Sahiwal and Harappa

1. Al Urooj Internet Cafe (E2)
2. Bus Station (E3)
3. Caresite Pharmacy (E2) (see 3) Christian Hospital (E2)
4. Daewoo Express (D3)
5. Harappa Archaeological Museum (A3)
6. Harappa Historic Site (A3)
7. Iris Hotel (E2)
8. Italian Pizza Hut (E2)
9. Parex Money Exchange (E2)
10. Post Office (E2)

Approximate scale
5km
Minor roads not shown.

Internet Cafe
Al Urooj Computers: 1 Al Arooj Street, off High Street *(map pg. 117)*

Money Exchange
Parex: 303 1/3 Block 2, Jinnah Chowk; *(map pg. 117)*

Post Office
Railway Road *(map pg. 117)*

Help in Sahiwal
Safety
Sahiwal is small and while it is more progressive than some other villages in the region, is still quite a conservative place. Dress and act conservatively for a warmer welcome.

Medical Services

Christian Hospital: the best in Sahiwal, corner of Mission Chowk & High St (+92) 040-4460133 *(map pg. 117)*

Caresite Pharmacy: associated with the Christian Hospital *(map pg. 117)*

Getting around Sahiwal and Harappa

A rickshaw around town costs Rs. 50 - Rs. 100, while to the Daewoo Terminal is Rs. 50.

Leaving Sahiwal

The Daewoo Express bus station is at the western end of town *(map pg. 117)*. The local bus station is on Multan Road, just a bit closer to the centre *(map pg. 117)*.

Lahore: Daewoo Express, 2 hours 30 minutes, Rs. 530
Faisalabad: Local buses; 2 hours, Rs. 300
Multan: Daewoo Express, 2 hours 30 minutes, Rs. 530
Okara: Local buses; 1 hour, Rs. 300
Pakpattan: Local buses, 45 minutes, Rs. 50

PAKPATTAN

Population: 1.5 million, Elevation: 152m, Telephone code: 0457

Out towards the Indian border from Sahiwal lies dusty Pakpattan, one of the oldest towns in Punjab. It's an important point of pilgrimage for many Pakistanis who come to pay their respects to the saint Baba Farid who was buried here, along with several other important Sufi mystics. Most travellers who come here do so on a day trip, either from Sahiwal, or further afield, Lahore or Multan.

What to see and do in Pakpattan

Shrine of Baba Farid

map pg. 119, Free, Open to public

"Baba Farid" is the affectionate name for Khwaja Fariduddin Masud Ganjshakar, a saint and poet who was born near Multan in 1179. He is highly respected as one of the subcontinent's most prominent early Islamic scholars. Through his life he studied and taught Islamic philosophy throughout the subcontinent, Central Asia and Middle East. When he passed away in 1265 he was living in Pakpattan, and a shrine quickly sprang up around his tomb. Constructed from marble, the small shrine continues to attract a constant stream of devotees who believe that the saint's presence has special healing powers. Women are not allowed to enter the inner sanctum of the tomb, but the grave itself is always covered in flowers thrown by pilgrims.

Shoes must be removed to enter the shrine (leave them with the minder at the gate for Rs. 10). The shrine (and Pakpattan generally) are especially crowded during the saint's *urs* (death anniversary) which in 2018 is expected to fall on around the 15th September, and moves about 10 days earlier each year. Note that the *urs* of Baba Farid falls between the 5th and 10th of Muharram, a time of heightened security across Pakistan (see page 21) and security in Pakpattan is particularly tight at during this time.

Waris Shah Mosque

map pg. 119, Free, Open to public

Waris Shah, the renowned Sufi poet from Jandiala Sher Khan (page 69) lived in a small town 15 kilometres northwest of Pakpattan called Malka Hans. While he was buried near his birthplace, the mosque next to his residence has become a place of pilgrimage and is referred to as Masjid Waris Shah (Waris Shah Mosque). The simple white and green building attracts a steady stream of visitors who pay their respects to the poet, philosopher and mystic. To get here, hire a rickshaw from Pakpattan (Rs. 200, incl. waiting time.)

Staying in Pakpattan

Most travelers who are not pilgrims to the Baba Farid Shrine do not stay in Pakpattan, rather visiting on a day trip from Sahiwal, Multan or even Lahore. If you choose to stay the night, the Mehran Hotel *(map pg. 119)* is one of the best places to rest your head – count on paying Rs. 900 – 1700 depending on the season.

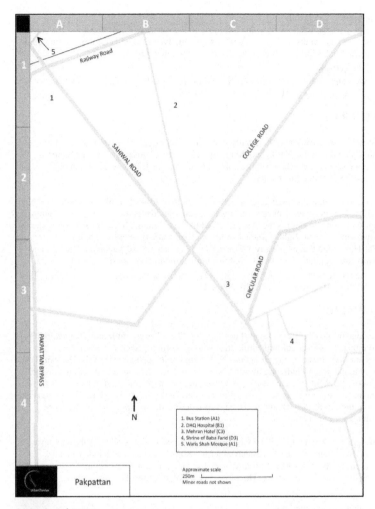

1. Bus Station (A1)
2. DHQ Hospital (B1)
3. Mehran Hotel (C3)
4. Shrine of Baba Farid (D3)
5. Waris Shah Mosque (A1)

Approximate scale
250m
Minor roads not shown

Pakpattan

Eating in Pakpattan

Mehran Hotel (mentioned above) is one of the better places to eat, but the surrounding streets (and streets near the Baba Farid Shrine) have plenty of cheap street eats.

Services in Pakpattan

Banks

No international banks have repreentation in Pakpattan.

Help in Pakpattan

Safety

Pakpattan is conservative, but considering the number of devotees who come to visit the shrine, it's also more accepting than the average Punjabi village. Note the issue of police officers described on page 109.

Medical Services

District Headquarters Hospital (DHQ Hospital) is the best in town *(map pg. 119)*.

Getting around Pakpattan
A place in a qingqi rickshaw from the bus stand to the shrine will cost about Rs. 10, but if there are less passengers the price will rise exponentially. Anywhere else in town, including to the Waris Shah Mosque, costs about Rs. 20 per spot in a qingqi.

Leaving Pakpattan
Buses, vans and wagons to Sahiwal leave from the bus stand at Pakpattan Chowk and cost Rs. 40 – 80 depending on comfort and air conditioning.

UCH SHARIF
Population: 21,000, Elevation: 103m, Telephone code: 06902
Uch Sharif , also known as Uch, is built on the site of Alexander the Great's city of Alexandria on the Indus. Hardly anything remains of that civilisation, but Uch Sharif is home to the spectacularly crumbling tombs of Sufi notables Bibi Jawindi, Baha'al-Halin and Sufi great Syed Jalaluddin Bukhari.

The octagonal tombs are three large structures, each two stories tall, tiled in a colourful blue and yellow Islamic style. Bibi Jawindi was the great granddaughter of Sufi saint Jahaniyan Jahangasght, and her tomb is the best preserved of the lot, dating back to 1493, while the other two tombs are in slightly worse condition. Signs mark the tombs of Sufi mystic Baha'al-Halim and that of Jahaniyan Jahangasht's architect. Syed Jalaluddin Bukhari and his family are also buried at this site, but in significantly more modest tombs.

There's nowhere to stay in Uch Sharif; take a day trip from Multan (Rs. 4,000, page 111) or a half-day from Bahawalpur (Rs. 2,500, page 122).

BAHAWALPUR
Population: 855,000, Elevation: 119m, Telephone code: 062
On the edge of the Cholistan Desert (known as the "Thar Desert" in India), Bahawalpur's location means it shares cultural similarities with the former princely states of Rajasthan. Palaces and forts make up the attractions here, with the imposing walls of the Derawar Fort dominating the desert landscape for miles around, and acting as something of an icon for this desert city. While the city itself is not much to look at, the mention of its name to Pakistanis conjures up imaginings of a princely state in the desert, lavish royal functions and time-honoured traditions. Being on the edge of a desert, It's also very hot in summer - temperatures routinely top 50C.

Bahawalpur was founded in 1748 by Nawab Mohammed Bahawal Khan Abbasi I whose son went on to found the state of Bahawalpur in 1802. After Pakistan's independence Bahawalpur retained its distinct princely state heritage for eight years before finally ceding power to the central government. The town is centred on Chowk Fawara.

What to see in Bahawalpur
Noor Mahal and other palaces
map pg. 121, Closed to the public
Built in 1872 for the *nawab* (prince) or Bahawalpur, Noor Mahal is a beautiful palace built in a fusion of Mediterranean and Islamic architecture styles. Unfortunately for travellers it is in the hands of the Pakistan Army who keep it closed unless a dignitary wants to have a gala dinner there. You can still see it from the outside. There is also a Dubai Palace in Bahawalpur, off limits to the public, where the Emir of Dubai apparently comes and spends his falconry vacations.

Derawar Fort and the Cholistan Desert
map pg. 121, Fort open sunrise to sunset daily, Entry: Rs. 500
Derawar Fort is one and half hours from Bahawalpur, and is a great way to visit the desert. The Cholistan Desert is a sandy expanse which straddles the border of India and Pakistan, and is named after the local nomads (*chol*) who tread the barren landscape.

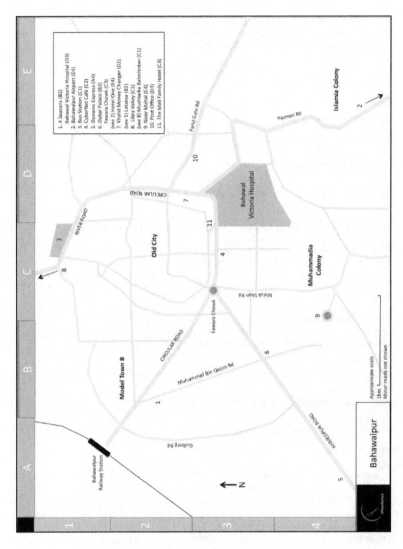

Legend (map):

1. 4 Seasons (B2)
2. Bahawal Victoria Hospital (D3)
3. Bahawalpur Airport (E4)
4. Bus Station (C1)
5. CyberNet Café (C3)
6. Daewoo Express (A4)
7. Dubai Palace (C3)
Fawara Chowk (C3)
[see 2] Hostel One (E4)
7. Khalid Money Changer (D2)
[see 11] Lataksa (B2)
8. Ubra Valley (C1)
[see 8] Mushtarka Balochistan (C1)
9. Noor Mahal (C4)
10. Post Office (D3)
11. The Mall Family Hotel (C3)

Islamia Colony

Yarman Rd

Fand Gate Rd

10

Bahawal Victoria Hospital

CIRCULAR ROAD

7

Old City

11

RIVER ROAD

8

4

Muhammadia Colony

9

Malik Shah Rd

Fawara Chowk

CIRCULAR ROAD

Model Town B

6

Muhammad Bin Qasim Rd

1

AHMEDPUR ROAD

Gulberg Rd

Bahawalpur Railway Station

5

Approximate scale
1km
Minor roads not shown

N

Bahawalpur

Derawar's huge circular ramparts stand 30 metres tall and can be seen from kilometres away. The square fort is 1.5 kilometres in circumference. A fort of some form is believed to have existed on this site for centuries before it came under Bahawalpur's rule in 1733. As you approach the fort, you pass under arches, before driving up the road to the final gate. Here you will probably be met by someone offering a camel ride around the fort - if you feel so inclined.

Into the fort, directly ahead of you in the centre, are the old living quarters, some with marble tiles on the floor - it's not clear how recently these were added. At the far end of the living quarters you can descend a spiral staircase to the old dungeon, but since one wall has yielded to the forces of nature, the airy room doesn't feel as menacing as it might have once upon a time. The fort is pretty much open to be explored – very little is off-limits. Clamber all over the ramparts, look out into the desert and imagine invading armies galloping across the sands. The nearby mosque is also quite pretty - reportedly modelled on the mosque in Delhi's Red Fort.

Derawar Fort is best reached with a day tour from Bahawalpur - see "Getting Around Bahawalpur" for details. The fort can also be reached from Rahim Yar Khan (2.5 hours one way, see pg. 123).

Staying in Bahawalpur
Economy
The Mall Family Hotel: Circular Road, Bahawalpur (+92) 062-2877698
map pg. 121, Dbl Rs. 5,000
A long-standing economic option with air-conditioning

Luxury
Hotel One: Yazman Road, near airport, Bahawalpur; (+92) 0341-2201111; www.hotelone.com.pk
map pg. 121, Dbl US$140
A budget-business venture by Pakistan's respected Pearl Continental chain.

Eating in Bahawalpur
There isn't one central gastronomical district in Bahawalpur like in Lahore or Islamabad, but there are lots of restaurants around. **Lataksa**, **4 Seasons**, **Mushtarka Balochistan** and **Libra Valley** are all nice (more upmarket) options, but the latter two are quite a distance out of town *(all on map pg. 121)*.

Services in Bahawalpur
Banks
No major international banks have representation in Bahawalpur.

Internet Cafe
CyberNet Café: is on Circular Road, near the Bahawal Victoria Hospital *(map pg. 121)*.

Money Exchange
Khalid Money Changers: Circular Road *(map pg. 121)*.

Post Office
The GPO is on University Chowk Road *(map pg. 121)*.

Help in Bahawalpur
Safety
A conservative place, Bahawalpur requires travellers to be sensitive to local customs and beliefs. Dress and behave appropriately. Note the issue of overzealous police officers described on page 109.

Medical Services
Bahawal Victoria Hospital (BVH): (+92) 062-9250411 *(map pg. 121)*.
24 Hour Pharmacies: are across the road from Bahawal Victoria Hospital *(map pg. 121)*.

Getting around Bahawalpur
A rickshaw around the centre of town should cost no more than Rs. 50 to Rs. 100, while the centre of town to the Daewoo Terminal is around Rs. 100, and to the airport would cost about Rs. 300. Tours to Derawar Fort can be arranged through your hotel or a travel agency, and should cost around Rs. 3000 for the day. **Travel agencies** can also organise day trips to Uch Sharif (page 120). Speak to your hotel about a recommended agency, or otherwise there are plenty to be found around Fawara Chowk.

Leaving Bahawalpur
The Daewoo Express bus station is to the southwest of town on Ahmedpur Road *(map pg. 121)*. The local bus station is at the northern end of town on River Road *(map pg. 121)*.

<u>Bus</u>
Lahore: Daewoo Express, 6 hours 40 minutes, Rs. 1,250.
Faisalabad: Daewoo Express, 6 hours 15 minutes, Rs. 1,050.
Multan: Daewoo Express, 1 hour 45 minutes, Rs. 300
Rahim Yar Khan: Daewoo Express, 3 hours, Rs. 470
Sukkur: Daewoo Express, 6 hours, Rs. 1,170
Karachi: Daewoo Express, 14 hours, Rs. 2,600

<u>Train</u>
Lahore: 6 to 7 hours, Rs. 450 (seat)
Islamabad: 11 – 13 hours, Rs. 840 (berth)
Karachi: 12 – 14 hours, Rs. 840 (berth)
Rohri/Sukkur: 5 – 6 hours, Rs. 370 (seat)

<u>Air</u>
Lahore: PIA, 1 hour, from Rs. 6500
Karachi: PIA, 1 hour 30 minutes, from Rs. 6500

RAHIM YAR KHAN
Population: 353,000, Elevation: 83m, Telephone code: 068
Rahim Yar Khan is, on the surface, a scruffy-looking town without any major tourist sites. Scratch the surface to reveal a newly-wealthy but comparatively conservative town whose richest inhabitants live in walled compounds on the outskirts, and who have vast business interests in Karachi, Dubai and beyond. Rahim Yar Khan (RYK) is known for being a centre of business, and despite being home to only 353,000 people, hosts an outlet of the Karachi Stock Exchange and an international airport. The rulers of more than one Arab Gulf state spend their holidays around here, on desert safaris and falconry retreats. The region is dusty and semi-arid, but the town is mostly clustered around a green park which is home to a government office - look for the large brick building set amongst gardens. Rahim Yar Khan's weather can be prohibitively hot in summer, and duststorms are not uncommon.

In 1881 the prince of Bahawalpur decided to rename the town of Naushera, and naturally he did so after his first son, Rahim Yar Khan. Despite being saddled with an odd name, RYK is now one of Pakistan's fastest growing cities, owing to its strategic location on the national highway, and in the southern agricultural region of Punjab. While it doesn't have the allure of Bahawalpur (a former princely state) or the size of Multan, Rahim Yar Khan is a great jumping off point for some beautiful tourist sites.

What to see in Rahim Yar Khan
Rahim Yar Khan doesn't have a lot of tourist attractions, but it's a great jumping-off point for Bhong Mosque (see below) and Derawar Fort and the Cholistan Desert (see page 120).

<u>Bhong Mosque</u>
map pg. 108, Open sunrise to sunset daily, Entry: free
Rahim Yar Khan's most famous icon is the sublime Bhong Mosque. Located in the small village of Bhong, fifty kilometres southwest of Rahim Yar Khan, this mosque is a constant work in progress. A local legend says that if construction work was to halt, then members of a local family would start dying. The result is an ornate construction that is perpetually being added to and maintained. The outrageous colours of the Bhong Mosque are an arresting sight; magenta, turquoise, maroon and straw, the riot of hues continues around every corner. Highlights of this elaborate mosque are the giant tiled Qur'an in the fountain at the entrance, the page at the *mihrab* which contains every single word of the Qur'an written in miniature, and the door handles shaped to resemble the Arabic spelling of the name "Muhammad". The best way to reach Bhong is on a half-day tour from Rahim Yar Khan - a tour to would usually cost around Rs. 2,000.

Staying in Rahim Yar Khan
Economy
Hotel Lamis: Shahi Road, Rahim Yar Khan; (+92) 068-5887244
map pg. 125, Dbl Rs. 3,500
Cheap in the centre of town, with an attached restaurant.

Luxury
Desert Palm Hotel: Businessmen Colony,; (+92) 068-5877615;
www.facebook.com/desertpalmhotel
map pg. 125, Dbl 8,400, Suite 10,900
The best hotel in town (3 - 4 stars), the Desert Palm is a fairly recent construction with comfortable rooms and a large restaurant downstairs.

Eating in Rahim Yar Khan
Fast food eateries of all sorts exist on the streets around the central park; Almaida and Hot Chicks *(map pg. 125)* are fast food joints, Cafe Lamis *(map pg. 125)* is more upmarket, and the restaurant at the Desert Palm Hotel is great *(map pg. 125)*. Walking away from the town hall's face, there are a bunch of cheap eateries at the next major junction; around here you'll find karahi, barbecue places and Lahore's Chaman Ice Cream.

Services in Rahim Yar Khan
Banks
Standard Chartered: 13 Town Hall Road, Rahim Yar Khan *(map pg. 125)*.

Internet Cafe
There are a couple of internet cafes in the streets around the central park, or otherwise the Royal Internet Cafe *(map pg. 125)* is on Shahi Road at the eastern end of town, near the railway station.

Money Exchange
NBP Exchange: 28 Shahi Road, Model Town, opposite City Park *(map pg. 125)*.

Post Office
The GPO is in the town centre, across the road from the central park *(map pg. 125)*.

Help in Rahim Yar Khan
Safety
Rahim Yar Khan is a conservative town and the areas around it are home to some very poor and conservative communities. Dressing appropriately is non-optional. This region has seen militant activity in the past, and while at the time of writing it was generally safe, there's no guarantee that it will always be peaceful. Make yourself aware of local conditions, and speak to authorities before setting out. Note the issue of overzealous police officers described on page 109.

Medical Services
Sheikh Zayed Medical College: (+92) 068-92301618 *(map pg. 125)*.
Pharmacies are available opposite Sheikh Zayed Medical College

Getting around Rahim Yar Khan
Rickshaws around the city centre should cost no more than Rs. 50 - Rs. 80 (tourist price), while a rickshaw to the airport is Rs. 100. Ask at your hotel for a tour, otherwise there are several tour agencies in the street surrounding the central park. A tour to Derawar Fort (page 120) should cost around Rs. 8,000.

Leaving Rahim Yar Khan
The Daewoo Express bus station is actually not in Rahim Yar Khan, but at Chowk Bahadarpur *(map pg. 108)*, a suburb to the west on the main highway. Daewoo Express

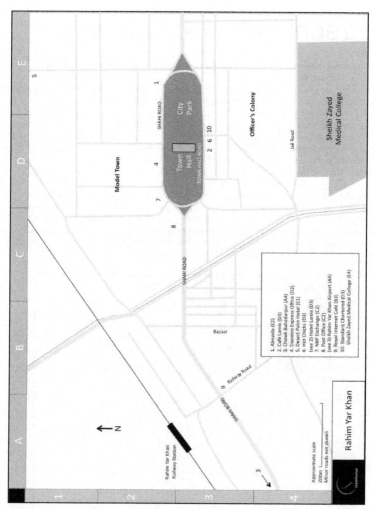

Rahim Yar Khan

1. Almaida (E2)
2. Café Lamis (D3)
3. Chowk Bahadarpur (A4)
4. Daewoo Express Office (D2)
5. Desert Palm Hotel (E1)
6. Hot Chicks (D3)
(see 2) Hotel Lamis (D3)
7. NBP Exchange (C2)
8. Post Office (C2)
(see 3) Rahim Yar Khan Airport (A4)
9. Royal Internet Café (B3)
10. Standard Chartered (D3)
    Sheikh Zayed Medical College (E4)

Approximate scale
200m
Minor roads not shown

operate a feeder minibus service from an office in Rahim Yar Khan's main street *(map pg. 125)* to Chowk Bahadarpur to meet departing or arriving buses.

Bus
Lahore: Daewoo Express, 10 hours, Rs. 1,700
Faisalabad: Daewoo Express, 9 hours 30 minutes, Rs. 1,600
Multan: Daewoo Express, 5 hours, Rs. 950
Bahawalpur: Daewoo Express, 3 hours, Rs. 470
Sukkur: Daewoo Express, 3 hours, Rs. 560
Karachi: Daewoo Express, 10 hours 30 minutes, Rs. 2,000

Air
Lahore: PIA, 1 hour 25 minutes, from Rs. 7,300
Karachi: PIA, 1 hour 25 minutes, from Rs. 7,300 one way.

Karachi *and surrounds*

Karachi is Pakistan's largest city, its economic and trading hub, and a focal point for business. This enormous metropolis sprawls out in all directions, but despite its size, has little in the way of tourist attractions; in fact most foreign travellers skip the city altogether, forsaking it for more-interesting Lahore or the more peaceful northern mountains. In many ways, Karachi doesn't even feel like Pakistan at all; it's much more cosmopolitan, liberal, secular and fast-paced than the traditional ethos of most of the rest of the country. The local Urdu-speaking population are a much more multicultural bunch than you'll find in any other city, and it's not unusual to see Hindus, Christians or "Parsis" (Zoroastrians) practicing their faiths or celebrating their festivals relatively openly. There's also a palpable Arabic influence here, reflected in the names of hotels, aiming to attract traders from the Gulf.

Around Karachi lie a handful of attractions; Hyderabad and Thatta (although both considered "Interior Sindh") are logical choices for day trips from the provincial capital. One of Karachi's defining features is the coastline, something of a treat in Pakistan where the majority of the population lives hundreds of kilometres inland. The beaches immediately around Karachi are not beautiful, but further afield there are options to swim, snorkel and even scuba-dive in the clear waters of the Arabian Sea.

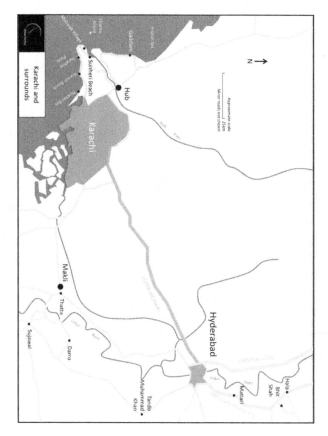

KARACHI

Population: 27 million, Elevation: 8m, Telephone code: 021

Set by a wide bay on the Arabian Sea, Karachi's climate is not dissimilar to that of Dubai or Mumbai. It's hot and humid for much of the year, with warm winters and stifling heat in summer, often offset by a welcome seabreeze (sometimes cool, sometimes warm, but a breeze nonetheless) in the evenings. It's streets are, admittedly, dirtier than the streets of any other city of Pakistan, a result of the heaving population (by some counts, Karachi is the 7th largest city in the world). However not all of Karachi is filthy, and while standing in the lovely seaside district of Clifton you can almost forget the squalor of places like Lyari. Away from the sea front, many middle class Karachiites live in towering concrete apartment blocks; an indicator of the city's urban mentality, unlike Lahore where entire extended families often live under one roof.

Karachi's urbane sensibility stands in stark contrast to the rural character of the rest of Sindh, and in fact Sindhi culture in Karachi is drowned out by the cacophony of Urdu-speaking immigrants. This disconnect between Karachi and the province of which it is the capital has led to many complaints over the years - from Sindhis who accuse Karachi of being out of touch, and from Karachiities who label rural Sindhis as "backwards". More than once the idea of a separate "Karachi Province" has been floated.

If Pakistan is, as British author Anatol Lieven once said, "a hard country", then Karachi is its hardest city. Karachi is a victim of its own story. There has been a settlement at or near the mouth of the Indus River for time immemorial. It is a logical location for a port; when you stand on any of Karachi's beaches, you're looking out towards ports in Oman, the UAE, Yemen, East Africa and the western coast of India. Like most ports with a transient population of traders, Karachi was an attractive base from which criminals could operate - and they continue to do so. In fact Karachi's crime rates are a point of national discussion, and although they have dramatically improved since a major police operation in 2013, they continue to be significantly above the average. Everything from petty theft and bag-snatching through to targeted killings and organised crime is an issue in Karachi.

Social issues in Karachi have been exacerbated over the years by the influx of millions trying to improve their lives; the "*mohajir*" refugees who fled India during partition in 1947 placed an enormous but inevitable strain on a fledgling but unprepared city. As the nation's business hub for the past seventy years, scores of northern Pakistanis migrated to the city in search of greener pastures, and the war in Afghanistan saw a third wave of migrants descend on the city in the hope of a brighter future. Perhaps inevitably, ethnic and sectarian-based political parties emerged and inhibited the progress of the city - the 1980s and 1990s saw particularly violent episodes of near-urban warfare between rival factions. In 1958 Karachi lost its status as the national capital, compounding the decline of a city which was fast outgrowing itself.

All of this makes for a mix which is simultaneously fascinating and horrifying - a dystopian Singapore, if you like. Gigantic apartment blocks marching into the deserted plains; huge, leafy parks once planned by the British but now home to squatters; businesses everywhere but perhaps more beggars than anywhere else in the country; smartly-dressed corporate high flyers (both men and women) making their way to work past armed-to-the-hilt security personnel; Pakistan's best restaurants and celebrity scene besieged by the worst traffic jams you might ever experience. If you're arriving from anywhere else in the world, you may well start counting the days until you leave - your enjoyment of Karachi will depend on your state of mind, and where and with whom you stay. If you're arriving from the northern cities of Lahore or Islamabad, you are about to experience a modern slice of Pakistan (warts and all) that you never knew existed.

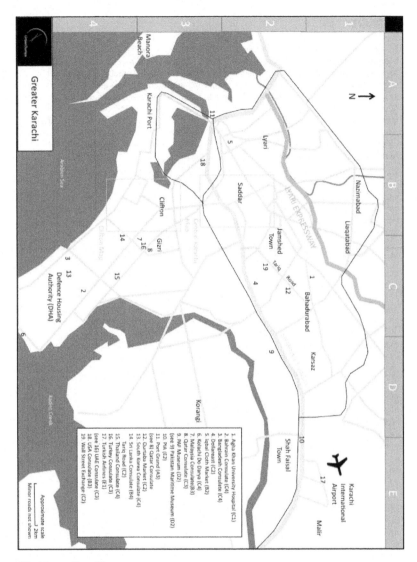

Greater Karachi

1. Agha Khan University Hospital (C1)
2. Bahrain Consulate (C4)
3. Bangladesh Consulate (C4)
4. Dollarsest (C2)
5. Iqbal Cloth Market (B2)
6. Kolachi Do Darya (C4)
7. Malaysia Consulate(B3)
8. Qatar Consulate (C3)
9. PAF Museum (D2)
(see 9) Pakistan Maritime Museum (D2)
10. PIA (E2)
11. Port Grand (A3)
(see 8) Qatar Consulate
12. Ourtaba Market (C2)
13. South Korea Consulate (C4)
14. Sri Lanka Consulate (B4)
15. Thailand Consulate (C2)
Tariq Road (C2)
16. Turkey Consulate (C3)
17. Turkish Airlines (E1)
(see 16) UAE Consulate (C3)
18. USA Consulate (B3)
19. Wall Street Exchange (C2)

Approximate scale
Minor roads not shown.

What to see Karachi
Mazar-e-Quaid (Muhammad Ali Jinnah's Mausoleum)
map pg. 130, Open 10am – 6:30pm, Closed Monday, Rs. 20

When the founder of Pakistan, Muhammed Ali Jinnah (usually referred to as Quaid-e-Azam, the "Great Leader") passed away on 11th September 1948, his mourning nation was just over a year old. Suffering from a lung condition, he had been staying at a retreat in Ziarat, Balochistan (near Quetta) whose summer climate was more agreeable. On the morning of the 11th September, at the urging of his doctors, he was flown to Karachi where the medical treatment was more advanced, but he succumbed to cancer-related pneumonia a few hours after arriving.

Jinnah was laid to rest in what was to become a huge mausoleum on the edge of Karachi's downtown. The tomb was completed in the 1960s, and was designed in a Central Asian style, constructed from white marble. The large park around the tomb is popular with picnickers and neighbourhood children who come to play cricket. Inside the tomb visitors are required to remove their shoes, and the atmosphere is suitably solemn. You may be lucky enough to witness the dramatic changing of the guard ceremony, which occurs every couple of hours in complete silence inside the inner sanctum of the grave. No cameras are allowed inside the grounds of the tomb.

Clifton Beach
map pg. 134
Clifton Beach isn't winning any awards for its beauty - the black sand, throngs of crowds and corresponding piles of trash make it one of the least visually appealing beaches you will ever see, and there's no way you'd swim here. So why do people still come? The answer lies in the beach's proximity to the city, and the fact that on a sweltering Karachi day people will do anything to catch the seabreeze (and, at a stretch, allow the water to wash over their feet). For visitors the scene is more about the crowds and the drama of watching the sun set into the Arabian Sea while camels and snack-sellers wander past; people-watching, not sunbathing is the order of the day. If you want to visit a beach for more traditional seaside pursuits, try French Beach or Charna Island (page 137).

Abdullah Ghazi Ziarat
map pg. 134, Open Dawn – late, Free
Something to make a trip to Clifton Beach more fruitful might be a visit to the Abdullah Ghazi Ziarat. Ghazi was a Muslim mystic born in Medina (in modern-day Saudi Arabia) in 720 AD and may have taken part in Muhammad bin Qasim's conquest of Sindh in the eighth century. As one of the first Muslims in the subcontinent he is highly regarded, especially in Pakistan. Upon his death he was buried at the seafront where he is believed to have first set foot in the region. 1,200 years later the shoreline has shifted and his grave now stands about a kilometre from the beach, upon a small ridge disguised by roads and flyovers. The tomb itself is housed amid a simple complex that, at the time of research, was getting a huge upgrade - expect the place to look like a construction site for months, or maybe years to come. Thankfully, the interior blue-and-white tilework of the actual grave site has been preserved.

Museums
As the largest city in Pakistan and one-time capital, it makes sense that Karachi would host its fair share of museums. Appropriately, the National Museum of Pakistan *(map pg. 128, Rs. 200, 10am-5pm, closed Wednesday)* is here, and although its intentions are in the right place, it's large collection of artefacts and posters feels a bit underwhelming. Nevertheless you might find the collections from northern Pakistan interesting, particularly the regional costumes and weapons.

Better maintained are the Pakistan Maritime Museum *(map pg. 128, Rs. 30, 8am - 10pm)* and the PAF (Pakistan Air Force) Museum *(map pg. 128, Rs. 50, 8.30am - 5pm except Friday 3pm - 5pm)*. Both are better updated than the National Museum, and present a wide range of artefacts and vignettes of the work of Pakistan's lionised military forces. Strangely, the Pakistan Air Force Museum has a "families only" policy, meaning that no single men, or groups of men can visit without the company of a woman.

Quaid-e-Azam House/Museum
map pg. 130, Open daily 9am - 5pm, Free
Flagstaff House, now known as Quaid-e-Azam House, was the residence of Muhammad Ali Jinnah from 1944 until his death in 1948. After his death his sister Fatima Ali Jinnah, herself a prominent figure in the Pakistan movement, continued to live here. In 1985 the house was converted to a museum and houses a few interesting curios from the leader's life.

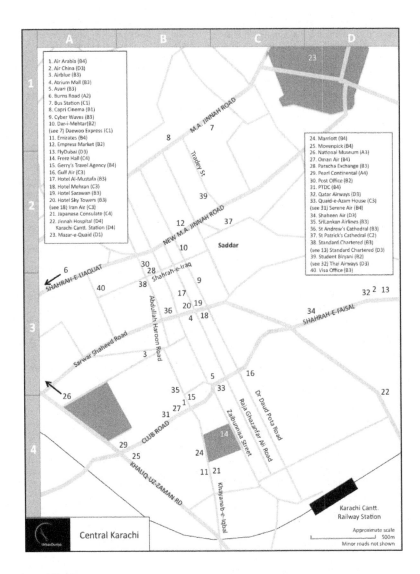

Central Karachi

Approximate scale
500m
Minor roads not shown

1. Air Arabia (B4)
2. Air China (D3)
3. Airblue (B3)
4. Atrium Mall (B3)
5. Avari (B3)
6. Burns Road (A2)
7. Bus Station (C1)
8. Capri Cinema (B1)
9. Cyber Waves (B3)
10. Dar-i-Mehtar(B2)
(see 7) Daewoo Express (C1)
11. Emirates (B4)
12. Empress Market (B2)
13. FlyDubai (D3)
14. Frere Hall (C4)
15. Gerry's Travel Agency (B4)
16. Gulf Air (C3)
17. Hotel Al-Mustafa (B3)
18. Hotel Mehran (C3)
19. Hotel Sarawan (B3)
20. Hotel Sky Towers (B3)
(see 18) Iran Air (C3)
21. Japanese Consulate (C4)
22. Jinnah Hospital (D4)
    Karachi Cantt. Station (D4)
23. Mazar-e-Quaid (D1)

24. Marriott (B4)
25. Movenpick (B4)
26. National Museum (A3)
27. Oman Air (B4)
28. Paracha Exchange (B3)
29. Pearl Continental (A4)
30. Post Office (B2)
31. PTDC (B4)
32. Qatar Airways (D3)
33. Quaid-e-Azam House (C3)
(see 31) Serene Air (B4)
34. Shaheen Air (D3)
35. SriLankan Airlines (B3)
36. St Andrew's Cathedral (B3)
37. St Patrick's Cathedral (C2)
38. Standard Chartered (B3)
(see 13) Standard Chartered (D3)
39. Student Biryani (B2)
(see 32) Thai Airways (D3)
40. Visa Office (B3)

Around Saddar

Saddar *(map pg. 130)* is one of the districts of Karachi's city centre, and as such is the busiest, most polluted, most congested part of town. It's also home to a handful of smaller sights that can be seen in a long day's walk around the centre, or alternatively, a hired rickshaw could run you around to avoid the worst of the heat. Walking really is a good option if you can bear it, however, because half the fun comes from engaging in daily Karachi life - the smells from the food vendors, the invitations to chai and the friendly bookshop owners who want to chat.

The most obvious sight near Saddar is <u>Empress Market</u>, the huge wholesale produce market directly to the north. You'll know when you're there because it's construction looks like a town hall facade, but through the arched door below lies rows and rows of fruit and vegetable sellers, proffering hundreds of varieties of produce that you mightn't have even heard of. Further inside are butchers (whole goat, anyone?), and beyond that, livestock and pets. It's difficult to measure the extent of the illegal bird trade here, but it's safe to say that some of the species sitting glumly in cages probably shouldn't be in Pakistan at all.

On opposite ends of Empress Market, but within a kilometre of each other, are two of Karachi's most historic churches. <u>St Patrick's Cathedral</u>, a Catholic church opened in 1881. It is believed to have replaced a smaller building on the site which was first church in Sindh, dating back to 1845. Meanwhile not far away sits the <u>St Andrew's Church</u>, an Anglican mission built in 1868. Both churches are still functioning places of worship and serve Karachi's Christian communities; services are given in Urdu, and private schools are associated with each. Security is tight, however foreigners are usually allowed to enter with the correct identification, the assumption being that all foreigners are Christian.

Back into the main part of Saddar, heading away from Empress Market on the left is <u>Dar-i-Mehtar</u>, the Zoroastrian Fire Temple, serving the small "Parsi" community in Karachi. Zoroastrianism is the traditional religion of Iran, and ideas of duality and balance in the universe feature heavily. "Parsi" is the common name given to this community in Pakistan and India, who arrived as traders and refugees in different lots both before and after the Muslim conquest of Persia. Their long history in this part of the world has given rise to a unique "Pakistani Parsi" or "Indian Parsi" identity, with associated linguistic features, food, festivals, dress and naming traditions. Dar-i-Mehtar is not open to non-Zoroastrians, but the building's traditional winged "Faravahar" embellishments can be seen from the street.

At the other end of Saddar, <u>Frere Hall</u> contains a collection of books and paintings from Karachi's history. The impressively tall building is a British colonial construction, and is at least a century and a half old. It was named after Sir Henry Bartle Edward Frere, once the Commissioner of Sindh (1851 - 1859), who was known for promoting the use of the indigenous Sindhi language in the region. You may be allowed inside, however this depends on the security climate of the time. If not, you can get a handsome view of the exterior of the building from across the adjacent park.

Sleeping in Karachi
Backpacker
<u>Hotel Al-Mustafa</u>: Raja Ghazanfar Ali Rd, Saddar; (+92) 021-35661047
map pg. 130, Sgl Rs. 800, Dbl Rs. 1,200
A centrally-located cheap option, popular with foreign travelers. In-room dining menu. A/C optional.

<u>Hotel Sky Towers</u>: Raja Ghazanfar Ali Rd, Saddar; (+92) 021-35675211; www.hotelskytowers.com
map pg. 130, Dbl Rs. 1,800
Another centrally-located option with air conditioning at the higher end of the budget category.

Economy
<u>Hotel Mehran</u>: Shahrah-e-Faisal; (+92) 111-909-909; www.hotelmehran.com
map pg. 130, Dbl US$102, Suite $210
A long-standing favourite in Karachi's mid-range bunch. 2 restaurants, a café and airport transfers.

<u>Hotel Sarawan</u>: Raja Ghazanfar Ali Rd, Saddar; (+92) 021-35216001; www.hotelsarawan.com
map pg. 130, Sgl US$48, Dbl US$53, Suite $57
It's old and run down, but it's cheap, clean(ish), centrally located and provides free transport to the airport. Breakfast included.

Luxury
Movenpick: Club Road; (+92) 021-35633333;
www.movenpick.com/en/asia/pakistan/karachi/hotel-karachi
map pg. 130, Sgl US$149, Dbl US$162, Suite US$185
One of the best places to stay in Karachi; four restaurants (including Lebanese, Italian and
Pakistani) and a 24-hour cafe, a pool, gym, sauna and spa. Great value too, at these prices.

Pearl Continental: Dr Ziaddin Ahmed Rd; (+92) 021-111505505;
www.pchotels.com/pckarachi
map pg. 130, Dbl US$174, Suite US$280
The Pearl Continental might be old, but it's awesome. Five resturants (choose from Chinese,
Japanese, Continental, Pakistani or a steakhouse) plus a cool café and a swimming pool.

There are also Marriott and Avari hotels among Karachi's 5-star bunch *(all on map pg. 130)*.

Eating in Karachi
Eating options in Karachi run the whole gamut from fried fish by the roadside to lobster
served in 5-star hotel restaurants. For the former - and other options like it - look no further
than the streets near where you are staying. The streets of Saddar in particular are filled with
cheap food vendors, selling dhal, vegetable dishes, biryani, tea, meat curries, samosas and
other snacks like *bhel puri* (fried rice puffs and vegetables in a tamarind sauce). One reliable
option is **Student Biryani** *(map pg. 130)*, which has been serving up chicken and beef
biryani, among other dishes, since the 1969. It has now grown into a chain, but the original
branch is still operating in a street behind Empress Market.

Middle range options exist at **Tariq Road** *(map pg. 128)* and **Burns Road** *(map pg. 128)*; the
latter stands more at the "cheap" end of mid-range. Both are well served in terms of eateries,
but Tariq Road has the popular **KebabJees** kebab shop. These are great places to try
Karachi biryani, regarded throughout Pakistan as among the best and spiciest.

For more upmarket options, try the selection of restaurants at **Boat Basin** *(map pg. 134)* (near
Clifton) and **Port Grand** *(map pg. 128)* (between Clifton and Saddar). One local favourite in
the past few years has been **Kolachi Do Darya** *(map pg. 128)*, on a deck overlooking the
mouth of the Kadiro Creek - a seafood grill by the sea. "Do Darya" as it's referred to is in
the Defence Housing Authority area, so bring your passport to pass the security checks.
Expect to pay Rs. 200 from Clifton, Rs. 300 from saddar in a rickshaw or taxi. If you've got
money to spend, Karachi's top hotels also have restaurants offering everything from Italian
to Japanese - try the Sheraton, Marriott, Movenpick, Avari or Pearl Continental. More
upmarket choices can be found at www.karachisnob.com.

Services in Karachi
Airlines
Air Arabia: 1&2 Lotia Building, Abdullah Haroon Rd; (+92) 021-111272242 *(map pg. 130)*
Airblue: Ground Floor PIIA Bldg, Moulana Deen Mohammad Wafa Rd; (+92) 021-
35693903 *(map pg. 130)*
Air China: 11 Business Ave, Shahrah-e-Faisal; (+92) 021-34301801 *(map pg. 130)*
Emirates: 2nd Floor, Faysal Bank Building, 16 Abdullah Haroon Rd; (+92) 021-35203377
(map pg. 130)
Etihad: Executive Tower, 7th Floor, Dolmen Mall, Clifton; (+92) 80090044017 *(map pg. 134)*
FlyDubai: Caesars Towers, National I.T Park, Shahrah-e-Faisal; (+92) 021-111225539 *(map
pg. 130)*
Gulf Air: Kashif Centre, Shahrah-e-Faisal, near Mehran Hotel; (+92) 021-35654483 *(map pg.
130)*
Iran Air: 10 Mehran Hotel, Shahrah-e-Faisal; (+92) 021-35215001 *(map pg. 130)*
Pakistan International: Shahrah-e-Faisal, Shah Faisal Colony, Malir Halt; 021-3343399213
(map pg. 128)
Oman Air: Qasar-e-Zainab, Club Road; (+92) 021-335693977 *(map pg. 130)*
Qatar Airways: Technology Park St 8, Shahrah-e-Faisal; (+92) 021-111310310 *(map pg. 134)*

<u>Saudia:</u> Emerald Tower, 14th Floor, Block 5, Clifton; (+92) 021-111747300 *(map pg. 130)*
<u>Serene Air:</u> Ground Floor, Shafi Chambers, Club Road opp. Qasar-e-Naz; 021-35631773 *(map pg. 130)*
<u>Shaheen:</u> Ground Floor, IEP Building, opp. Regent Plaza, Shahrah-e-Faisal; 021-111808080 *(map pg. 130)*
<u>SriLankan Airlines:</u> 50C State Life Building #10, Abdullah Haroon Rd; 021-35643801 *(map pg. 130)*
<u>Thai Airways:</u> 7th Floor, Technology Park, Shahrah-e-Faisal; (+92) 021-32788000 *(map pg. 130)*
<u>Turkish Airlines:</u> Jinnah Int'l Airport Terminal Complex Lvl 2, Departure Hall; 021-34604692 *(map pg. 128)*

Banks
<u>Citibank:</u> 15th Floor, The Harbour Front, Dolmen City, Block 4, Scheme 5, Clifton *(map pg. 134)*
<u>Standard Chartered:</u> Snowhite Center, Shop 3, Plot 285-A, Main Abdullah Road, Saddar *(map pg. 130)*
<u>Standard Chartered:</u> Commercial Plot No. ST-10, Caesars Tower, Shahrah-e-Faisal *(map pg. 130)*

Cinemas
<u>Dolmen Mall</u> in Clifton *(map pg. 134)* and <u>Atrium Mall</u> in Saddar *(map pg. 130)* both show a selection of local, Bollywood and Hollywood movies. For the original Karachi movie experience, try the historic <u>Capri Cinema</u> *(map pg. 130)* – somewhere between nostalgic and just plain old, it usually shows crowd-pleasing Bollywood flicks to a whooping crowd.

Internet Cafe
Hotels usually offer wifi, otherwise there are a few run-down places around the city. <u>Cyber Waves</u> in Haroon Castle *(map pg. 130)*, on Dr Dawood Pota Rd, Saddar is notable, and the owner is friendly.

Money Exchange
Being a trading hub, Karachi is littered with money exchanges. This is just a selection;
<u>Dollar East:</u> 9 Ground Fl, Amber Castle, 21-A, Block 6, opp. Lal Kothi, Shahrah-e-Faisal *(map pg. 128)*
<u>Paracha Exchange:</u> Mehboob Cloth Market, Shahrah-e-Iraq, Saddar *(map pg. 130)*
<u>Wall Street Exchange:</u> 1st Floor, Above Mustafa Jewellers, Tariq Road *(map pg. 128)*

Post Office
Abdullah Haroon Rd, Saddar *(map pg. 130)*. Several others throughout the city.

Shopping
Karachi has so many local markets that it would be impossible to mention them all here. Instead, you might be best advised to ask at your hotel regarding what you want to buy, and let them point you in the right direction. <u>Empress Market</u> in Saddar *(map pg. 130)* has just about every conceivable type of locally-produced food you could imagine. <u>Iqbal Cloth Market</u> *(map pg. 128)* or <u>Qurtaba Market</u> *(map pg. 128)* are where the fabric for all of those colourful ladies' shalwar kameez are sourced, although the ready-made variety is sold at the boutiques and shops on the <u>Tariq Road</u> shopping strip *(map pg. 128)*. Zainab Market *(map pg. 128)* also has a good reputation for leather, silver and gold goods.

For the shopping mall experience, the fabulous <u>Dolmen Mall</u> *(map pg. 134)* is a mall by the beach in Clifton with a Hyperstar supermarket and a food court. <u>Emerald Mall</u> *(map pg. 134)* is another option in Clifton. <u>Atrium Mall</u> *(map pg. 130)* has been around for ages, and has a cinema and food court in the heart of Saddar.

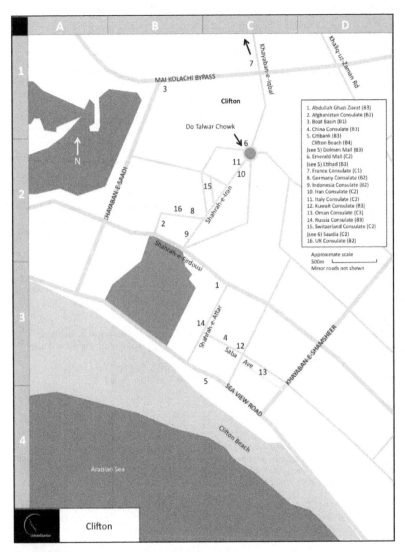

Clifton

1. Abdullah Ghazi Ziarat (B3)
2. Afghanistan Consulate (B2)
3. Boat Basin (B1)
4. China Consulate (B3)
5. Citibank (B3)
   Clifton Beach (B4)
   (see 5) Dolmen Mall (B3)
6. Emerald Mall (C2)
   (see 5) Etihad (B3)
7. France Consulate (C1)
8. Germany Consulate (B2)
9. Indonesia Consulate (B2)
10. Iran Consulate (C2)
11. Italy Consulate (C2)
12. Kuwait Consulate (B3)
13. Oman Consulate (C3)
14. Russia Consulate (B3)
15. Switzerland Consulate (C2)
    (see 6) Saudia (C2)
16. UK Consulate (B2)

Approximate scale
500m
Minor roads not shown

Supermarkets
The best bet for foreign goods in Karachi is Hyperstar at Dolmen Mall *(map pg. 134)*

Tourist Information
PTDC: Shafi Chambers, Club Road, Saddar; (+92) 021-99202971 *(map pg. 130)*

Travel Agency
Gerry's Travel Agency has the best reputation in town; Hotel Metropole, Abdullah Haroon Rd; (+92) 021-35685017; www.gerrystravel.com *(map pg. 130)*. Lots more in the area.

Visa Office
Shahrah-e-Iraq, Saddar *(map pg. 130)*

Help in Karachi
Safety
There's no two ways about it, Karachi is a big, bad-ass city. Organised crime, petty crime, drug-related crime, violent crime – it's all here. Rarely is it targeted squarely at travellers, although it's often aimed at the rich and elite, which includes how foreign tourists are perceived. Keep your wits about you everywhere – be wary of accepting random invitations, stay aware of what's happening in the news, and follow locals' advice. Don't flash your relative wealth unnecessarily, especially in places like Saddar. If you're not a seasoned Pakistan or India traveller, you're advised to take registered taxis everywhere – avoid rickshaw drivers, who are sometimes involved in shakedowns for cash or valuables.

Amid the jumble that is Karachi, there is always the small possibility for something to go seriously wrong – smaller crime rackets are known to be in cahoots with bigger, politically-motivated groups. There are simply so many people, so many groups and so many issues in Karachi that the police barely keep track of it all, let alone keep things under control. Kidnappings and shootings occur at a higher rate than in any other major city of Pakistan.

All that said, however, greater Karachi is still a safe enough place for around 27 million people to live and go about their daily business. Many foreigners visit here and leave with nothing but praise for Karachiites and their big-city confidence and street-smart friendliness. One thing you'll appreciate in Karachi is the relatively liberal atmosphere. Stay in a secure hotel (the ones we have listed are all approved by Karachi Police), use common sense, try not to stand out, listen to local advice and you should be fine.

Medical Services
Agha Khan University Hospital offers the best private health care in Karachi *(map pg. 128)*.
Jinnah Hospital is the biggest government hospital in Karachi *(map pg. 130)*.
Pharmacies are everywhere around Karachi – just ask your hotel for the nearest. Otherwise both of the above hospitals have several 24-hour pharmacies.

Getting around Karachi
Autorickshaws and local taxis: Karachi has beaten-up old taxis, autorickshaws and qingqi rickshaws to get you around town. The prices that follow are averages; expect to pay slightly more for a taxi, and slightly less for a chartered qingqi. Getting around Saddar, Cantt railway station, or Mazar-e-Quaid should cost around Rs. 100. From Saddar to Clifton, expect to pay Rs. 150 - 200. The airport costs Rs. 350 from Saddar, or Rs. 500 from Clifton - you are advised to hire a chartered taxi for this journey, particularly at night time, for security reasons (see below).

Bus and train: Karachi's bus system is like a rolling stock of tin cans on wheels - it's almost unbelievable that it works at all. If you manage to figure out a way to make it useful to foreign travellers, we'd love to hear from you - until then, it's probably better to stick to the autorickshaws and taxis. Similarly, Karachi's "Circular Railway" is great in theory, but in total disrepair.

Taxis: To hire a chartered taxi, Metro Radio cabs operates in Karachi. Call 111-222-787.

Uber and Careem ride-sharing services have landed in Karachi, with the former also offering female-driver and rickshaw services. Download the applications to your phone and get a quote easily! Both take cash.

Karachi International Airport
Karachi's Jinnah International Airport is the country's largest airport with the greatest array
of flights and airlines operating. Few travelers have negative reports of the airport, although
it's no palace. Security is tight, especiallty after a shooting attack in 2014 – don't be
surprised to see a Pakistan Army tank stationed outside the terminal.

The districts around the airport are known to be a bit lawless, so you're advised to take a
registered Metro Radio Cab to the city, even during daylight hours. There's a red Metro
Radio Cab stand outside at arrivals.

Leaving Karachi
Karachi's local bus station is at Taj Complex, just to the northeast of Saddar *(map pg. 130)*.
The Daewoo Express terminal is next door *(map pg. 130)*. The most convenient train station
is Karachi Cantt *(map pg. 130)*.

Bus
Lahore: Daewoo Express, 21 hours, Rs. 3,750
Rawalpindi/Islamabad: Daewoo Express, 24 hours, Rs. 4,400
Faisalabad: Daewoo Express, 20 hours 35 minutes, Rs. 3,550.
Multan: Daewoo Express, 14 hours, Rs. 2,850
Bahawalpur: Daewoo Express, 14 hours, Rs. 2,600
Rahim Yar Khan: Daewoo Express, 10 hours 30 minutes, Rs. 2,000

Hyderabad: Daewoo Express; 2 hours; Rs. 300
Bhit Shah: A handful of small buses full of pilgrims go directly from Karachi to Bhit Shah,
but most visitors go to Hyderabad first, then get another bus to Bhit Shah. 3 hours, Rs. 400
for a direct bus.
Sehwan Sharif: Most buses which go to Larkana stop enroute in Sehwan Sharif – this costs
Rs. 500 and takes 5 hours. Otherwise travelers go to Hyderabad and change for another bus
to Sehwan.
Larkana: Local buses, 7 hours; Rs 800
Sukkur: Daewoo Express, 7 hours 30 minutes, Rs. 1,510

Train
Lahore: 18 to 20 hours, Rs. 1,250 (berth)
Rawalpindi/Islamabad: 25 - 27 hours, Rs. 1,440 (berth)
Faisalabad: 17 – 19 hours, Rs. 1,060 (berth)
Multan: 13 – 15 hours, Rs. 910 (berth)
Bahawalpur: 12 – 14 hours, Rs. 840 (berth)
Hyderabad: 2 hours, Rs. 250 (seat)
Sukkur/Rohri: 6 – 8 hours, Rs. 480 (berth)

Air
Islamabad: PIA, Shaheen, AirBlue and Serene Air, 2 hours,: from Rs. 7,400 one way.
Lahore: PIA, Shaheen, AirBlue and Serene Air, 1 hour 45 mins, from Rs. 7,400 one way.
Faisalabad: PIA, 1 hour 40 minutes, from Rs. 8,200 one way. Serene Air have also
expressed interest in this route, but operations had not begun at the time of research.
Multan: PIA and Shaheen, 1 hour 30 minute, from Rs. 6,500 one way
Bahawalpur: PIA, 1 hour 30 minutes, from Rs. 6,500 one way
Rahim Yar Khan: PIA, 1 hour 25 minutes, from Rs. 7,300 one way
Sukkur: PIA, 1 hour, from Rs. 6,600 one way
Mohenjodaro (Larkana): PIA, 1 hour 15 minutes, from Rs. 5,600 one way

Around Karachi
BEACHES and CHARNA ISLAND
Beaches get progressively better the further you get from Karachi. Don't expect the
Maldives here - the coast is backed by barren hills, and the beaches are desolate - they
scream "potential" rather than "paradise". The road eventually leads to Balochistan, and the

scenery is a preview of that province - miles and miles of empty, dry, rocky mountains, hemmed in by the warm, calm Arabian Sea. The coastline itself resembles parts of Oman, or perhaps the UAE had it not been blessed with oil - long stretches of rocky beaches, punctuated sporadically by crumbling, isolated forts and lonely fishing villages that might be quaint were they not so poor.

These beaches are mostly places to wade in the ocean - with the exception of French Beach no-one sunbathes, no-one surfs, and there are definitely no bikinis visible. If you visit any of these, expect to dip in the ocean semi-clothed, then relax with a spicy seafood meal and a (non-alcoholic) cold drink by the sea - this is beach-going Pakistan-style.

Hawkes Bay *(map pg. 126)* is a suburb of Karachi, and the first beach out of Karachi that you might consider stepping in. It's nothing special, and only marginally nicer than Clifton Beach (page 129), but if you're short on time it's easy and quick to get to. An autorickshaw will cost Rs 400 from Clifton or Saddar (30 to 45 minutes, depending on traffic) - ask to be dropped by the beach near a restaurant or hotel.

French Beach *(map pg. 126)* is a designated 'resort beach', meaning that access is restricted and there are restaurants and facilities dedicated to visitors. This is the best option for swimming within close range of Karachi, and is probably the most comfortable place for women to take a dip. A chartered taxi for the day to French Beach will cost about Rs. 1,500 including waiting time - speak to your hotel in Karachi to organise this. French Beach is about 45 minutes drive from Karachi.

Paradise Point, Mubarak Village and Sunheri Beach *(map pg. 126)* are all further away and less developed than French Beach. Although they're quite nice, they're a bit sparse and more likely a place where you'll go for water sports or to take a boat to Charna Island, rather than swimming or chilling out. Ask your Karachi hotel for advice, and expect to pay about Rs. 1,500 to Rs. 2,000 for a car for the day to each of them (all about 1 hour drive from Karachi).

Gaddani Beach *(map pg. 126)* is actually in Balochistan, but only 25 kilometres from the border with Sindh at the Hub River. It's quite a pleasant, if exposed beach, popular with day-trippers from Karachi. It's a lovely place to take a dip on a hot day, and there are a handful of small restaurants turning out grilled and fried fish. To the southern end of the beach is the Gaddani ship breaking yard, a place where boats come to be wrecked and picked over for spare parts. The handful of dilapidated boats by the coast are quite a photogenic, if rather bleak sight. Ask to be taken here by your taxi driver - it's too far to walk from the main part of the beach. Gaddani Beach is approximately one and a half hours from Karachi, and a hired car for the day will cost about Rs. 2,000. Ask your hotel in Karachi to arrange transport, and bargain hard.

Charna Island *(map pg. 126)* is a rocky outcrop 6 kilometres off the coast of Mubarak Village, near the provincial border with Balochistan. The island is uninhabited, rocky and dry, but startling in its size; what appears to be a rock in the ocean is actually over a kilometre long and rather tall when seen up close. It has been used as a practice firing range by the Pakistan Navy, but nowadays it's better known as a destination for water sports like sailing, jet skiing, snorkelling, cliff diving and scuba diving, one of the few places in Pakistan to offer such activities. Under the sea is a plethora of marine life, from colourful fish and jellyfish to coral and underwater caves. A whole range of people come here for day trips from Karachi - fishermen, rich private yacht owners, divers. However the overwhelming majority of visitors come on a pre-arranged package tour from Karachi, usually including a light breakfast, bus and boat transfers, snorkelling equipment, photography and lunch.

One excellent and cheap company that offers these tours is SportsDivers (+92-3343275132 www.facebook.com/sportsdivers). Tours usually operate on Saturdays and Sundays and are led by the affable but no-nonsense Razzak - he comes highly recommended.. He can also organise scuba diving if that's your thing, and can even organise PADI-certified instructors to get your scuba license. Pakistan might be one of the cheapest (and most unexpected) places on earth to get scuba certified! Another, better-known (but slightly pricier) group offering similar packages is the Karachi Water Sports Club (+92-3111882442).

THATTA
Population: 220,000. Elevation: 13m, Telephone code: 0298

Pronounced *tuttah* (the first "T" is aspirated), this town's best days have long since passed. It was the capital of Sindh from the 14th to the 17th century, during which time the city's most famous attraction was built, the Shah Jahan Mosque (1647). One major contributing factor too Thatta's decline was the change in the course of the Indus River, leaving the town stranded on the edge of a dusty desert. Nowadays Thatta *(map pg. 126)* is a regional town attracting day trippers from Karachi who come to see the Shah Jahan Mosque's beautiful tilework. Another attraction in Thatta is the World Heritage-listed Makli Hill necropolis, where at least 100,000 local rulers, Sufi saints, clergy and nobility were buried during the Mughal dynasty. The site is huge - 8 kilometres across, necessitating a car to visit properly - and unless you are really enthusiastic about the history of the region, you might find it a long way to travel for the few tomb structures that remain intact.

Thatta can be reached from Karachi by crowded local bus (2 hours, Rs. 250 one way), and then rent an autorickshaw or qingqi for Rs. 100 to get around the major sites. Alternatively you can hire a car from Karachi for the day for about Rs. 3,500 - speak with your Karachi hotel to organise this. Overnight stays in Thatta are not usually necessary, but if you choose to stay ask for the SRO Guesthouse Hotel; it's the best place to lay your head (around Rs. 2,500 for a double room).

HYDERABAD
Population: 3.4 million, Elevation: 13m, Telephone code: 0221

Big, hot, featureless and busy; Hyderabad is hardly enticing. The main reason to visit here is the Qadam-e-Ali, the footprint and handprint of the son-in-law of the prophet Muhammad (pbuh), Ali ibn Talib. Hyderabad was the briefly the capital of Sindh from 1739 to 1742, and while Urdu-speaking Karachi is the provincial capital, Hyderabad is the true Sindhi metropolis - the largest Sindhi speaking city, and a centre for Sindhi culture. Unfortunately, for all of this, the city of Hyderabad doesn't have much to show, perhaps a reflection of just how rural-based Sindhi culture is. If you're in search of something Sindhi, go shopping in the bazaar for *ajrak* (traditional Sindhi shawls), Hyderabadi sandals or bangles, or eat spicy Sindhi biryani and traditional Hyderabadi *rabri* (sweet milk-based dessert). There's also a fort in the centre of town which dates back to 1768 and is in surprisingly good condition - but it's closed to the public. Hyderabad would usually be considered part of "Interior Sindh", but for a traveller is best done as a day trip from Karachi, so is included in this section. Depending on the prevailing security situation, you may be assigned a guard by the local police - check with your hotel before leaving Karachi. This is more likely if you choose to stay in Hyderabad (see page 144 for more information about police registration in Interior Sindh).

What to see and do in Hyderabad
The Shrine of Qadam-e-Ali
map pg. 139, Open sunrise to sunset, Free

On the other side of the fort from the train station is Qadam-e-Ali, a small shrine to the handprint of the son-in-law of the prophet Muhammad (pbuh), Ali ibn Talib. Hazrat Ali, or Imam Ali as he is known by the Shia, is said to have prayed in or around Hyderabad in the seventh century, and left the impression of his hand in the sand. The piece of earth has been preserved and is now contained within a glass box in the centre of this shrine. For a non-Muslim, the handprint is really only interesting for those interested in the history of the culture and faith of Pakistan, but the shrine is rather pretty and it's a good place for people-watching; devotees kiss and press their faces against the cabinet in an effort to draw closer to the imam, while others spontaneously break out into devotional songs.

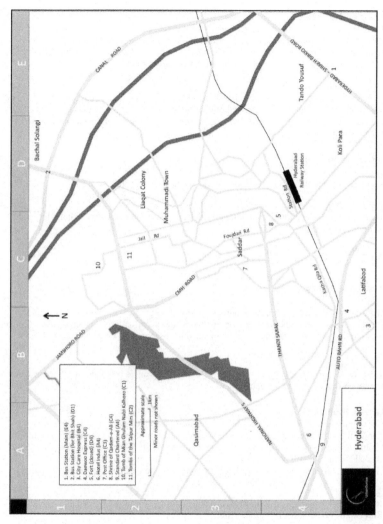

Hyderabad

1. Bus Station (Main) (E4)
2. Bus Station (for Bhit Shah) (D1)
3. City Care Hospital (B4)
4. Daewoo Express (C4)
5. Fort (closed) (D4)
6. Hotel Indus (A4)
7. Post Office (C3)
8. Shrine of Qasam-e-Ali (C4)
9. Standard Chartered (A4)
10. Tomb of Mian Ghulam Nabi Kalhoro (C1)
11. Tombs of the Talpur Mirs (C2)

Approximate scale
1km
Minor roads not shown

This shrine is particularly busy on the birthday and martyrdom day of Ali ibn Talib, which in 2018 are expected to fall on around the 31st March and the 6th June respectively, and move about 10 days earlier each year. Visitors to the shrine are required to remove their shoes (pay about Rs. 20 to the shoe-minder) and behave with appropriate reverence.

Other sights

Hyderabad is home to two crumbling shrines; the Tomb of Mian Ghulam Nabi Kalhoro *(map pg. 139)*, an 18th century ruler of Sindh, and the Tombs of the Talpur Mirs *(map pg. 139)*, a complex of the tombs of the Talpir dynasty who ruled Sindh in the 19th century.

Staying in Hyderabad

With Karachi and its plentiful options just two hours away, there might not be much reason to sleep the night in Hyderabad, but if you do the Hotel Indus on Thandi Sarak *(Rs. 9,000, map pg. 139)* accepts foreigners.

Eating in Hyderabad
There are multiple cheap eating options around the train station. If you are looking for something more upmarket, your best option is probably the Hotel Indus (see "Staying in Hyderabad"). There are a couple of Western fast food chains like Pizza Hut and KFC near the Hotel Indus, and a McDonalds near Standard Chartered Bank *(all on map pg. 139)*.

Getting around Hyderabad
Nowhere in Hyderabad costs more than Rs. 100 in an autorickshaw or qingqi rickshaw - and short hops around the town centre will only cost Rs. 30 - 50. The Careem ride-sharing service is in Hyderabad. Download the application to your phone and get a quote! Careem operates with cash.

Services in Hyderabad
Banks
Standard Chartered: Autobhan Road near the junction with Thandi Sarak *(map pg. 139)*.

Internet Cafes
There are not a whole lot of great internet cafes in Hyderabad – ask at your hotel for local recommendtions.

Post Office
The General Post Office is in Saddar *(map pg. 139)*

Help in Hyderabad
Safety
Hyderabad sees hardly any casual tourists, local or foreign, so it's important to try not to stand out too much. Although it's a bit lawless, it's not a particularly dangerous place. Police may require you to register and be accompanied by a security guard – see page 144.

Medical Services
The private City Care Hospital *(map pg. 139)* is one of the city's best facilities. Serious cases should consider going to Karachi.

Leaving Hyderabad
The Daewoo Express terminal is on the city's western fringe. There are two local bus stands; the main one is a large station to the southeast. Some smaller destinations (like Bhit Shah) are served from is a dusty, chaotic junction at the city's northern end at a place called Bachal Solangi. You'll need to explain to your rickshaw driver that you want to go to "Bachal Solangi Chowk" – it's the intersection next to the canal on the National Highway.

Bus
Karachi: Daewoo Express 2 hours, Rs. 300
Bhit Shah: Local buses 1 hour, Rs. 100
Sehwan Sharif: Local buses, 2 hours, Rs. 300
Sukkur: Daewoo Express, 5 hours, Rs. 1,070
Larkana: Local buses, 5 hours, Rs. 500
Lahore: Daewoo Express, 19 hours, Rs. 3,380
Rawalpindi/Islamabad: Daewoo Express, 18 hours, Rs. 4,030

Train
Karachi: 2 hours, Rs. 250 (seat)
Sukkur/Rohri: 4 hours, Rs. 350 (seat)
Lahore: 15 to 17 hours, Rs. 1,700 (berth)
Rawalpindi/Islamabad: 22 - 24 hours, Rs. 1,330 (berth)
Multan: 10 – 12 hours, Rs. 800 (berth)

BHIT SHAH

Population: 20,000, Elevation: 26m, Telephone code: 02289

A mess of a town is Bhit Shah, an overgrown village whose importance outweighs its size. Not a lot of people stay in Bhit Shah except for in the shrine of Shah Abdul Latif Bhittai - which is the main reason to visit. Unless you are here on a pilgrimage, Bhit Shah is a place to get in, see, and get out again - there's little to recommend hanging around for. On the other hand, Bhit Shah and the journey there is a great opportunity to experience rural Sindh within a stone's throw of Karachi. Like Hyderabad, Bhit Shah would normally be considered part of "Interior Sindh", but is easily and most conveniently done as a day trip from Karachi, so is included here. Depending on the prevailing security situation, you may be assigned a guard by the local police - check with your hotel before leaving Karachi. This is more likely if you choose to stay in Hyderabad (see page 144 for more information about police registration in Interior Sindh).

What to see and do in Bhit Shah
Tomb of Shah Abdul Latif Bhittai
map pg. 142, Open sunrise to sunset, Free

Abdul Latif (1689 - 1752) was one of the Sindhi language's most celebrated poets, and was also a Sufi saint and mystic who continued to amass devotees and followers long after his death. So highly regarded were his spiritual writings that he has often been compared to the legendary Persian poet Rumi. Ten years after his burial his shrine was completed, resplendent in white and blue tilework, and a wide courtyard designed for the public recitation of his poetry. Today his shrine is no less popular than before - the courtyard is indeed used for poetry recitation, often to the strains of qawwali-inspired tunes. Inside the shrine devotees hug, kiss and pray on the tomb itself, and many sit down in quiet contemplation to simply spend time and get lost in the atmosphere. Several other tombs of his family members and other local spiritual leaders lie to the rear of the shrine. He is usually given the honorific title "Shah", and the suffix "Bhittai" is often added to his name to identify his native village of Bhit Shah.

The shrine is packed on the the *urs* (death anniversary) of Shah Abdul Latif Bhittai, which in 2018 is expected to fall on around the 25th October, and moves about 10 days earlier each year. Visitors to the shrine are required to remove their shoes (pay about Rs. 10 to the shoe-minder) and behave with appropriate reverence.

Staying and eating in Bhit Shah
The lack of other attactions and proximity to Hyderabad and Karachi means you probably won't need nor want to stay in Bhit Shah the night. Being such a small village, security is also a concern.

There aren't a whole bunch of places to eat in Bhit Shah – the canteens near the central junction (outside the shrine's entrance) *(map pg. 142)* are probably the best bet for cheap curries and cold drinks.

Getting around Bhit Shah
Getting from the highway to the centre of town will cost Rs. 20 in a shared qingqi. The centre of town is small enough to navigate on foot.

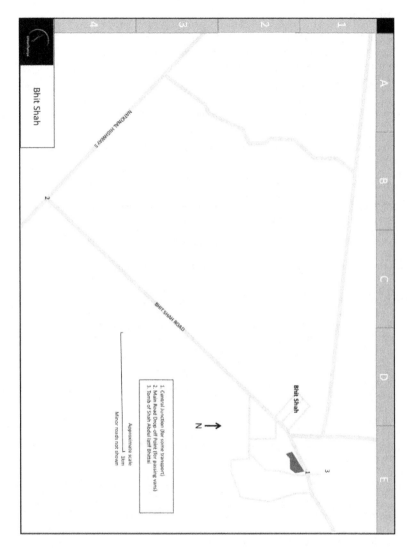

Leaving Bhit Shah

Qingqi rickshaws leave from the junction directly outside the shrine *(map pg. 142)* and take about 10 minutes to reach the main road, from where you can catch a passing van. Some vans leave directly from the junction to their destination – ask when you get there.

Hyderabad: Local buses, 1 hour, Rs. 100
Karachi: Local buses, 3 hours, Rs. 400
Sehwan Sharif: Local buses, 2 hours, Rs. 250 - last vans leave at about 4pm, and even then are highly dependent on pilgrimage traffic. Otherwise you will need to go via Hyderabad.
Sukkur: Local buses, 4 hours, Rs. 350.

Sukkur
and Interior Sindh

Interior Sindh (including Hyderabad; page 138 and Bhit Shah; page 141) is a wide, dry, baking hot, open land defined by its villages and farms. Even the scattering of cities in this region are inextricably linked to their surrounding agricultural communities; they exist as trading hubs, service centres, and irrigation points. Throughout Interior Sindh lie some of Pakistan's least developed regions, places where life has barely changed since partition in 1947, if not Mughal times. Landlords, feudal families, workers and their 'owners', caste and indigenous beliefs aren't just realities in this area, they are the basis on which society operates. Islam blends with traditional beliefs and superstition in places like Sehwan Sharif where Sufi devotion sometimes even resembles certain Hindu practices. This region provides a window on traditional Sindhi culture in a way that Karachi never will. Be prepared to witness mind-bending displays of religious conviction at shrines, a tapestry of religions including significant numbers of Hindus and even Jains, and a guarded hospitality in a society often completely unfamiliar with foreign tourists. Many foreigners who come to Pakistan are apprehensive about engaging in a culture vastly different from their own; many urban Pakistanis feel similarly about visiting Interior Sindh.

Predictably, travelling in an area so untouched by development and globalisation comes with its challenges, and this is one of the toughest areas of Pakistan to visit. Not a lot of English is spoken; illiteracy in local languages is shockingly common. However those who dare, and who persevere with Interior Sindh, leave with vivid memories to last a lifetime.

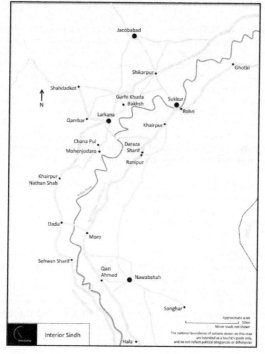

Police registration

Depending on the prevailing security situation, foreigners who visit Interior Sindh may be assigned an armed guard from the local police force, free of charge.

Why?
Interior Sindh is home to some of Pakistan's least developed communities, as well as strategic national infrastructure and the sensitive border with India. Guards are assigned to act as a buffer between you and a region unfamiliar with tourists, and to keep an eye on you as you pass landmarks critical to the nation's security.

How?
After checking in at any hotel in Interior Sindh, the hotelier will inform the local police of your arrival. If it is deemed necessary, two police officers will then visit the hotel to welcome you to the region and discuss the security situation with you. If a guard is required, he will be sent to your hotel to accompany you on your travels through the region. If you travel a long distance between cities, such as from Sukkur to Sehwan Sharif, then he will probably leave you at the bus station and call the next place for a colleague to meet you there and "take over the duty". Guards can act as your travel companion, tour guide, friend, or simply your shadow - if the security situation is stable, it will most likely be your choice as to how closely you will travel together. Do not cause any problems by running away or being disrespectful - he is simply doing his job, and interfering with the official process could cause problems for your travel plans, and land your guard in trouble. You are not required to pay anything for him; if you befriend him and choose to buy a cold drink or ice cream then this is appreciated as a kind gesture, but definitely not expected.

SUKKUR and ROHRI
Population: 905,000 (Sukkur City), Elevation: 67m, Telephone code: 071

While Sukkur isn't a place you'll likely fall in love with, its (slightly) more cosmopolitan character is a breath of fresh air after the rigours of rural Sindh. If you're arriving from Punjab, you might detect a shift from Seraiki to Sindhi culture, but it's not obvious - Sukkur is a trading city of Punjabis, Saraikis, Sindhis and more. Built by the Indus River, the city is strategically located at the headworks of the entire province's irrigation system. The river seems extra wide near Sukkur, and it is; the Sukkur Barrage forms a reservoir of sorts, and the proceeding water is then distributed through wide canals to elsewhere in Sindh. Needless to say, the barrage is therefore a very sensitive piece of infrastructure - you are advised not to spend time hanging around here, or attempt to photograph it. Irrigation aside, Sukkur is home to a few historic sites and an important Hindu temple. The Indus River, polluted though it is, is home to the endangered Indus River Dolphin, a light-pink coloured animal that is known to be completely blind. You'll be lucky to see one though - sightings are famously rare.

Near Sukkur is the town of Rohri, unremarkable if it wasn't one of the most important railway junctions in the country. Nearly every train running between Karachi and the rest of the country stops here. In local parlance Rohri and Sukkur are two completely separate cities, however for a traveller they can be conveniently treated as one metropolis - they compliment and serve each other.

What to see and do in Sukkur
Due to the requirement of a security guard, and the importance of the Indus River at this point, a police guard may discourage you from visiting the sits associated with the river (such as Sadh Belo, Sathiyan jo Asthan or the Ayub and Lansdowne Bridges). If you are visiting Sukkur as a base to see other places (such as Mohenjodaro), then don't arrive with high expectations to see much of the river - you may only be disappointed. If seeing the riverside attractions is really important to you, you are advised to contact a local travel agency ahead of your arrival to confirm your visit to these places.

The Minaret of Masoom Shah
map pg. 143, Open sunrise to sunset, Rs. 15
This pretty, if not spectacular minaret is the most easily visited of Sukkur's attractions. Standing near the centre of the town, it is the final resting place of Masoom Shah, a Muslim historian who was the governor of Sindh under the Mughal ruler Akbar. When he died in 1610 construction began on the shrine to honour him. The 31-metre minaret was completed in 1617, and stands across a bougainvillea-covered courtyard about 30 metres from Masoom Shah's actual tomb. There are 84 steps to reach the top of the minaret, from where almost of all of Sukkur can be viewed (but ask your guard before taking pictures from here).

Sadh Belo
map pg. 143, Open sunrise to sunset, Free
Sadh Belo is the name of an island in the Indus River that is home to the largest Hindu temple in Pakistan. Established in 1823 by prominent local Hindu Swami Brakhandi Maharaja, the temple continues to attract pilgrims from around Pakistan, and even from India, especially on the anniversary of his death in late November every year. Non-Hindus are not allowed to visit without prior permission - speak to a local travel agency to organise, but be aware that in amny case most travellers are only allowed to view it from the outside, or from the river bank. If you are allowed to cross the river to the island, expect to pay Rs. 30 to the boat driver.

Sathiyan Jo Asthan
map pg. 143, Open 10am – 6pm, Rs. 200
No-one really knows the truth about why, or even if, seven women (*"sathiyan jo asthan"*) were buried here, but legend has it that they were fleeing political oppression. Unable to continue living as they were, they threw themselves on their husbands' funeral pyres, becoming martyrs; their ashes were scattered in the Indus River near this point. Tombs were then built to memorialise the band of ladies who died for the cause. What is known, however, is that the complex was built in 1554 AD and was given most of its embellishments by local ruler Mir Abu Al-Qasim Namkeen who was buried here. A visit to this evocative site at sunrise or sunset affords a perfect view of the city of Sukkur and the Indus River, as well as the Ayub and Lansdowne Bridges. You may not be allowed to take photographs of the bridges from this location.

Ayub and Lansdowne Bridges
map pg. 143
These two parallel bridges are an icon for Sukkur, but are much grander in importance than in aesthetics. Connecting the railway and road lines from Balochistan (and therefore Iran and Turkey) to the main north-south route at Rohri, The Lansdowne Bridge was constructed by the British in 1889, and is the trapezoidal vehicular bridge to the north. The taller, arched Ayub Bridge was completed in 1962 and named after Pakistan's first military leader, General Ayub Khan, and carries trains. Photography of the bridges is technically illegal, however we have heard stories of photography being candidly permitted from the site of Sathiyan jo Asthan. Ask your guard, and respect his instructions.

Staying in Sukkur
Backpacker
Sindh Faran Hotel: Chandni Cinema Road; (+92) 03337156370
map pg. 143, Cost: Rs. 2,000
A basic, passable choice – in-house restaurant makes not-bad Pakistani and Pakistani Chinese dishes.

Mehran Hotel: Station Road; (+92) 071-5613792
map pg. 143, Cost: Rs. 2,000
A better budget option with a restaurant that makes Pakistani staples.

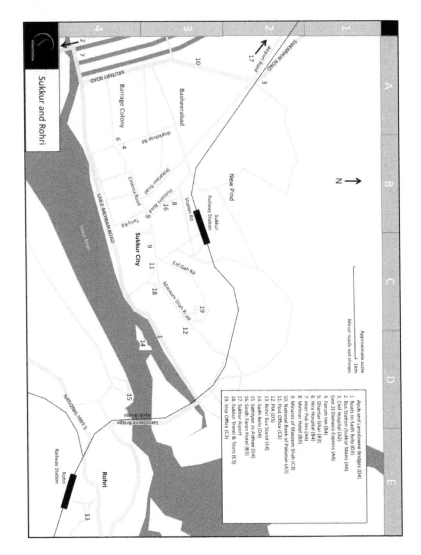

Sukkur and Rohri

Ayub and Landsdowne Bridges (D4)
1 Boats to Sadh Belo (D3)
2 Bus Station (Sukkur Main) (A4)
3. Civil Hospital (A2)
(see 2) Daewoo Express (A4)
4. Forum Inn (B4)
5. Ghantar Ghar (B3)
6. Hira Hospital (B4)
7. Inter Pak Inn (A4)
8. Mehran Hotel (B3)
9. Minaret of Masoom Shah (C3)
10. National Bank of Pakistan (A3)
11. Post Office (C3)
12 PIA (D3)
13 Rohri Bus Stand (E4)
14. Sadh Belo (D4)
15. Sathiyan Jo Asthan (D4)
16. Sindh Faran Hotel (B3)
17. Sukkur Airport
18. Sukkur Travel & Tours (C3)
19. Visa Office (C3)

Economy
Forum Inn: Workshop Road; (+92) 071-5613013
map pg. 143, Cost: Rs. 4,500
Not a bad option, and the most popular choice with foreigners. Good location near eateries.

Luxury
Inter Pak Inn: Barrage Rd
map pg. 143, Cost: Rs. 10,000
The Inter Pak's glory days are behind it, but the prices don't reflect that. The location is not great either – you might be better just to go to the Forum. It has a restaurant and function room.

Eating in Sukkur
The best restaurants are to be found in the better hotels. You can also find lots of good eating options in the vicinity of the Hira Hospital, and Western fast-food outlets near the National Bank on Military Road just out of the centre.

Services in Sukkur
Airlines
Pakistan International: 50 Masoom Shah Minar Road; (+92) 111-786-786 *(map pg. 143)*

Banks
No international banks are represented in Sukkur.

Internet cafes
There's a glut of internet cafes on the road between Ghantar Ghar and Masoom Shah Minar. *(map pg. 143)*

Money exchange
National Bank of Pakistan: Military Road *(map pg. 143)*

Post office
The GPO is on Masoom Shah Minar Road *(map pg. 143)*

Travel agency
Sukkur Travel & Tours: Masoon Shah Minar Rd, Behind Makki Masjid; (+92) 071-5622010 *(map pg. 143)*

Visa office
C-628 near Local Board, Mules Road *(map pg. 143)*

Help in Sukkur
Safety
Sukkur isn't a dangerous place, but the areas around Sukkur are particularly undeveloped. Police in Sukkur are paranoid about the city's reputation, and any potential incident that might affect it, and therefore are known for being overbearingly protective of travelers who come here. While it is probably unwarranted, you have no choice but to cooperate with the local authorities requirements, so if they say you need an armed guard by your side, it's easier just to do as you're told. See page 141.

Medical Services
Hira Hospital is a good private option in the centre. *(map pg. 143)*
Civil Hospital is the biggest government hospital. *(map pg. 143)*
Pharmacies are associated with both of the above hospitals.

Getting around Sukkur
A rickshaw or qingqi ride around Sukkur will cost about Rs. 80, while out to the airport or bus stations will cost about Rs. 100. A ride to the train station in Rohri is around Rs. 200.

Leaving Sukkur
Bus
The Daewoo Express terminal is on the east side of the river, near a large junction, about 6 kilometres from the Inter Pak Hotel. Local buses depart from the same junction *(map pg. 143)*. Some local buses to nearby destinations also leave from a junction near Rohri Station, but they are less frequent, and usually stop by the Sukkur stand on their way anyway.

Larkana: Local buses, 1 hour 30 mins, Rs. 150
Hyderabad: Daewoo Express, 5 hours, Rs. 1,070
Bhit Shah: Local buses, 4 hours, Rs. 350
Sehwan Sharif: Local buses, 4 hours, Rs. 350

Karachi: Daewoo Express, 7 hours 30 minutes, Rs. 1,510
Lahore: Daewoo Express, 13 hours, Rs. 2,400
Rawalpindi/Islamabad: Daewoo Express, 16 hours 30 minutes, Rs. 3,070
Rahim Yar Khan: Daewoo Express, 3 hours, Rs. 560
Bahawalpur: Daewoo Express, 6 hours, Rs. 1,170
Multan: Daewoo Express, 8 hours 20 minutes, Rs. 1,570

Train
Trains depart Rohri with high frequency. The small train station at Sukkur isn't very useful.
Karachi: 6 – 8 hours, Rs. 480 (berth)
Hyderabad: 4 hours, Rs. 350 (seat)
Lahore: 10 to 12 hours, Rs. 1,400 (berth)
Rawalpindi/Islamabad: 18 - 20 hours, Rs. 1,140 (berth)
Bahawalpur: 5 – 6 hours, Rs. 370 (seat)
Multan: 6 – 7 hours, Rs. 430 (seat)

Air
Karachi: PIA, 1 hour, from Rs. 6,600 one way
Lahore: PIA, 1 hour 50 minutes, from Rs. 7,900 one way
Islamabad: PIA, 1 hour 20 minutes, from Rs. 7,900 one way

East or west of the Indus?
From Sukkur, in the north of Sindh, the main road divides and travels either side of the
Indus River before the two branches meet at Hyderabad. On the western branch of the
road lie Larkana and Sehwan Sharif, while the busier eastern branch threads past Daraza
Sharif and Bhit Shah. A few minor roads link the two parallel highways, but they do not
carry a lot of traffic and getting from one side of the river to the other sometimes involves
doubling back to either Sukkur or Hyderabad.

Around Sukkur
Most people come to Sukkur to visit places further afield, including Mohenjodaro and Garhi
Khuda Baksh (both near Larkana, page 149) and Daraza Sharif (below).

DARAZA SHARIF
Population: 9,900, Elevation: 46m, Telephone code: 0243
Home to an important shrine, Daraza Sharif makes an easy day trip from Sukkur *(map pg.
140)*. The village is actually a small hamlet near the larger town of Ranipur in a region
noted for its date palms.

In 1827 Daraza Sharif became important as the final resting palce of Abdul Wahab Farooqi,
better known as Hazrat Sachal Sarmast. With a name meaning "the ecstatic saint of truth",
Sachal Sarmast was a Sufi poet who is considered a master of Sindhi poetry. Like the shrine
at Bhit Shah, Daraza Sharif draws in devotees from all around who come to be in the saint's
presence.

The shrine is a work of art, with yellow, blue, white, turquoise, green and indigo tiles and
paintwork all competing for space on the square building. Outside, in the courtyard, lie the
graves of Sachal Sarmast's relatives and devotees.
The shrine is packed on the the *urs* (death anniversary) of Sachal Sarmast, which in 2018 is
expected to fall on around the 1st June, and moves about 10 days earlier each year. Visitors
to the shrine are required to remove their shoes (pay about Rs. 10 to the shoe-minder) and
behave with reverence.

To get to the shrine you can get in a packed minivan at Sukkur's local bus stand – ask to be dropped off at Daraza Sharif. They'll drop you on a highway turnoff about 500 metres from the shrine – ask for directions if you're not sure which way to go. Getting back is a matter of flagging down a Sukkur-bound van at the same highway turnoff. They'll slow down, you shout out the name "Sukkur", and they'll let you know if they're going your way. The journey takes about 1 hour and costs Rs. 150 each way.

LARKANA
Population: 270,000, Elevation: 147m, Telephone code: 074

Larkana is a typically rural Sindhi city; filled with produce markets, dust and traffic, and with a certain agricultural sensibility that pervades every street and conversation. It's a jumping off point to visit Mohenjodaro and Garhi Khuda Bakhsh. It's advisable to visit both places as a day trip from Sukkur due to the lack of tourist facilities in Larkana, and indeed your guard may recommend you to do this.

Things to see and do in Larkana
Mohenjodaro

map pg. 140. Open sunrise to sunset. Site entry: Rs. 300, Museum entry: Rs. 300

Approximately 30 kilometres south of Larkana, Mohenjodaro is the best preserved example of the Indus Valley Civilisation, one of the world's first known urban civilisations. Although the site is extensive for a 4,500 year-old ruin it's not as spectacular as some other world-famous attractions, and anyone who comes expecting structures to rival Angkor Wat, Petra or Macchu Picchu will be quite disappointed.

The Indus Valley Civilisation inhabited these plains (and those at Harappa, page 112) from approximately 3,300 BC to 1,700 BC, when the city was mysteriously abandoned. It is thought that changes in the course of the Indus River forced the evacuation of the city, although some historians have suggested that changes in climate could have forced its inhabitants to migrate elsewhere in the subcontinent. In 2016 an Indian movie called Mohenjodaro portrayed a fictional love story in the time of the Indus Valley Civilisation.

The Indus Valley Civilisation is believed to have had a highly developed social structure, involving a cryptic written language, defined social strata and prehistoric religion (perhaps early Hinduism). At some point in history, however, Buddhism is known to have visited the site, evidenced by a Buddhist stupa which remains standing to this day. The stupa in the middle of the site stands atop a mound from which Mohenjodaro takes its name; "Mound of the Dead".

The site is divided into three main sections; workers quarters, the elites' residences, and the main section of the city centre. Pay the entry fee at the front gate on the main road. Coming from the main entrance, there is a small museum down a path to the right - you'll no doubt be hustled towards it anyway by overenthusiastic guides. The museum contains a collection of artefacts recovered from the site, including some small statues and cooking and building instruments. Continuing down the main path from the entrance, pass through a leafy park before the main mound appears ahead of you. Through the gates, the path climbs the mound to the stupa in the centre. At the top of the steps, behind and to the left are the remains of what were once the monks' or priests' quarters. Circumnavigating the stupa, you are afforded a wide view of the whole site; to the northeast, the elite residential area, to the southeast the workers' residences, and directly below the stupa to the west, the city centre.

Descending from the stupa and turning to the right, the path leads to the great bath, a bathing area for the ancient Mohenjodarans. Beyond this, on the western edge of the site, lies the city's granary. Directly south of the stupa, and separated from the main site by a small open area, is an assembly hall, possibly once used for the administration of the city.

The elite's residential area is still in a process of being excavated, but visitors are still welcome. The workers' residential area, however, is exposed and recommended for anyone with a particular interest in the historic civilisation. Although not as visually interesting as the central site, the workers' residential area still has the footprints of the houses, along with still-intact public wells and even evidence of a public drainage system.

To get to Mohenjodaro from Larkana, take a Qingqi to the Chowdagee bus stand south of the city. From there, get in a van bound for Dadu, but make it clear to the driver that you are going to Mohenjodaro (30 mins, Rs. 50). You will be dropped off at a junction known as Chana Pul, from where you can take a qingqi to Mohenjodaro (Rs. 100 for the whole qingqi, divided among passengers, 10 mins). Coming back is roughly the same process in reverse, but qingqis don't wait at the front of Mohenjodaro - you'll need to be patient and flag one down as it passes. Similarly, you may need to wait at Chana Pul for some time before finding a van to Larkana. Be patient, and leave Mohenjodaro well before sunset. If you want to hire a car from Sukkur for the day, please see page 144.

Garhi Khuda Bakhsh

map pg. 140. Open sunrise to sunset. Free

Garhi Khuda Bakhsh is the name of a small village to the north of Larkana where Pakistan's Bhutto dynasty are buried. Known as Mazar-e-Zulfiqar Ali Bhutto, Mazar-e-Shaheed or Mazar-e-Bhutto, the family's shrine's political, emotional and even spiritual importance dominates any discussion of the local area; for many, just the name Garhi Khuda Bakhsh simply refers to the shrine. Whether or not the shrine warrants a visit depends on your knowledge of Pakistani politics; those who understand the dominance of the Bhutto family in Pakistan since the 1970s, and who understand the gravity of the title "*shaheed*" (martyr), may find the shrine an integral piece of the nation's history; a casual visitor may find it a long way to travel for little visual appeal.

The shrine itself is rather broad and grand on the outside; visitors must traverse a huge but desolate courtyard for a few hundred metres before reaching the building itself. The building has two main levels, and is broad and flat, topped by three gleaming white domes. Visitors enter from the main door beneath the largest dome, depositing their shoes with the minder outside (free service, small donations appreciated). Inside, the building is both touching and underwhelming. The front hall is adorned with politically-charged posters, mostly depicting the late Benazir Bhutto either working studiously among party members, grinning triumphantly at her supporters, or smiling benevolently at her children. It's no doubt an emotional sight, but the parallels drawn between her maternal instincts and her custodianship of the nation might be a bit overblown.

Further inside lie the actual tombs of Benazir (who died in a terrorist attack in 2007) and her father Zulfiqar (who was hanged after a politically motivated court case in 1979); the other tombs belong to other members of the Bhutto family, including Benazir's brothers Shahnawaz and Murtaza, both of whom died unnatural (and perhaps suspicious) deaths in 1985 and 1996 respectively. The graves, particularly those of Benazir and Zulfiqar, are adorned with flowers and special shrouds, and visitors spend hours in quiet contemplation or even prayer for the departed souls. It's important to understand that the Bhutto family don't just represent politics in the region, but the hope of millions of rural Sindhis. However for the sanctity and importance of the shrine, it's unfortunate that so much of the interior is simply dusty exposed concrete - children run around playing, and some families even come in simply to seek respite from the day's heat, or even to sleep on the floor.

Getting to Garhi Khuda Bakhsh is a two-step process. From Larkana's Purana bus stand, take a van towards Naudero (Jacobabad is a common destination, so ask to be dropped at Noudero). This will cost Rs. 30 and take 20 minutes. From Naudero, take an autorickshaw or qingqi to Garhi Khuda Bakhsh (Rs. 20, 5 minutes). Coming back is basically the same thing in reverse, but transport doesn't run from Garhi Khuda Bakhsh very frequently, so it makes sense to ask the autorickshaw or qingqi to wait for you while you explore the inside

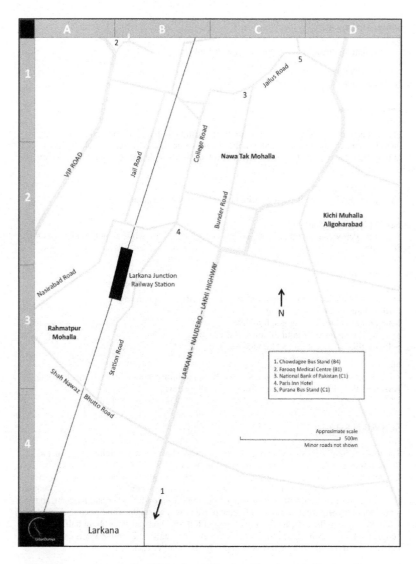

Map legend:
1. Chowdagee Bus Stand (B4)
2. Farooq Medical Centre (B1)
3. National Bank of Pakistan (C1)
4. Paris Inn Hotel
5. Purana Bus Stand (C1)

Approximate scale
500m
Minor roads not shown

Larkana

of the shrine - pay an extra Rs. 100 for the waiting time. If you want to hire a car from Sukkur for the day, please see page 144 for details of a travel agency.

Eating in Larkana
There's a whole lot of eating options, including Pakistani, Chinese and even a KFC, along the main street near the Paris Inn Hotel *(map pg. 148).*

Staying in Larkana
If you do need to stay in Larkana, one recommended hotel is the Paris Inn Hotel *(Rs. 2,000, map pg. 148).*

Services in Larkana
Banks
No international banks have representation in Larkana.

Money exchange
National Bank of Pakistan: Bunder Rd *(map pg. 148)*

Help in Larkana
Safety
Larkana is a rough and ready rural Sindh town. Although it's not particularly dangerous, there isn't much reason to hang around here, and a lone foreigner would stick out like a sore thumb. If you really want to spend time in Larkana dress and behave appropriately – this is a conservative place.

Medical services
Farooq Medical Centre is one of Larkana's better private hospitals *(map pg. 148).*

Getting around Larkana
A spot in a crowded qingqi around Larkana costs Rs. 20 - 50, while an autorickshaw is Rs. 50 – 100.

Leaving Larkana
Bus
Intercity buses leave from "Purana Stand" on the city's northern edge.
Hyderabad: Local buses, 5 hours, Rs. 500
Karachi: Local buses, 7 hours, Rs. 800
Sukkur: Local buses, 1 hour 30 mins, Rs. 150
Sehwan Sharif: Local buses, 4 hours, Rs. 350

Air
The airport is actually at Mohenjodaro, an attempt to promote tourism to the historic site.
Karachi: PIA, 1 hour 15 minutes, from Rs. 5,600 one way

SEHWAN SHARIF
Population: 41,000, Elevation: 28m, Telephone code: 025
The town of Sehwan, usually referred to as "Sehwan Sharif" ("noble Sehwan"), is draws in thousands of pilgrims every day visiting the shrine of Lal Shahbaz Qalander, one of the region's most prominent Sufi mystics. Other than the main shrine, there is another shrine and a fort to visit, both of which are related to the epic story of the life and times of Shahbaz Qalander. Sehwan stands about four and a half hours from both Sukkur and Karachi, so it's a very long day trip from either, or a logical place to stay the night while passing through. Every year on the the *urs* (death anniversary) of Lal Shahbaz Qalandar about half a million people pack the rooms, streets and shrines of Sehwan Sharif. In 2018 the *urs* is expected to fall on around the 4th May, and moves about 10 days earlier each year.

Shrine of Lal Shahbaz Qalander
map pg. 151, Open from sunrise to midnight, Free
Syed Muhammad Usman Marwandi, popularly known as Lal Shahbaz Qalander, was born in a small town in Afghanistan in 1177, but his legend is inextricably linked to the town of Sehwan. It was here that, already aged in his 70s, he ended his travels around the Muslim world and settled and devoted his life to the teaching, philosophy and mysticism. Devotees claim that he lived to the age of 150 in health and celibacy, and preached understanding, tolerance and forgiveness. He is said to have performed miracles such as resurrecting a slain follower, and destroying a fort with the palm of his hand. Unreal though these might seem, the miracles and the spiritual healing power of Lal Shahbaz Qalander are taken very

seriously by his followers, who in vast numbers visit the shrine to pay their respects, make spiritual promises, engage in *dhamaal* (an ascetic spiritual trance/dance) and seek salvation and cure from ailments. You will see the full spectrum of religious conviction; men who voluntarily walk in chains as "slaves" to their God, women shrieking as they have evil spirits driven from their souls, entire families splayed out on the floor in complete submission to the higher power... it's essential to keep an open mind.

The shrine, which was built in 1356, has two main entrances; one from the main bazaar, and another, smaller entrance near the mosque at the back. The inner sanctum is home to the tomb itself, sitting below a spectacularly elaborate chandelier, and a dome clad in pretty Sindhi tilework. The interior of the shrine is particularly stunning at night, when the lights reflect of the tiles and the shimmering chandelier. Occasionally the wooden cabin housing the casket may be opened, allowing devotees to actually enter and touch the tomb. On one corner of the tomb hangs a silver flask, through which water is poured by devotees; some believe that the water which passes out of the flask is blessed. The shrine of course has special significance for Sufis, some Shia and anyone who has faith in the saint, however even other visitors (Muslim or otherwise) have reported feeling an overwhelming sense of peace when there. Take a place in the corner of the shrine, sit on the floor and watch the spectacle unfold... see what effect it has on you.

Shoes must be removed to enter the shrine - give Rs. 20 to the shoe minders at either gate. Security is tight after a bombing here in February 2017. Thursday evenings are a special time to visit as this is when *dhamaal* takes place - the courtyard at the main entrance is filled with spiritual types dancing and spinning to the beat of drums, lost to the love of God. The shrine is packed on the the *urs* (death anniversary) of Lal Shahbaz Qalandar, which in 2018 is expected to fall on around the 4th May, and moves about 10 days earlier each year.

Shrine of Bodla Bahar
map pg. 151, Open sunrise to late night, Free
Bodla Bahar Sikander was a devotee and contemporary of Lal Shahbaz Qalander, whose history is shrouded in myth and legend. One story is that he used to sweep the floor with his beard while waiting for the saint to arrive in Sehwan. Another states that he was brutally murdered by an enemy, only to have his mutilated body parts sewn back together and then resurrected by his guru. Whatever the truth, his legend earned him a place in the hearts of Lal Shahbaz Qalander's followers, who consider him a saint in his own right. His shrine is nowhere near as grand as that of his master, but is subtly memorable. The small courtyard leads to the dim inner sanctum where devotees pray and kiss his casket. Outside and to the left is a tree filled with colourful threads; each left behind by a visitor who tied it with a wish and a prayer.

To get here, walk past the Shrine of Lal Shahbaz Qalander on Bodla Bahar Street – it enters a covered market. About 100 metres along a slightly larger laneway to the left leads out of the bazaar - take this, and the shrine is just outside on a corner on the right. Visitors must leave their shoes with the minder outside the front gate for Rs 10. Each night a small *dhamaal* group dances and spins in the courtyard at sunset; the shrine is also suitably busy during the *urs* of Shahbaz Qalander (see above).

Purana Qila (Alexander's Fort)
map pg. 151, Open 24 hours, Free
The *Purana Qila* (meaning Old Fort), has many names; it is rarely referred to by its English name, "Alexander's Fort" (because it was apparently built by Alexander the Great). It's occasionally referred to as *Kafir Qila*, "unbeliever's fort", as some say it was built during Hindu rule. Some other's call it *Sehwan Qila*. Usually however it's just referred to as Purana Qila, or just "qila" ("the fort"). Not a lot is left of it, but the road into the centre still has to weave its way through the rocky walls. Its said that Lal Shahbaz Qalander, in an effort to prove his miracle-working powers, picked up the entire fort in the palm of his hand, flipped it over and smashed it down again, resulting in the fort's present crumbling, stout structure. Inside the fort is a small *imambargah* (Shia memorial house) and a military post - so don't

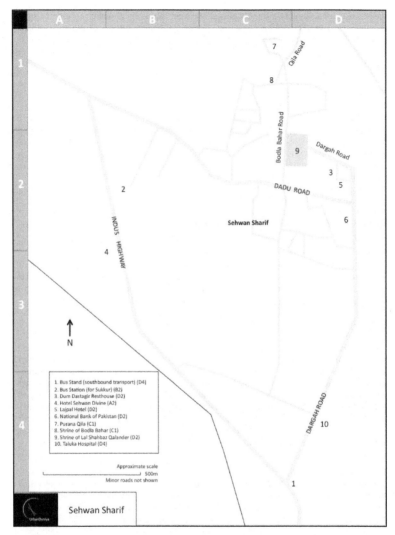

	A	B	C	D
1			7 Qila Road	
			8	
2		2	Bodla Bahar Road 9 Dargah Road	3 5
		INDUS HIGHWAY	DADU ROAD	6
			Sehwan Sharif	
3		4		
	↑ N			
4			DARGAH ROAD	10
				1

1. Bus Stand (southbound transport) (D4)
2. Bus Station (for Sukkur) (B2)
3. Dum Dastagir Resthouse (D2)
4. Hotel Sehwan Divine (A2)
5. Lajpal Hotel (D2)
6. National Bank of Pakistan (D2)
7. Purana Qila (C1)
8. Shrine of Bodla Bahar (C1)
9. Shrine of Lal Shahbaz Qalander (D2)
10. Taluka Hospital (D4)

Approximate scale
⊢————————————⌐ 500m
Minor roads not shown

Sehwan Sharif

wave your camera around too freely. You also get a spectacular view of the shrine of Lal Shahbaz Qalander from across the rooftops of Sehwan, and a good perspective on the surrounding dusty plains and farmland.

To get here, go to the Shrine of Bodla Bahar (see above). Turn down the street next to Bodla Bahar, and continue down the hill and through the archway; the fort is in front of you.

Staying in Sehwan Sharif
Backpacker
Dum Dastagir Resthouse: Dargah Road Bazaar; (+92) 03072195833
map pg. 151, Dbl Rs. 70
Bare bones and basic, but with a friendly owner and right near the shrine and bazaar. It's

almost impossible to find amid the bazaar – ask at the Lajpal Hotel restaurant, and they will point you in the right direction.

Economy
Hotel Sehwan Divine: Indus Highway, Sehwan Bypass; (+92) 03420350341
map pg. 151, Dbl US$48
Sehwan Divine has the cleanest, most comfortable rooms in town; a little bit of comfort while in rural Sindh. The attached Sehwan Restaurant is great too!

Eating in Sehwan Sharif
Bodla Bahar Road, directly outside the shrine is packed with cheap eateries selling Pakistani staples. The best kitchen in town belongs to the Lajpal Hotel *(map pg. 151)*, in a laneway near the shrine. The only mid to top-end option is the Sehwan Restaurant (attached to the Hotel Sehwan Divine) out of town on the bypass road.

Services in Sehwan Sharif
Banks
No international banks have representation in Sehwan Sharif.

Internet services
At the time of writing there were no reliable internet cafes in Sehwan Sharif – the best option would be to have a meal at the Sehwan Restaurant (above) and ask politely to use the hotel's wifi.

Money exchange
National Bank of Pakistan *(map pg. 151)* on Dargah Road is able to change money, but practicalities (like a lack of foreign cash) sometimes present difficulties.

Help in Sehwan Sharif
Safety
Sehwan is a small town which is used to seeing all types of people coming and going, foreigners included, so it might be one of the safest places in interior Sindh. That said, still use common sense when it comes to valuables and not flashing your (relative) wealth. There are a lot of beggars in Sehwan Sharif. Security in Sehwan has been tightened after a bombing at the shrine claimed over 70 lives in February 2017.

Medical services
Taluka Hospital: Dargah Road. Serious cases will be taken to Hyderabad, Sukkur or Karachi. *(map pg. 151)*

Getting around Sehwan Sharif
From the bypass road to the centre of town costs Rs. 30 in a qingqi or rickshaw. Most of the centre of the town is best navigated on foot.

Leaving Sehwan Sharif
The bus stands are on the bypass road – buses go from the southern junction to Larkana, Hyderabad, Karachi (and Bhit Shah, when it's running). Buses leave from the northern junction (ie – the proper bus stand) to Sukkur.

Bhit Shah: Local buses, 2 hours, Rs. 300 - last vans leave at about 4pm, and even then are highly dependent on pilgrimage traffic. Otherwise you will need to go via Hyderabad.
Hyderabad: Local buses, 2 hours, Rs. 300
Karachi: Local buses, 5 hours, Rs. 500
Sukkur: Local buses, 4 hours, Rs. 350
Larkana: Local buses, 4 hours, Rs. 350

Abbottabad
and the Kaghan Valley

Pakistanis, particularly Lahoris, love the Kaghan Valley. In fact for many Lahori tourists the the village of Naran in the north of the valley practically *is* the northern areas. While the scenery here is not quite as dramatic as it is in Gilgit-Baltistan, it's still very spectacular, and there's no denying the ease of access. What's remarkable about travelling in the Kaghan Valley is how abruptly the temperature drops - from warm Balakot to the frozen peaks around Naran, it's easy to see why this is currently one of the favoured summer getaways for "downland" Pakistanis.

The valley begins as a crease between the foothills of the Himalayas north of Islamabad near the garrison city of Abbottabad. Driving upstream beside the Naran River, the valley walls become increasingly taller and steeper, until they open out to a wide valley at Naran - here you are 2,500m above sea level. The road continues to climb, cutting a swathe through glaciers until it eventually reaches Babusar Top, and the border with Gilgit-Baltistan. Culturally the valley's inhabitants are closely related to Kashmiris, despite being in Khyber Pukhtoonkhwa province.

Police registration

Foreigners who visit the Kaghan Valley outside of Abbottabad are sometimes required to register with the local police force on arrival. However many report happily entering and leaving the region without ever encountering a policeman. The Kaghan Valley has not experienced unrest of the sort which has troubled other parts of Pakistan, however many foreign countries' travel advisories still advise against travel due to the situation in other parts of the provice.

Registration usually consists simply of noting your name, passport details, accommodation details and travel plans in a book at the local police station. If it is deemed necessary, you may also be assigned an armed police guard. This guard is free of cost, and will accompany you, especially on trips into the mountains or forests. The guard can be a source of local knowledge, and is not intended to impede your travel - some travellers report befriending their guard and staying in touch afterwards.

ABBOTTABAD

Population: 1.4 million, Elevation: 1,256m, Telephone code: 0992

Abbottabad is a military town surrounded by hills with little to attract foreign visitors. It shot into the headlines on 2nd May 2011 as the place where Osama bin Laden had apparently been hiding. The "hideout" has long since been bulldozed, photography of the site is strictly prohibited, and a curious foreigner in the neighbourhood would probably draw the attention of security forces - so stay away. Aside from this chapter in history, Abbottabad is a reasonably safe city - the strong military presence means a higher level of security than in many other Pakistani cities. Abbottabad is the gateway to the lovely Kaghan Valley which begins just to the north. It is an important stop on the Karakoram Highway, and it is the spot where the Murree/Nathia Gali road loops back around towards Islamabad, so while you might not need to stay here, it's conceivable that you might travel through at some point.

Staying in Abbottabad

Economy

Royal Hotel: 203 The Mall Road; (+92) 03009115490
map pg. 158, Dbl Rs. 3,200
Wifi and breakfast at this hotel in the city centre, but it's not spick and span like Alaf Laila Guest House.

Alaf Laila Guest House: Bilqias Town Road, Kaghan Colony; (+92) 03459566871;
map pg. 158, Dbl Rs. 1,500, Suite Rs. 2,000
Quite a distance out of the centre, this comfortable guest house comes recommended for its quiet location. There are a few eateries around too, such as the Usmania Restaurant chain.

Hotel De Ville: Opposite Mirpur police station, Main Mansehra Road; (+92) 0992-381932
map pg. 158, Dbl Rs. 2,500, Suite Rs. 3,600
One of the best economy options, also north of the centre. Free wifi, a restaurant and cable television.

Luxury

Sarban Hotel: The Mall, near Sarban Chowk; (+92) 03454644666
map pg. 158, Dbl Rs. 5,000
An old building with clean, if dated rooms, free wifi and 24 hour room service.

Hotel De Manchi: Main Mansehra Road; (+92) 0992-381835;
www.hoteldemanchi.com/abbottabad
map pg. 158, Dbl Rs. 4,000, Suite Rs. 7,000
De Manchi is the best place to sleep in Abbottabad with well-appointed, clean rooms and a buffet restaurant offering Pakistani and Chinese dishes.

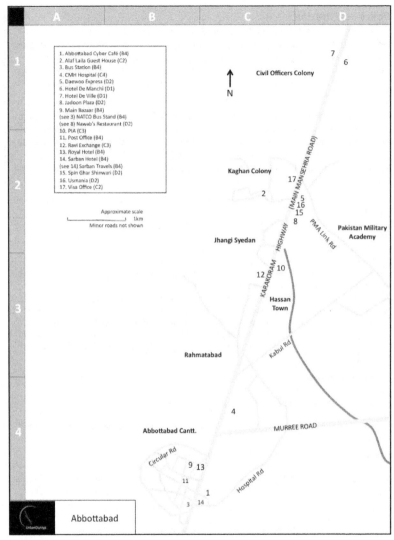

1. Abbottabad Cyber Café (B4)
2. Alaf Laila Guest House (C2)
3. Bus Station (B4)
4. CMH Hospital (C4)
5. Daewoo Express (D2)
6. Hotel De Manchi (D1)
7. Hotel De Ville (D1)
8. Jadoon Plaza (D2)
9. Main Bazaar (B4)
(see 3) NATCO Bus Stand (B4)
(see 8) Nawab's Restaurant (D2)
10. PIA (C3)
11. Post Office (B4)
12. Ravi Exchange (C3)
13. Royal Hotel (B4)
14. Sarban Hotel (B4)
(see 14) Sarban Travels (B4)
15. Spin Ghar Shinwari (D2)
16. Usmania (D2)
17. Visa Office (C2)

Approximate scale
1km
Minor roads not shown

N

Civil Officers Colony

Kaghan Colony

(MAIN MANSEHRA ROAD)

KARAKORAM HIGHWAY

PMA Link Rd

Pakistan Military
Academy

Jhangi Syedan

Hassan
Town

Rahmatabad

Kabul Rd

MURREE ROAD

Abbottabad Cantt.

Circular Rd

Hospital Rd

Abbottabad

Eating in Abbottabad

There are plenty of cheap canteen-style eateries in the main bazaar on Circular Road. For a proper sit-down meal go to **Nawab's Restaurant**, **Usmania** or **Spin Ghar Shinwari** restaurants, all in a cluster out of the centre. The **Hotel De Manchi** also has a nice multi-cuisine restaurant. **Jadoon Plaza** has a couple of fast food outlets, although no foreign chains *(all map pg. 158)*.

Services in Abbottabad

Airlines

Despite not having an airport for commercial flights, <u>Pakistan International</u> has an office here on the Karakoram Highway; (+92) 111-786-786 *(map pg. 158)*.

Banks
No international banks are represented in Abbottabad

Internet cafes
Abbottabad Cyber Café *(map pg. 158)* is a well-known option in the centre – otherwise ask at your hotel.

Money exchange
Ravi Exchange: Shop 1-2 Madina Market, Main Mansehra Road *(map pg. 158)*

Post office
Allama Iqbal Road, Cantt Area *(map pg. 158)*

Travel agent
Sarban Travels is associated with the Sarban Hotel; (+92) 0992-335011 *(map pg. 158)*

Visa office
Abdullah Market, Missile Chowk, Main Mansehra Road *(map pg. 158)*

Help in Abbottabad

Safety
Aside from the headlines of 2011, Abbottabad is actually one of Pakistan's safest cities. The normal precautions apply, but there's a certain air of calm here which is no illusion.

Medical services
Combined Military Hospital (CMH): Main Mansehra Road *(map pg. 158)*
There's a 24-hour pharmacy at the hospital.

Getting around Abbottabad
There aren't as many autorickshaws plying the streets of Abbottabad as in other cities of Pakistan. Instead Suzuki vans run circuits around the city. Stand at a major road junction and wait for one to approach you. When it's near, shout the name of the hotel/district/mall/junction that your're going to, and they'll let you know if they're headed your way. Bolan Suzukis charge between Rs. 50 and 100 to anywhere in the city.

Leaving Abbottabad
The Daewoo Express bus terminal is north of the city on the Main Mansehra Road *(map pg. 158)*, while the local bus stop is in the centre near the Hotel Sarban. NATCO Buses stop at the local bus stand *(map pg. 158)*.

Transport from Abbottabad to Gilgit usually travels via the Karakoram Highway. If you want to travel via Naran, you might find direct transport available, but otherwise you will need to change in Naran and Chilas. Note the seasonal closure of the Babusar Pass (page 170)

Rawalpindi/Islamabad: Daewoo Express, 2 hours 15 minutes, Rs. 330
Murree: Local buses, 2 hours 30 minutes, Rs. 250
Nathia Gali: Local buses, 1 hour 30 minutes, Rs. 100
Mansehra: Local buses, 45 minutes, Rs. 50
Kiwai: Local buses, 3 hours, Rs. 150
Naran: Local buses, 4 hours, Rs. 500
Gilgit (via Karakoram Highway): NATCO buses, 9 hours, Rs. 2,000
Chilas (via Karakoram Highway): NATCO buses, 7 hours, Rs. 1,800
Lahore: Daewoo Express, 6 hours and 10 minutes, Rs. 1100
Peshawar: Daewoo Express, 3 hours 15 minutes, Rs. 530

Around Abbottabad

The road to Nathia Gali climbs 33 kms before beginning its gradual descent to Murree and looping back around to Islamabad. Just outside of Abbottabad, a smaller road climbs the hill towards Thandiani. Khanpur Dam is a popular day trip for water sports from either Abbottabad or Islamabad, or at a stretch, Lahore.

NATHIA GALI

Population: 5,000, Elevation: 2,500m, Telephone code: 0992

While there are plenty of places around the world where you can see forested ridges, there's something special about wrapping your hands around a cup of hot Pakistani *chai* on a chilly evening at Nathia Gali (also spelled Nathiagali). And that's what you come to Nathia Gali, or any of the galis for - to unwind and allow the drama of 'mainland' Pakistan to unfold miles away in the distance.

Nathia Gali is not as built-up as Murree, owing in part to its location further away from the capital. It is part of a group of settlements - Changla Gali, Kuza Gali, Dunga Gali - known collectively as "The Galis". *'Gali'* means 'mountain pass' in the local Hindko language, and each village is built at or near a strategic ridge-top location. The Galis are a really lovely place to get away from it all, and take in some gorgeous alpine views.

It gets very cold here in winter - and even in May or October the nights can be seriously chilly, so come prepared. During the day you can stroll the bazaars, shopping for woollen shawls which are a specialty of this region.

Staying in Nathia Gali

Due to the nature of tourism in Nathia Gali a lot of the accommodation is aimed at the economy bracket, without many options for backpackers (who would stay in Murree, or camp), or luxury-lovers (who would rent a private villa for their stay).

Economy
K International Hotel: Nathia Gali - Abbottabad Road; (+92) 0992-555231
map pg. 161, Dbl: Rs. 4,000
Previously known as the Hotel Kamran International, this is a pure mid-range hotel; comfortable and clean but not much more. In the heart of Nathia Gali's bustling bazaar, and with wifi.

Hotel Elites: Hotel Road, Bhurban; (+92) 0992-0355045; www.hotelelites.com
map pg. 161, Dbl: $80
About a kilometre from the centre of town, Hotel Elites has a classy restaurant, comfortable rooms and great views across the valley, making it the pick of the bunch.

Eating in Nathia Gali

The main bazaar is lined with places to eat - one very popular (although not particularly upmarket) option is Red Onion, serving pizzas and other tasty staples. Finer dining options are more likely to be found in expensive hotels, such as Hotel Elites *(map pg. 161)*.

Services in Nathia Gali

Banks
There are ATMs here, but no international banks are represented

Internet Cafe
Internet cafes can be found along the main bazaar, and wifi at better eating and accommodation establishments

Post Office
Nathia Gali - Abbottabad Road, near the main bazaar *(map pg. 161)*.

———

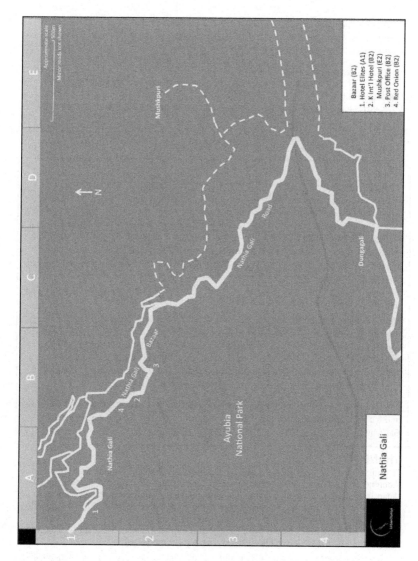

Map legend:
Bazaar (B2)
1. Hotel Elites (A1)
2. K Int'l Hotel (B2)
Mushkpuri (E2)
3. Post Office (B2)
4. Red Onion (B2)

Help in Nathia Gali

Safety
Nathia Gali is a safe destination, however the usual precautions apply here. Don't underestimate how cold the mountain air can get at night, even in spring and autumn.

Medical Services
The nearest hospital is CMH Hospital in Abbotabad, while serious cases would be treated in Islamabad. There are some pharmacies in the Nathia Gali bazaar *(map pg. 161)*.

Getting around Nathia Gali
You probably won't need to 'get around' Nathia Gali too much - there's not far to go, and most visitors either bring their own transport or enjoy walking. If you do need a lift somewhere, you'll need to walk to the bazaar and hail a rickshaw (around Rs. 50 from one end of town to the other).

Leaving Nathia Gali
Local buses leave from Nathia Gali's bazaar, picking up passengers from the main road *(map pg. 161)*.

Murree: Local buses, 30 minutes, Rs. 70.
Abbottabad: Local buses, 1 hour 30 minutes, Rs. 100

Hike to Mushkpuri

If you're more physically inclined, you can take a walk through the pine forests up to Mushkpuri (also spelled as Mukshpuri *(map pg. 161)* a sparsely vegetated ridge affording views of the Jhelum River and to Azad Jammu and Kashmir. The track begins from a street above the main bazaar in Nathia Gali - be sure to ask for directions, as the start of the track isn't very well signposted. Once you're on the track, it's a short but moderately strenuous climb up to a small wildlife park which hosts a couple of pheasants, a bear, and a snow leopard in only passable conditions. Entry costs Rs. 200 for foreigners, and there is a small cafeteria just inside the gate. Because the park is built around the track, you're obliged to pay the entry fee even if you don't want to stop. To avoid this, you could start from Dunga Gali and join the main track half way up.

From the other end of the park, the gate leads back on to the track, and it's another moderately strenuous climb of 2 and a half hours before reaching Mushkpuri. There's little shelter up there, and virtually zero tourist facilities, so pack enough water and sun protection for the day. Visitors can either walk back down the way they came, or about halfway down the hill there's a path off to the left which takes you down into Dunga Gali. The trip back down the hill takes approximately 2 hours via either route.

If you start in Dunga Gali, get a local bus from Nathia Gali (Rs. 30, 20 minutes) to drop you in the centre of town. Ask around for the track's start – there's a blue sign near Dunga Gali's bazaar.

THANDIANI
'Thandiani' *(map pg. 156)* literally means 'cold place'. It's a small hill station high above Abbottabad from where you can see the snow-capped peak of Nanga Parbat on a clear day. Apart from drinking a hot chai and walking around the unclean bazaar, there's not a lot to do here, but the scenery of the surrounding mountains is indisputably pretty. There is a small church, which is quaint if only for its colonial appeal. A sign prohibiting foreigners from entering Thandiani didn't appear to be having its desired effect when we visited - there were no checkpoints, and we haven't heard of anyone being turned away.

From Abbottabad's bus station a bus should cost Rs. 100 and will take 1 hour 30 minutes. Buses to Thandiani aren't frequent, and they don't fill up very quickly - ask at your hotel in Abbottabad or Nathia Gali for a rental car if you want to speed things up – an afternoon's round trip will cost around Rs. 3,000.

KHANPUR DAM
This large dam is actually much closer to Islamabad than Abbottabad (just 40 kilometres north of the capital), but is nevertheless in Khyber Pukhtoonkhwa *(map pg. 156)*. Swimming, waterskiing, jet skiing and cliff diving are all possible here, and a welcome respite from the city in the middle of summer. A car with driver for the day from either Islamabad or Abbottabad is about Rs. Rs. 3000 - ask at your hotel.

MANSEHRA

Population: 1.1 million, Elevation: 1,088m, Telephone code: 0997

Mansehra *(map pg. 156)* is a small city with little to attract the casual visitor. Most buses from "downland" Pakistan towards the north ends here, from where travellers transfer into smaller vans more suited to the hilly road conditions. The road from Islamabad and Abbottabad splits in to two main branches - one heads north towards the Kaghan Valley, while the Karakoram Highway travels further west with a turn off for the Swat Valley.

While Mansehra and Abbottabad are close enough to be thought of as twin cities (only about 20 kilometres apart), they are remarkably different in character - while Abbottabad is a stately garrison town, Mansehra leaves no doubt that you have arrived in Pakistan's rough-and-ready northwestern frontier province.

Most travellers who come to Mansehra are on the way elsewhere, and there's little reason to hang around. If you need to stay here, there is the Hotel Royal City near the bus station. Around the bus station there are also lots of cheap eateries, or otherwise try at the Hotel Royal City hotel for a proper restaurant meal.

Mansehra's bus station is known as the Lari Bus Station and is on the city's northern edge. Buses heading towards Gilgit depart from the separate bus stand closer to the city centre.

Leaving Mansehra

Transport from Mansehra to Gilgit usually travels via the Karakoram Highway. If you want to travel via Naran, you might find direct transport available, but otherwise you will need to change in Naran. Similarly, transport to Murree, Nathia Gali or Peshawar usually requires a change in Abbottabad.

Rawalpindi/Islamabad: Local buses, 3 hours, Rs. 400
Abbottabad: Local buses, 45 minutes, Rs. 50
Kiwai: Local buses, 2 hours, Rs. 100
Naran: Local buses, 3 hours, Rs. 300
Chilas (via Karakoram Highway): NATCO buses, 6 hours, Rs. 1,700
Gilgit (via Karakoram Highway): NATCO buses, 8 hours, Rs. 1,900
Peshawar: Local buses, 4 hours, Rs. 550
Lahore: Local buses, 9 hours, Rs. 900

BALAKOT

Population: 30,000, Elevation: 975m, Telephone code: 0985

Balakot *(map pg. 156)* was close to the epicentre of the 2005 earthquake which devastated much of northern Pakistan. As a result the town is mostly the result of reconstruction efforts over the past decade, and is filled with ugly masks of concrete. For those passing through towards Naran there's not a lot to stop for, but this is where most travellers notice the temperature beginning to drop as the road ascends.

KIWAI

Population: 3,400, Elevation: 1,512m, Telephone code: 0985

This small service town is a great place to stop on the way to Naran. At the bend in the road there is a small cafe *(map pg. 165)* where you can sit on benches in a stream, let the flow from the glacial melt wash over your weary feet, and chill your Coca Cola in the icy water. A handful of guesthouses face on to the main road - the Tourist Inn Hotel and Restaurant *(map pg. 165)* near the turnoff for Shogran Road is one cheap option.

Kiwai is the main transport junction for Shogran (see below).

Leaving Kiwai

To go further south then Mansehra, or further north than Naran, you'll need to change your transport in either town.

Mansehra: Local buses, 2 hours, Rs. 100
Naran: Local buses, 1 hour 30 minutes, Rs. 150
Shogran: Jeeps to Shogran leave when full and cost about Rs. 2,000 one way (for the whole jeep - this cost is divided among six passengers). The journey takes 20 minutes. The return jeeps leave from the main intersection in Shogran. The price doubles in peak season June - August.

SHOGRAN
Population: nomadic/seasonal, Elevation: 2,400m, Telephone code: 0985
Shogran is a small village on a hill high above the Naran Road. The main attraction is enjoying the cool environs and watching the fickle weather weave its way through the folds of the pine-filed valley below.

What to see and do in Shogran
Siri Pae
Siri Pae ("Head and Foot") is the name of an area on the mountain above Shogran, a bumpy jeep ride from the village centre. Exactly what people come here for is unclear - there are many more beautiful places nearby - but its accessibility is easy and its popularity is for certain. Siri is the name of the small, muddy lake on the left as you approach the end of the road, although most people don't stop here. More popular are the meadows and lake at Pae which, despite being known as "the foot", are actually higher up the hill than "Siri". The rolling meadows lead past pine-filed escarpments, and are filled with picnickers, day-trippers from Islamabad and Rawalpindi, and local tribesmen offering horse rides.

Follow the hordes of local visitors past the snack vendors towards the bottom of Makra Peak, and look back along the valley towards Balakot. On the other side, the snow-capped peaks near Naran can be seen peeping over the folds in the Kaghan Valley.

There are hiking opportunities up Makra Peak (4,000m). From Pae meadows its a constant, steep, 4 hour climb to the top, but once you reach there the views across the Kaghan Valley and over into Kashmir are tremendous. Don't attempt this walk alone, or ill prepared - the weather can change quickly, and more than a few visitors have set out for a casual stroll and got stuck halfway in a sudden rainstorm.

To get to Siri Pae, hire a jeep from the main junction in Shogran. The price for the return journey is approximately Rs. 2,500 for the whole jeep - bargain hard. This price is split among the passengers of the jeep - usually about 6 people). The cost doubles in peak season, from June - August. The jeep ride is approximately 45 minutes on a cliff-edge road, and is very rough - anyone afraid of heights or prone to motion sickness, be warned.

Day-tripping groups often rent out entire jeeps for themselves, so if you're travelling alone be prepared to either shell out the whole cost, or wait for a jeep to fill up with similarly independent travellers. If you're really stuck, hang around the intersection in Shogran and perhaps get talking with a group of people who are also waiting - see if they wouldn't mind sharing the cost with you.

Occasionally it's possible to rent a jeep all the way from Kiwai (page 163) to Siri Pae. This costs about Rs. 3,500 return in off peak season, Rs. 6,000 in peak season.

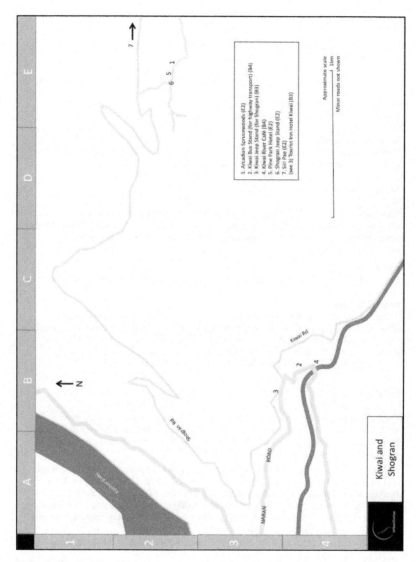

The map shows:

1. Arcadian Sprucewoods (E2)
2. Kiwai Bus Stand (for highway transport) (B4)
3. Kiwai Jeep Stand (for Shogran) (B3)
4. Kiwai River Café (B4)
5. Pine Park Hotel (E2)
6. Shogran Jeep Stand (E2)
7. Siri Paie (E2)
(see 3) Tourist Inn Hotel Kiwai (B3)

Approximate scale — 1km
Minor roads not shown

Kiwai and Shogran

Eating in Shogran

With only a handful of small eateries offering up standard Pakistani dishes, the best eating options are in any of the hotels around town.

Staying in Shogran

Shogran is not a cheap place to stay - locals are going for the "elite hill station" feel, and cottages and chalets are much more common than hotels and guest houses. Out of the peak summer season you could walk into any hotel and ask for discounts, which you will probably get. However between late May and August the cheapest place to stay is not in Shogran at all, but instead at the guest house on the main road in Kiwai (page 163).

<u>Pine Park Hotel:</u> Shogran Road: (+92) 3465633947
map pg. 165, Dbl: Rs. 3,000, Suites Rs. 5,000, prices double in summer
Not a cheap option, but one that gets good reviews. Well appointed and has a good restaurant.

<u>Arcadian Sprucewoods:</u> Shogran Road; (+92) 051-8436972 www.arcadian.pk/sprucewoods
map pg. 165, Dbl: Rs. 3,500, Deluxe cottage Rs. 12,500, prices double in summer
One of the most luxurious places to stay in Shogran - wifi, a lovely restaurant, and a stunning lawn where you can promenade as much as you like.

Services in Shogran
A resort town, Shogran has few basic services; basic services like post are normally located in Kiwai, while internet is usually provided by the hotels.

Help in Shogran
Safety
Shogran is very safe, and the main danger comes from the environment - make sure you are carrying enough warm clothes in case the weather turns. Don't forget that although Shogran seems to be a tourist hot spot, you are still in conservative Khyber-Pukhtoonkhwa - dress and act appropriately.

Medical services
Shogran has basic medical services, but serious cases are likely to be treated in Abbottabad.

Leaving Shogran
There is little, if any transport between Shogran and anywhere but Kiwai. To get to Shogran, take the jeeps which depart from the junction with Naran Road in Kiwai. The jeeps leave when full, cost about Rs. 2,000 one way (for the whole jeep - this cost is divided among six passengers) and take 20 minutes. The return jeeps leave from the main intersection in Shogran. The price doubles in peak season June - August.

NARAN
Population: nomadic/seasonal, Elevation: 2,500m, Telephone code: 0997
Cool in summer, frozen in winter - Naran's climate is the stuff of dreams for many Pakistanis who swelter through June and July. Accordingly, no small number of Pakistanis try to make their dream come true, and on holiday weekends (like Eid) the region is so crowded that authorities close the roads for fear of gridlock.

Naran's main road is its bazaar, and it's nothing special - cheap eateries, mediocre hotels and throngs of domestic tourists - from entire extended families to squads of bachelors. Imagine a popular ski resort, without the ski runs, but lots of apres-ski scene, but without alcohol. In winter the town is snowbound and virtually shuts down for four to five months between October or November and April or May; check with tourist officials in Islamabad or elsewhere if the road and town are open.

The attractions of Naran (apart from the halal apres-ski scene) are the gorgeous alpine lakes and their pretty, snowy settings nearby.

What do see and do in Naran
Jheel Saif-ul-Malook (Lake Saif-ul-Malook)
This lake, 3,224 metres above sea level, is absolutely worth a visit *(map pg. 156)*. The colour of the lake seems to change with the light and the season; in sunny May and June it melts into bright turquoise, and when the sun is not out its darkness shimmers with the reflection of the surrounding mountains. It remains frozen until at least mid-May, but sometimes later, so check before heading here.

Folklore and mystery surrounds the history of Lake Saif-ul-Malook. 19th century poet Mian Muhammad Baksh wrote a story about an Arabian prince who travelled to the lake and fell madly in love with a fairy who inhabited the nearby mountains. Like everything in Pakistan the lines between reality and fantasy are blurred, and the "haunting" of Lake Saif-ul-Malook is considered a fact by more than a few locals.

It's possible to walk the circumference of the lake (about 3 hours), but consult locals before setting out - the weather changes quickly in the mountains, and tourists sometimes get stuck. You can also try to climb up the slippery snow-covered slopes of Malika Parbat - that's the 5,290 metre mountain on the left as you approach the lake from Naran. Watch out for shrieking domestic tourists sliding back down to their hysterical families, using their backsides as toboggans.

Try to visit when it's not busy - that way, you'll avoid the hordes of local tourists and their accompanying litter. If you want to stay the night at Lake Saif-ul-Malook, there is one hotel whose view makes up for the lack of luxury. The Lake View Hotel charges Rs. 7,000 per night during the summer season, and is on the road to Lake Saif-ul-Malook, about 200 metres from the shore of the lake.

Further afield, it's possible to hike to Ansu Lake in one very long day. Ansu means 'tear drop', and this beautiful, remote lake is indeed shaped like an eye shedding a tear. This lake is said to have been formed by one of the teardrops shed by the Arabian prince in the Saif-ul-Malook of folklore. Speak with your hotel in Naran before undertaking this hike - it's strenuous and can only be taken in late July or August when the snow drifts have receded. Stories exist about bandits near Ansu Lake, so its important to travel in a group - again, speak with your hotel in Naran.

A seat in a jeep to Lake Saif-ul-Malook costs Rs. 200 one way, but prices might double or even triple in peak season (June - August). The journey is a rough 1 hour - jeeps leave from the main intersection in Naran.

Lalazar
map pg. 156
Lalazar (not to be confused with Lulusar, below) is a pretty pine-dotted plateau 21 kilometres northeast of Naran. The road here gets snowed over during the winter months, but in summer it's open for trekkers and picnickers with an adventurous bent. Most visitors come for the day from Naran by hiring a jeep - ask at your hotel in Naran for rates, but expect to pay around Rs. 4,500 for the return one day trip. Pack comfortable shoes, water and snacks - there's a lot of walking involved.

The more adventurous can hike to Lalazar from Lake Saif-ul-Malook (above). This trek takes approximately 6 hours; ask at your hotel for guidance, as the track conditions change very frequently. Never trek unprepared or alone - more than a handful of travellers have run into trouble here, falling prey to either extreme weather conditions or bandits.

A handful of services, including basic food shops, can be found in the bazaar on the road in Batakundi, the small service town on the main road from Naran.

Lulusar-Dudipatsar National Park
map pg. 156
Lulusar is the name of a group of mountains in the far north of the Kaghan Valley, and the lake which they surround. Here, 50 kilometres northeast of Naran, you are almost at the top of the valley; there's not much further to climb before the road spills over Babusar Pass and into Gilgit-Baltistan. The mountains are almost always capped with snow, and the melt feeds the clear Lulusar Lake in the valley. Much further up the mountain is Dudipatsar Lake, another, smaller high-altitude lake which at 3,800m will leave you feeling on top of the world. All of these attractions are part of the Lulusar-Dudipatsar National Park, which extends all the way up to Babusar Pass (page 170).

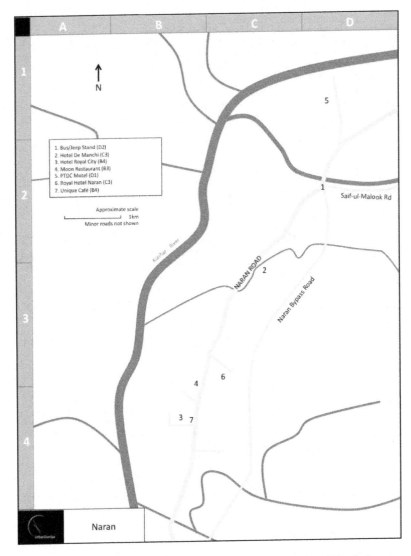

1. Bus/Jeep Stand (D2)
2. Hotel De Manchi (C3)
3. Hotel Royal City (B4)
4. Moon Restaurant (B3)
5. PTDC Motel (D1)
6. Royal Hotel Naran (C3)
7. Unique Café (B4)

Approximate scale
1km
Minor roads not shown

Saif-ul-Malook Rd

Kunhar River

NARAN ROAD

Naran Bypass Road

Naran

These spectacular mountains and lakes provide ample opportunities for trekking. Lulusar Lake (3,400m) sits right by the roadside, so is easily accessed by the casual traveller. Other lakes require a lot of walking, perhaps even an overnight camping - including Dudipatsar. The national park is also home to several interesting species, including snow leopard, marmot, snow partridge and markhor.

To get to Lulusar-Dudipatsar National Park, hire a jeep from your hotel in Naran. Expect to pay about Rs. 6,000 for a day's trip, in which you will see Lulusar Lake, Lulusar peaks, and maybe one or two other sights (ask if you have time for Babusar Pass or Lalazar). If you plan to trek into the national park, you can make the necessary arrangements in Naran - seek local advice and never trek alone.

Just before the entrance to the park, town of Jalkhand had some basic services - it's worth stopping near here anyway even if just to admire the spectacular mountains which stand ahead of you. At the entrance of the park is the smaller village of Besal (sometimes called Basel), from where the trail to Dudipatsar Lake begins. A few kilometres further along the main road, Lulusar Lake appears on the left.

Sleeping in Naran
Prices shown here as much as quadruple in the high season (June - August), or on long weekends.

Backpacker
Hotel Royal City: Naran Road; (+92) 0997-430019
map pg. 168, Dbl: Rs. 500
Very basic - electricity for 5 hours per day, hot water is provided by the bucket and no heating or eating facilities... but it's one of the cheapest in town. It's on a side street just behind the Unique Cafe

Economy
PTDC Motel: Naran Road; (+92) 0997-430002
map pg. 168, Dbl: Rs. 5,000
Pleasant, if not luxurious cabins set around a clearing in the forest, all within earshot of the gushing river.

Luxury
Royal Hotel Naran: Main Bazar, Naran Road; (+92) 0997-430133; www.royalhotel.pk
map pg. 168, Dbl: Rs. 3,000, Suites Rs. 5,000, prices double in summer
There's a generator here, so you'll never be left without power! There's also wifi and good heating.

Hotel De Manchi: Naran Road; (+92) 03125510000; www.hoteldemanchi.com/home-naran
map pg. 168, Dbl Rs. 8,000, Suite Rs. 11,000
De Manchi is the best place to sleep in Naran with warm clean rooms, two restaurants and a coffee shop.

Eating in Naran
"Spoilt for choice" is not the phrase that comes to mind here. Choose from any number of eateries on the main street turning out the standard parathas for breakfast, or naan and oily meat curries for lunch and dinner. **PTDC Motel** is one of the more reliable "upmarket" options. **Unique Café** and **Moon Restaurant** seem popular with locals *(all map pg. 168)*.

Servives in Naran
There are few services in Naran. Most banking is done in Abbottabad, and internet services are restricted to the better hotels.

Help in Naran
Safety
Naran is fairly safe for travelers, but do not underestimate the cold weather, even in summer.

Medical services
There are limited medical facilities in Naran. Serious cases will be sent to Abbottabad.

Getting around Naran
Naran is small but hilly, so if you'd like to catch a lift anywhere around the town it will cost around Rs. 50 for a seat in a shared jeep.

Leaving Naran
Local buses and vans usually drum up business at the junction of the Naran Road and the road to Lake Saif-ul-Malook. When they're about to leave they might drive through the bazaar looking for a final few passengers.

Kiwai: Local buses, 1 hour 30 minutes, Rs. 150
Mansehra: Local buses, 3 hours, Rs. 300
Chilas and Gilgit (via Babusar Pass): There is no direct transport to Gilgit – you need to change in Chilas (see page 191). The journey to Chilas takes about 2 hours 30 minutes, and costs Rs. 500. From Chilas, transport to Gilgit is either by NATCO buses or local minivans. It costs Rs. 600 and takes about 3 hours. The road is closed from November to May every year (see below).
Fairy Point/Jhel (for Fairy Meadows): You need to go to Chilas first. See above, and page 190.

Babusar Pass
North of Lulusar Lake (page 167), the road begins to switchback up the mountain as the Kaghan Valley comes to its northern end. Also referred to as "Babusar Top", the mountain pass also represents the northeastern most point of Khyber-Pukhtoonkhwa - beyond the pass, you are in Gilgit Baltistan. Freezing in summer, and snowbound in winter, the highest point of the pass is at 4,173m, so altitude sickness is also a concern if you hang around here for too long.

The top of the pass affords spectacular views back down the Kaghan Valley, and on the other side, over towards Nanga Parbat in Gilgit-Baltistan (page 187). The mountain sides immediately before and after the pass are barren - a consequence of the bleak climate. There are opportunities for high-altitude trekking around here; get professional advice from an experienced trekking group in Gilgit or Naran, as the conditions are extreme. Most transport stops at the top of the hill for a short break.

The pass is closed from about October to May due to heavy snowfall. At other times it may be closed due to a lack of maintenance, security officials, or landslide. Check the conditions before setting out.

A proposed tunnel would bypass the high-altitude road, allowing for year-round access on the Naran – Chilas – Gilgit Road. Although this has been discussed for at least ten years, construction has not begun.

The Chitral Valley

In the knot of valleys that twist northwards to the Hindu Kush mountain range, Chitral is cultural anomaly. Unlike the regions further to the south, Chitral speaks Khowar, a local tongue related to Farsi. In the north of the valley, people are mostly Ismaili Muslims - a legacy perhaps of their proximity to Ismaili-dominated Gilgit-Baltistan. Towards the south of the valley lie the Kalasha people, an indigenous community of non-Muslims whose culture is said to be related to ancient Hinduism. All of this is watched over by the iconic Tirich Mir, the highest point of the Hindu Kush Range at 7,708m. What this peak lacks in beauty and ranking (it's "only" the 33rd highest mountain in the world), it makes up for in reputation - Tirich Mir is a kind of majestic feature of the entire region, visible from almost everywhere in the central valley.

Chitralis are at pains to distinguish themselves from the Pashto-speaking Pathans further south; no doubt an effort to distance their society from the perils of war and terrorism which have ravaged other parts of Khyber-Pukhtoonkhwa province. The dramatic Hindu Kush range forms a virtual wall separating this region from Afghanistan (although you're never really far from the border); the arduous Lowari and Shandur Passes to the south and east provide the only real linkages to the rest of Pakistan. All of this means that only a steady trickle of tourists make their way to this landlocked cultural "island" every year.

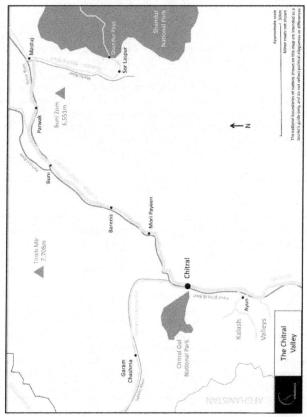

Compulsory registration and guard

All foreigners who visit the Chitral Valley (as defined by the borders of the Chitral district) must register upon arrival, and are automatically assigned an armed guard from the local police force, free of charge. There are no exceptions to this rule.

Why?

The registration is required to monitor who is visiting this sensitive border region, where Pakistan, Afghanistan, Tajikistan and China are all within a few hundred kilometres of each other. International politics aside, the roads to the north are believed to act as a route for illegal drug trade from Afghanistan.

The guard serves three purposes; firstly to act as a buffer between you and a fragile culture that is largely isolated from the rest of Pakistan (let alone the rest of the world). Secondly, they keep an eye on you (remember why you registered with the police). And thirdly, the guard ensures your security; while Chitral has been almost completely untouched by the problems which have plagued the tribal regions to the south, the main road through Chitral links regions which were held by the Taliban until relatively recently .

How?

If you arrive by air, a guard at the airport will ask you which hotel you're staying in as you leave the terminal. If you arrive by road, you'll be asked about this as you enter Chitral District. Either way, within 30 minutes of arriving at your hotel, you will be met by one or two men who identify themselves as "intelligence". They will ask for your details - who you are, why you're in Chitral, how long you'll stay. As intimidating as this sounds, it's usually a very cordial process - sometimes they even bring lunch for you.

After this, they arrange for someone at the hotel to take you to the local police station to register - take your passport, passport-sized photos and photocopies of your passport photo page and Pakistani visa. If you don't already have this organised, you can ask your hotel manager about where to get them done. The process at the police station takes about 10 minutes - again, everyone is rather friendly. You'll leave with a registration paper that you must keep with you at all times until you exit the district.

When you leave the police station, your guard might be assigned to you straight away, or you will meet him at your hotel within half an hour. The guards are local police officers who usually do whatever it takes to make sure you are happy and comfortable in Chitral. How you interact with them is up to you - they can be your travel companion, your tour guide, or your shadow - as you like. You aren't expected to pay anything for them, although some travellers make friends with their guards and invite them to meals together, where the traveller pays. It's totally up to you. Some travellers stay in touch with their guard after the trip, swapping Facebook IDs and getting in touch on return visits.

Your guard will not be with you all the time - sometimes you might be free to walk around the bazaar on your own, and the guard goes home at night, making a plan to meet the next day at a time of your choosing. That said - don't run away from your guard - that will cause problems and raise suspicions about your real intent for visiting Chitral. Your guard will accompany you on any excursions throughout the Chitral Valley, although the guard will not join you on long, one-way trips. On a trip from Chitral to Mastuj, for example, the Chitral guard will say goodbye at the Chitral bus station, and then call the police station in Mastuj to tell a colleague to meet you there.

CHITRAL

Population: 20,000, Elevation: 1,517m, Telephone code: 094

Chitral (sometimes referred to as "Chitral Town") is the administrative capital of the Chitral Valley. Arriving here by road, you may well wonder why you bothered - the scenery surrounding the town is nowhere near as beautiful as that to the north and south. While the steep slopes around Chitral are no doubt impressive, the dusty, frontier-like downtown of Chitral is much more "interesting" than "beautiful". Turbans bob up and down the main street, vendors proffer their plethora of goods from basic shopfronts and groups of men sit cross-legged in teashops as the fragrant steam wafts from the *samovar*. Chitral is the most common entry point to the valley, a logical place from which to start adventures in the region, and not a bad place to sip chai with the locals and get stuck for a few days.

What to see and do in Chitral

Shahi Bazaar

Chitral's bazaar *(map pg. 174)* is intriguing for the mix of cultures it attracts. Wander around the bazaar, meet the locals, pick up some dry fruits or handicrafts, or just take your place in one of the many canteens serving up *kabuli pulao* (Afghan-style rice with mutton) and tea. Don't forget to stop by the beautiful Shahi Mosque, built by the local royal family in 1924.

Birmoghlasht

Birmoghlasht *(map pg. 174)* is the mountain 'behind' Chitral's town centre to the west. The terrain rises steeply while still within the town limits; it's not uncommon to see locals striding up or down the hill, on their way to or from work. About a five minute drive up the hill, a bend in the road affords spectacular views over the valley, both north towards the airport and Tirich Mir, and south over the bazaar. Further up the mountain, about 30 minutes drive towards the Afghan border is the entrance to the relatively unspoilt Chitral Gol National Park, where you might spot a markhor (a type of wild goat) if you're really lucky.

To get to the lookout point, either follow the road up the hill on foot (strenuous - about 30 minutes), or hire a car from the bazaar (ask your guard to negotiate a good price - Rs. 400 for a return trip plus waiting time while you take photos is fair).

To travel further up the hill and into the national park, expect the price of a rented car to climb with the altitude - a return day trip should cost around Rs 4,000 for the car with a driver.

Polo Ground

About a kilometre south of Chitral is the town's polo ground *(map pg. 174)*, a long expanse of struggling grass with a lovely alpine backdrop. When there's no match on this place is deserted, but when the game of kings is being played (commonly between May and July), the ground and its long flat stands are filled with locals cheering on their favourite team. Ask the locals or your guard if there is a tournament going on while you are there.

Staying in Chitral

Backpacker

Al-Farooq Hotel: Shahi Bazaar; (+92) 0943-412726
map pg. 174, Sgl Rs. 600, Dbl Rd. 1,000
Basic rooms and even more basic bathrooms; friendly young staff make this place the best cheap choice.

Economy

PTDC Hotel: Shahi Bazaar; (+92) 0943-412683
map pg. 174, Sgl Rs. 2,900, Dbl Rd. 4,600
Functional rooms, obliging staff but a so-so restaurant.

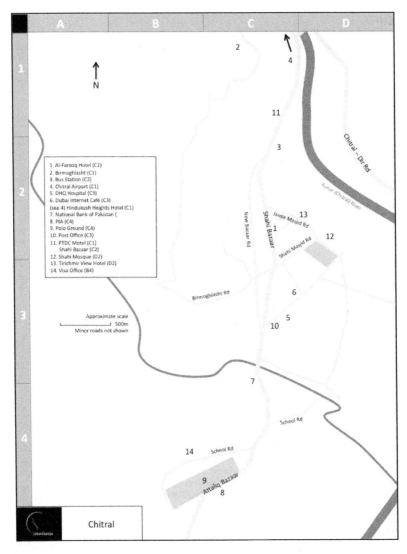

1. Al-Farooq Hotel (C2)
2. Birmoghlasht (C1)
3. Bus Station (C2)
4. Chitral Airport (C1)
5. DHQ Hospital (C3)
6. Dubai Internet Café (C3)
   (see 4) Hindukush Heights Hotel (C1)
7. National Bank of Pakistan (
8. PIA (C4)
9. Polo Ground (C4)
10. Post Office (C3)
11. PTDC Motel (C1)
    Shahi Bazaar (C2)
12. Shahi Mosque (D2)
13. Tirichmir View Hotel (D2)
14. Visa Office (B4)

Approximate scale
500m
Minor roads not shown

N

Chitral

Trichmir View Hotel: Shahi Masjid Road; (+92) 0943-414545
map pg. 174, Sgl Rs. 3,900, Dbl Rd. 5,600
Another centrally located budget choice, although rack rates are inflated – ask for a discount.

Luxury
Hindukush Heights: Shahi Masjid Road; (+92) 0943-413151; www.hindukush.com.pk
map pg. 174, Sgl US$84, US$90
More of a lodge than a hotel, well-appointed rooms and lovely views but the location 7 kilometres from the town centre might be an issue.

Eating in Chitral

Chitral doesn't abound with fine eateries like some other towns. Instead, walk the bazaar in search for local, Afghan or Pakistani dishes, and go where the crowd is. The PTDC Motel's *(map pg. 174)* restaurant is the best option for a proper "restaurant dinner", but the food isn't anything to write home about.

Services in Chitral

Airlines
Pakistan International: Attaliq Bazaar; (+92) 111-786-786 *(map pg. 174)*

Banks
No international banks have representation in Chitral.

Internet cafes
Dubai Internet Café: on the road leading from the bazaar to the Shahi Masjid *(map pg. 174)*

Money exchange
The National Bank of Pakistan doesn't always change money – so come prepared. *(map pg. 174)*

Post office
The GPO is near the corner on the road leading from the bazaar to the Shahi Masjid *(map pg. 174)*

Travel agency
There aren't a lot of specialized travel agencies in Chitral aimed at travelers; most hotels offer their services for whatever further travel arrangements you might need.

Visa office
Attaliq House, School Road, Attaliq Bazaar *(map pg. 174)*

Help in Chitral

Safety
Chitral is a fairly peaceful part of Pakistan, but the regular precautions apply - and in any case, your guard will be with you to smooth over any issues that may arise.

Medical services
The DHQ Hospital near the police station *(map pg. 174)* is the best place for medical attention, but serious cases are taken to Islamabad or Peshawar. Some pharmacies are in the bazaar, and one at the hospital.

Getting around Chitral

Most of the town can be covered on foot, but a taxi costs about Rs. 100 in the centre, Rs. 200 to the airport.

Leaving Chitral

Connections from Chitral are relatively simple - there's one main road that goes through the town, so you can approach from the south (Peshawar) or the north-northeast (Mastuj and Gilgit). The bus stand is to the north of town *(map pg. 174)*.

Bus and jeep
Mastuj (for Gilgit): Jeeps and minibuses, 4 hrs, Rs. 300. Also read the boxed on pg 194.
Peshawar: Minibuses travel this route daily in the summer; in winter the Lowari Pass is snowbound. The journey takes 14 hours and costs about Rs. 750. This road has also been closed due to tribal conflict in the recent past, and most travel advisories do not recommend taking this route due to security concerns.

Air
Islamabad: PIA, 45 minutes, from Rs. 10,500 one way. 4 flights per week. Note the boxed text on page 88.
Peshawar: PIA, 45 minutes, from Rs. 10,500 one way, 4 flights per week. Note the boxed text on page 88.

Chitral to Gilgit transport
There are no direct transport services from Chitral to Gilgit-Baltistan. All transport from
either Chitral or Gilgit terminates in Mastuj (see page 181). Note that NATCO buses from
Gilgit-Baltistan offer a service to "Chitral", but this refers to Mastuj as the gateway to
Chitral Valley.

The road from Chitral to Mastuj begins as a sealed, two-lane road, but about halfway
through turns to semi-smooth compacted earth, and in the final half-hour before Mastuj it
becomes rather rough.

Around Chitral
GARAM CHASHMA

Population: 5,000, Elevation: 2,550m, Telephone code: 0943

Garam Chashma literally means "hot spring", and sure enough, there's a hot spring in town!
The spring is connected to a couple of hotels, and the town is dotted with fruit orchards set
against a backdrop of the snow-capped Hindukush ranges. This small town by the border
with Afghanistan is rarely visited by outsiders, but if you fancy soaking in a hot tub in
paradise (and really, who doesn't?), then this might be the place for you. Don't forget to
sample some of the local trout while you're here - it's delectable.

What to see and do in Garam Chashma
The hot spring, of course! Go to the Injigan Hotel *(map pg. 177)* (or any of the other
guesthouses nearby the Injigan) and ask to use the pools - they'll know why you're there,
and charge a small fee to bathe for an hour or two.

Stroll around the town - the environs are simply stunning, and the locals are warm and
friendly - a walk through the bazaar will inevitably end in countless invitations for chai and
conversation with shopkeepers.

Staying in Garam Chashma
Injigan Hotel: Garam Chashma Road
map pg. 177, Sgl Rs. 5,000
Unlikely though the price of this place may seem, it all makes sense when you realise that a
stream of the town's hot spring is fed right into this hotel's swimming pool. Basic facilities,
but clean and comfortable.

Eating in Garam Chashma
Your hotel will probably have the best option - in fact you might even be hosted by the
family who owns the accommodation. Otherwise there are some basic options available in
the bazaar.

Services in Garam Chashma
Garam Chashma has few services for travellers – most local go to Chitral town for banking
and trade.

Help in Garam Chashma
Garam Chashma is a small, conservative town on the Afghan border with Pakistan which
sees hardly any foreigners. With your guard, you'll have no problems - it's a peaceful and
friendly place - but remember where you are and behave accordingly.

Likewise, medical facilities are severely limited, and anyone needing proper medical
attention will be taken to Chitral town or Peshawar.

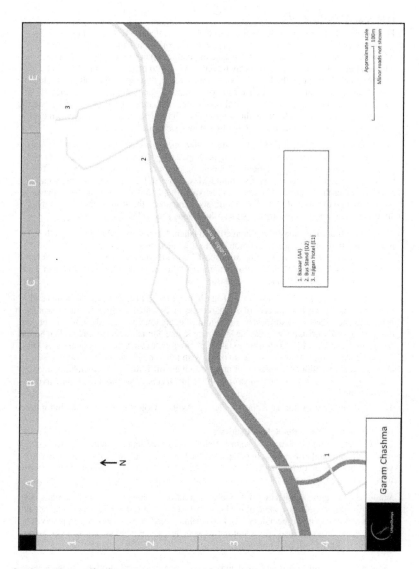

Garam Chashma

N

1. Bazaar (A4)
2. Bus Stand (D2)
3. Injigan Hotel (E1)

Approximate scale
100m
Minor roads not shown

Getting to Garam Chashma

Shared cars leave from Chitral's bus stand when full - say "Garam Chashma" and you'll be hustled in the right direction. The journey takes 2 hours and costs Rs. 200.

THE KALASH VALLEYS

The Rumbur, Bumboret and Birir valleys, collectively called the Kalash Valleys *(map pg. 179)*, are three tight creases in the mountains which separate the Chitral Valley from Afghanistan. They are home to some spectacular natural scenery and several farming villages, but by far the main reason why travellers visit is to observe the unique local culture. It is believed that the Kalash people have lived in this region for millennia. Their faith is said to be related to an ancient form of Hinduism, and has endured centuries of cultural onslaught from the outside world - Alexander the Great, the arrival of Islam and the British Raj have all failed to break the community. The Kalash language is considered a relative of, but still separate from the Khowar language spoken in Chitral.

The Kalash are easily identified by their distinctive outfits, which include long robes and head pieces for women, dyed in a riot of hypercolour red, orange, yellow, pink, green and black. You'll see them working fields, maintaining their homes and gardens, and staffing local shops including souvenir stores. In mid-May, June - July, September - October and mid-December the Kalash hold exuberant festivals complete with music, dancing, even more elaborate outfits and food. These festivals, particularly the Joshi festival (in May), attract large numbers who come to witness the unique spectacle.

About three thousand Kalash have converted to Islam, leaving around 4,000 who still practice the indigenous Kalasha religion. There is some debate within the Kalash community as to whether these "Muslim Kalash" are still considered Kalash at all. At least one Kalash leader has explained that if a member of the community converts to Islam, he or she will not be considered part of the Kalash society.

Tourism has begun to take its toll on the Kalash; heightened interest from Pakistanis and foreign travellers has led to a certain defensiveness in the villages which see most visitors. It is unfortunate to see the disrespectful behaviour of many tourists (including, it must be said, many Pakistani tourists), who treat the local people like animals at a zoo, rather than human beings in the real world. If you want to take a photograph of a person, it is imperative that you ask permission first, and respect anyone's wish not to be photographed. Do not joke around, wear revealing clothes or enter areas which are off limits, and remember that as intriguing as the culture may be, most Kalash are just trying to go about their daily lives uninterrupted.

The main service town for the Kalash Valleys is Ayun, 20 kilometres south of Chitral town.

What to see and do in the Kalash Valleys

The main attraction of visiting the Kalash Valleys is to experience a culture so different from your own, and also unique in this part of the world. If you are visiting on a day trip you may not be able to "get under the skin" of the villages, but if you spend some time you may be lucky enough to be taken to a community or family event by your host.

While respecting the sensitivities of the local populace, you are free to wander around any of the villages, stopping by some of the local craft shops and visiting the small vendor-style eateries serving up local specialties. Look for walnut bread, local cheese, fruit preserves and yogurt. A local wine is made from mulberries - you are welcome to sample it if you are not Muslim, but beware - it packs a punch.

Concepts of religion, spirits and good and evil are intertwined with daily life in the Kalash societies. Rituals are common and routinely practiced. Local families worship at their family's group of shrines or altars, located at various point through the villages and the countryside of the valleys. These shrines represent a weaving of family lineage traditions with religious belief and daily spirituality. Other traditional customs involve marriage and childbirth; both are associated with unique rituals, including a common practice of "wife-elopement", whereby a wife leaves her husband for another man, and the resulting divorce is settled (often semi-amicably) within the community. Menstruating women spend their days in a special "menstruating house", separate from wider society, although this is one of only a few examples of women and men being segregated in Kalash culture. After a

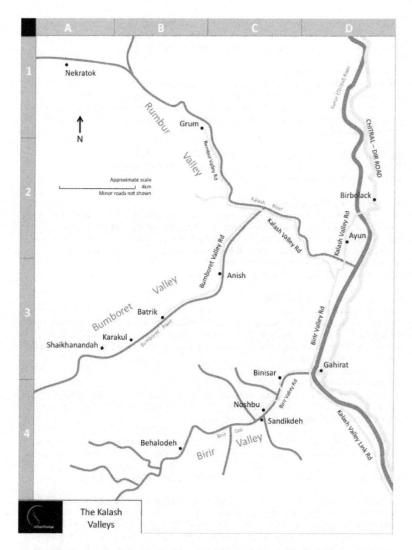

The Kalash
Valleys

person's death, several elaborate rituals are held in community halls, including one in a men's temple which involves dancing to invoke good spirits and banish bad spirits. Graveyards are sensitive areas that some Kalash people avoid, due to their belief about spirits.

Your access to any of these rituals or buildings will depend a lot on who you meet, how long you spend with them, and your general attitude towards the society. Always ask before entering a building of cultural significance. If you are not allowed to enter - for whatever reason - do not force the matter, and do not enter without permission. Some buildings, areas and events are off-limits to certain groups of people - such as men who are forbidden to enter the women's menstruating house.

If you visit during a festival time, be prepared for lots of music, singing, dancing, food, worship and even animal sacrifices. Again, your host or police guard will guide you on how best to experience the festival, and where you can and can't go.

Staying in the Kalash Valleys
Your hotel in Chitral (from where you organise the Kalash trip) would be able to recommend a hotel, and in many cases might include your nights as part of the "jeep and accommodation" price package. Hotels vary in cost and comfort, but most are basic. If you would prefer (or are required) to make your own choice, we recommend the following hotels in each valley:

Rumbur: Kalash Guesthouse, Grum Village; (+92) 0333-7731189
Bumboret: PTDC Motel Bumboret, Brun Village; (+92) 0943-404066
Birir: Irfan Guesthouse, Guru Village

Services in the Kalash Valleys
Bumboret and Rumbur are the most commonly visited valleys of the Kalasha. Birir is more remote and traditional. A handful of villages in each valley provide the most basic of services - hotels, eateries, supplies, first aid and telephone. Internet is less easily available. Your guard, or your hotel manager, will be of more assistance to locate the nearest necessities. Be prepared to travel out of the valley to Ayun, or even Chitral, for some services like medical treatment or onward travel bookings.

Getting around the Kalash Valleys
Most foreigners who visit the Kalasha valleys have rented their own vehicle. If you are without a vehicle while you are there, the local public transport isn't frequent or developed. It tends to be a mixture of jeeps which sometimes run the lengths of each valley, as far as the road condition allows (negotiate a price before you get in), or hitching a lift with traders, locals or other travellers.

Getting to and from the Kalash Valleys
Visitors often take a day trip or an overnight trip to one of the Kalash valleys from Chitral, although there is nothing to prevent a longer stay in any of the communities. Your guard from Chitral will accompany you the whole time.

A rented jeep from one of the hotels in Chitral should cost Rs. 4,000 - Rs. 6,000 per day. This price includes petrol and driver, but nothing more. Therefore, a day trip would cost Rs. 4,000 - Rs. 6,000, plus meals and Rs. 200 entry fee (see below). Speak with your hotel about visiting the Kalash valleys, and plan a trip which suits your interest and budget.

Alternatively, you could reach the valleys by a combination of public transport and hitching lifts. From Chitral's bus station take a jeep to Ayun *(map pg. 179)*; Rs. 300, 1 hour. From the quiet main street of Ayun, you'll need to ask around for anyone heading towards Rumbur, Bumboret or Birir - and negotiate the price. It's a gamble, as not a lot of traffic regularly heads to the valleys, and its quite possible to get stuck in Ayun for the night - in which case ask for the Ayun Fort Inn to lay your head at.

The roads from Ayun into the valleys are not in good condition. Expect to spend up to 2 hours on the dusty, unpaved road before reaching Kalash villages. At the time of writing there were two checkpoints along the way - first, a police checkpoint at the entry to Ayun, and a border force checkpoint at the entrance to each valley. At each one you will be required to show your passport and registration paper.

At the Border Force checkpoint you will be asked to pay Rs. 200 for a permit to enter.

MASTUJ

Population: 20,000, Elevation: 2,359m, Telephone code: 0943

Mastuj, for many travellers, will be the most isolated place they have ever been. Four hours drive from Chitral along a steadily deteriorating road, and a long day's drive from Gilgit, Mastuj isn't really close to anywhere except the Afghan border, about 50 kilometres away. Even then, across the border lies the Wakhan Corridor, the spectacular but lonely part of Afghanistan that was once the home of Northern Alliance leader Ahmad Shah Massoud.

The main reason to come to Mastuj is to break the journey between Chitral and Gilgit, although the mountains around the village are spectacular, snow-capped peaks and if you have the time to wander, do. There are also a handful of picturesque villages around the valley which, if you have the time and energy, will lend you an additional Marco Polo feeling of being an intrepid explorer.

What to see in Mastuj
Mastuj Fort
map pg. 182, Open 24 hours, Free

The only real tourist attraction in Mastuj is its fort, and you can't enter it anyway. It stands proud on a rise of land above the rest of the valley, set amid a pretty floral garden. The fort is in the garden just beyond the Hindukush Heights Hotel.

Sleeping in Mastuj
Budget
NATCO Retiring Rooms
map pg. 182, Dorm Rs. 150, Sgl Rs.450

Perhaps these rooms should have retired a long time ago - concrete floors, dimly lit bathrooms and a heap of old quilts on each string bed. Nevertheless they are right at the bus stop (the reason why most people stop in Mastuj), and the likeable manager Fateh Aman cooks each night for the busload of weary passengers who are stopping over.

Economy
Hot Spring Hotel: Yarkhun Valley Road; (+92) 0943-486119
map pg. 182, Dbl Rs. 2,200

Simple but clean(er), and yes, there's a hot spring to relax in! Expect good hospitality in spartan surroundings.

PTDC Motel: Yarkhun Valley Road; (+92) 0943-486034
map pg. 182, Dbl Rs. 3,500

Everything here is good except the location - a long walk from the town centre, but with great views over the valley. Restaurant attached.

Hindukush Heights: (+92) 0943-413151; www.hindukush.com.pk
map pg. 182, Dbl Rs. 9,000

A group of cabins facing on to an idyllic alpine garden, and just metres from the Mastuj Fort (above). A restaurant is attached here but it didn't seem to be open when we visited, and the location is even further away than the PTDC, perhaps a little too secluded?

Eating in Mastuj
Mastuj doesn't abound with eating options - there's a handful of vendors along the main road which come to life after dark, and a small Chinese eatery *(map pg. 182)* which serves basic snacks. Ask your hotel what's cooking, or otherwise there's the restaurant at PTDC.

Help in Mastuj
Mastuj is so far from anywhere that probably nothing will bother you here. Behave and dress appropriately in this conservative region.

Medical facilities are very limited. Serious cases will be taken to Chitral, Gilgit or Peshawar.

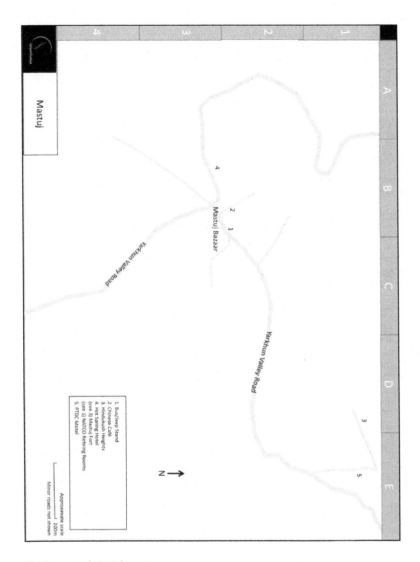

Mastuj Bazaar

Yarkhun Valley Road

Yarkhun Valley Road

1. Bus/Jeep Stand
2. Chinese Café
3. Hindukush Heights
4. Hot Spring Hotel
(see 3) Mastuj Fort
(see 1) NATCO Retiring Rooms
5. PTDC Motel

N →

Approximate scale
200m
Minor roads not shown

Getting around Mastuj

Apart from the PTDC Motel, Hindukush Heights and the fort, everything in Mastuj is within about 1 kilometre of each other, negating the need for a taxi. If you need to get dropped anywhere, ask your hotel manager, or anyone on the main street if they're heading your way.

Leaving Mastuj

Chitral: Jeep from the main street of Mastuj, Rs. 300, 4 hours

The road from Mastuj to Chitral begins as a rough track, but soon improves. After about 2 hours of driving the sealed road to Chitral begins.

Gilgit (via Ghizer Valley): NATCO Bus operates daily from Mastuj to Gilgit via Shandur Pass, Phander, Gupis, and Gakuch. The bus departs at 5am from the NATCO office *(map pg. 182)*, and runs until Gakuch where passengers need to change into a smaller bus for the final trip to Gilgit. The fare from Mastuj to Gakuch is Rs. 600, and another Rs. 120 is paid on the final stretch between Gakuch and Gilgit.

This road is closed from November to May every year. For more information on the intermediate stops of this bus and related fares, see page 194.

Gilgit-Baltistan

The jewel in Pakistan's crown is Gilgit-Baltistan, formerly known as the "Northern Areas". North of Punjab and Khyber Pukhtoonkhwa the Karakoram Range climbs with ever taller and more jagged peaks. Jutting in from the west is the Hindu Kush mountain range from Afghanistan from the north west Tajikistan's mountain range bears down on the region, while the eastern flank comprises the tail end of the Himalayas. High altitude lakes and cascades, snow-capped ranges, fruit orchards, glaciers and secret mountain passes all await the intrepid visitor.

The Karakoram Highway, 1,300 kilometre-long from Islamabad to Kashgar in China, is the backbone of this region. The highest paved road in the world crosses from Pakistan to China at the Khunjerab Pass, at a height of 4,693 metres. Built from 1959 to 1979, but only opened to the public in 1986, over one thousand lives were lost during its construction, and when you see the terrain it crosses, it's easy to see why. Road travel is smooth and easy, thanks to a network of Chinese and Pakistani-built roads to encourage trade.

'Intrepid' is the key word here, not 'brave' - things here are not as much 'scary' as 'unreliable', and road blockages of days aren't uncommon, especially during the monsoon (July - September) and in the snowy winter (November - March). Much of the northern part of Gilgit - Baltistan (Gojal, or Upper Hunza) shuts down between November and May; check with local authorities.

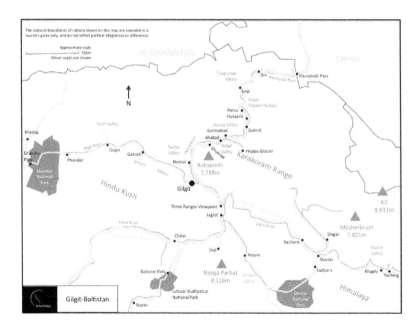

Compulsory police registration and guard

All foreigners who visit Gilgit-Baltistan must register upon arrival. This is done by way of a small card handed to the traveller at the airport, provincial border checkpoint, or at the Chinese border. Travellers must keep the card with them at all times until they leave Gilgit-Baltistan, and present it along with their passport at the regular police security checkposts.

While in Chilas (page 191), and on the road between Chilas and the Babusar Top (on the way to Naran), it is compulsory for an armed police guard to accompany you. An armed guard is also required for any travel towards Fairy Meadows and Nanga Parbat (page 190). This is free of cost.

It is not unheard of for foreign guests at a hotel to receive a visit from "intelligence officers" after checking in. This usually consists simply of a short discussion of travel plans and a noting of details. Presumably these measures are twofold; first, to ensure the safety of the traveller, but secondly, to monitor anyone passing through this geopolitically sensitive region, sandwiched between China, Afghanistan and Indian-held Kashmir.

GILGIT

Population: 300,000, Elevation: 1,500m, Telephone code: 05811

Gilgit is the capital of the territory of Gilgit-Baltistan, and is a logical place to start or end a journey in the northern areas. Besides having the most conveniently located airport for the region, it is also the largest town and has the widest range of travel and hiking services for miles.

Gilgit is a small, unexpectedly busy place, whose typically Pakistani streets look all the more shabby when compared with the otherwise gorgeous high-altitude setting. Winters get cold here, but days, especially in summer, can still be hot; Gilgit might be in the mountains, but it's not at the top. The bazaar dominates the centre of town, while just east of that is the airport. Beyond the airport is the upmarket district of Jutial, technically a separate town, but almost a suburb, and considering the bus station is beyond Jutial, you'll probably pass by it at some point.

What to see in Gilgit
Polo Ground

map pg. 186, Officially opens for tournaments, Entry: ticket price

Gilgit-Baltistan's most popular sport is not cricket but polo, the game of kings. Every year in late October thousands of people descend on Gilgit to attend the Shandur Polo Cup, and it all happens here at Gilgit's polo ground.

Walks, hikes and excursions

The mountains south of the Gilgit valley are home to several attractions, including a Buddha carving, a victory monument to 14th century Ismaili preacher and commander Taj Mughal; lookouts with views of Rakaposhi and the Gilgit Valley, charming forests and streams, and pretty mountain lakes.

Kargah Buddha is a 7th century carving of Buddha's face hewn from a cliff face in Kargah Nala, a valley six kilometres west of central Gilgit. Continuing up this valley, you can also reach some lovely villages and view points. To get here take a rickshaw to "Kargah" (Rs. 200), then ask locals for directions. Kargah Buddha is easily reached with a 30 minute walk from the main road. A longer walk through Kargah Nala is a lovely way to spend a morning or afternoon, or even a day if you carry a picnic. Be careful of loose rocks and precarious drops, and don't wander away from settled areas without a guide.

East of Gilgit, the hills behind the Serena Hotel are home to Taj Mughal's Victory monument, and views of Rakaposhi, the 12th highest mountain in Pakistan with its broad, velvety, snow-covered peak. The monument is about 30 minutes from the Serena Hotel –

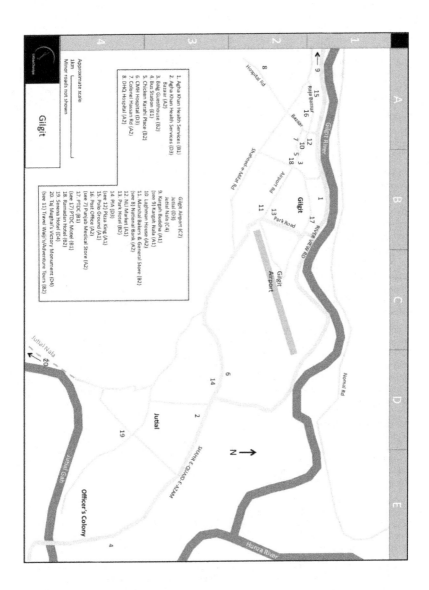

Gilgit

1. Agha Khan Health Services (B1)
2. Agha Khan Health Services (D3) Bazaar
3. Baig Guesthouse (B2)
4. Bus Station (E1)
5. Chicken Karahi Place (B2)
6. CMH Hospital (D3)
7. Colonel Hassan Rd (A2)
8. DHQ Hospital (A2)
9. Kargah Buddha (A1)
   (see 9) Kargah Nala (A1)
10. Laghman House (A2)
11. Marshal Bakers & General Store (B2)
   (see 8) National Bank (A2)
12. NLI Market (A1)
13. Park Hotel (B2)
14. PIA (D3)
   (see 12) Pizza King (A1)
15. Polo Ground (A1)
16. Post Office (A2)
   (see 7) Punjab Medical Store (A2)
17. PTDC (B1)
   (see 17) PTDC Motel (B1)
18. Ramadan Hotel (B2)
19. Serena Hotel (D4)
20. Taj (Mughal's Victory Monument (D4)
   (see 11) Travel Walji's/Adventure Tours (B2)

1. Agha Khan Health Services (B1)
Gilgit Airport (C2)
Jutial (D3)
Jutial Nala (C4)

Approximate scale
1km
Minor roads not shown

Hospital Rd

Raja Bazaar

Bazaar

Shahrade Millat Rd

Airport Rd

Gilgit River

RIVER VIEW RD

Gilgit

Park Road

Gilgit Airport

Normal Rd

Jutial Nala

Jutial

SHAHR E QUAID E AZAM

N →

Officer's Colony

Hunza River

Jutial Gah

you begin your way up Jutial Nala (Jutial Valley) but then bear right onto a smaller stream after about 15 minutes - ask for detailed directions before you leave. Meanwhile, two hours further up Jutial Nala is an alpine forest, Rakaposhi viewpoints, and a couple of hours beyond that, icy lakes. Ask at your accommodation, Travel Walji's/Adventure Tours Pakistan (see page 188) or PTDC for a driver and/or guide to take you to these places.

'Gilgit-Baltistan' or 'The Northern Areas'?

The 'Northern Areas' was officially renamed Gilgit-Baltistan in 2010 when it achieved upgraded 'territory' status (although crucially, not a fully fledged province of Pakistan). It is one of the country's most stable regions, but also one of the most hotly contested, as India still considers Gilgit-Baltistan to be part of Kashmir, to which Delhi lays claim.

Many Pakistanis still refer to the region as "the Northern Areas", while confusingly, more still imagine "the Northern Areas" to be anything north of west of Islamabad, including not only Gilgit-Baltistan but also Khyber-Pukhtoonkhwa.

Staying in Gilgit
Backpacker
Baig Guesthouse: Airport Road; (+92) 05811-59845
map pg. 186, Sgl Rs. 500, Dbl Rs. 600
Cheap but clean and comfy – no-fuss rooms come with private toilet and an old TV but no air conditioning.

Park Hotel: Airport Road; (+92) 05811-452379; www.parkhotel.pk
map pg. 186, Dbl Rs. 1,200, Suite Rs. 2,500
Conveniently located between the airport and the town centre, the Park Hotel's rooms are old but well furnished, but the prices are probably bit inflated – ask for a discount. There's a decent restaurant here too.

Economy
PTDC Motel: Babar Road; (+92) 05811-454262; www.tourism.gov.pk
map pg. 186, Dbl Rs. 2,850, Suite Rs. 3,800
The PTDC's Motel in Gilgit is probably the best midrange option - TV in every room, laundry facilities, a pleasant lawn and a restaurant. Conveniently located near the airport.

Luxury
Serena Hotel: Sherullah Beg Road, Jutial, Rais Road; (+92) 05811-455894; www.serenahotels.com/serenagilgit
map pg. 186, Dbl US$175, Suite US$250
The best hotel in town (4 stars) with a gym, conference facilities, multi cuisine restaurant and complimentary wifi. The downside? It's 5 kilometres to the centre.

Eating in Gilgit
The best places to eat in Gilgit are in hotels; particularly the abovementioned hotels. Additionally, there are quite a few places around NLI Chowk, including a great **chicken karahi place** on the corner, and the friendly **Ramadan Hotel** on the main street. There's also the fast-food style **Pizza King** in NLI Market, and in the vicinity, **Laghman House**, serving up Uyghur (Turkish-Chinese) cuisine *(all map pg. 186)*.

Services in Gilgit
Airlines
Pakistan International: CSD Complex, Gilgit (+92) 05811-920348 *(map pg. 186)*.

Banks
No international banks have branches in Gilgit.

Internet Cafe
There are a couple of internet cafes in and around NLI Market *(map pg. 186)*.

Money Exchange
National Bank *(map pg. 186)* at NLI Market can change major currencies (US Dollars, UK Pounds, Euros), but check the rate against what your hotel is offering. You may also find independent money change offices on the streets of the bazaar - use common sense if you choose to use these.

Post Office
Gilgit's General Post Office *(map pg. 186)* is just west of the centre of town, in Saddar Bazaar.

Shopping
Gilgit's bazaar *(map pg. 186)* is a treasure trove of carpets, shawls, clothes, foodstuffs - even animals! It's a real melting pot, true to Gilgit's position on the crossroads of Asia.

Supermarkets
For a wide variety of groceries (including a number of imported products) go to Coronet in NLI Market *(map pg. 186)*.

Tourist Information
The PTDC Office is connected with the PTDC Motel on Babar Road *(map pg. 186)*.

Travel Agency
Travel Walji's (represented in Gilgit by Adventure Tours Pakistan) is a reliable agency which organise trekking, rafting and other adventures, as well as car hire. Airport Chowk (+92) 05811-52663 *(map pg. 186)*.

Help in Gilgit
Safety
Gilgit is a fairly safe city. Tension between Sunnis and Shias has in the past erupted into violence, although this is thankfully rare and not aimed at foreigners (although there is always the "wrong place wrong time" possibility). If unrest occurs while you are in Gilgit, stay away.

Be aware of altitude sickness if you are travelling to higher altitudes.

Medical Services
CMH Hospital: Shahr-e-Quaid-e-Azam *(map pg. 186)*.
DHQ Hospital: Hospital Road *(map pg. 186)*.
Agha Khan Health Services have two locations around Gilgit *(map pg. 186)*.

24 Hour Pharmacies are at the CMH and DHQ Hospitals (listed above). The Punjab Medical Store *(map pg. 186)* on Colonel Hassan Road is also well established. Pharmacies also in NLI Market.

Getting around Gilgit
There are technically no autorickshaws in Gilgit, but instead "Suzuki" vans and pick up trucks ferry people around. A lift around town costs no more than Rs. 20, Rs. 30 from the bazaar out to Jutial. Taxis go to the airport - expect to pay something around Rs. 100 to the airport from the bazaar, and a taxi to the general bus stand could cost up to Rs. 300 (although it really shouldn't).

Leaving Gilgit
The bus station is 7 kilometres away, east of Jutial *(map pg. 186)*, from where NATCO buses leave. You'll need to hire a rickshaw to the centre. The airport is at one end of the town centre, although the terminal is about a kilometre down the road. Vans to Hunza and Gojal, Skardu, the Ghizer Valley, Raikot (for Fairy Meadows) and Chilas leave from a chaotic small stand in the centre of town.

NATCO buses to Islamabad and Abbottabad go via the Karakoram Highway; routes via Naran will require a change in Chilas. Note the Babusar Pass is closed for part of the year (see page 170). The Karakoram Highway between Gilgit and Islamabad has been the target of sectarian attacks, making the option of air travel more attractive. For more information about getting to Fairy Meadows, see page 190.

There are no direct transport services from Gilgit-Baltistan to the town of Chitral. All transport from either Chitral or Gilgit terminates in Mastuj (see page 181). NATCO buses from Gilgit-Baltistan offer a service to "Chitral", but this refers to Mastuj as the gateway to Chitral Valley.

Bus and jeep

Rawalpindi/Islamabad (via Karakoram Highway): NATCO, 10 hours, Rs. 1,500 – Rs. 2,200, depending on bus class

Abbottabad (via Karakoram Highway): NATCO buses, 9 hours, Rs. 2,000

Mansehra (via Karakoram Highway): NATCO buses, 8 hours, Rs. 1,900

Skardu: Minivans, 7 hours, Rs. 500 - sit on the right if you'e a keen photographer, on the left if you're scared of heights. About an hour's drive southeast of Gilgit, a short way along the Skardu Road, there is a great view of the sheer face of Nanga Parbat from the right side.

Karimabad (Hunza Valley): Minivans, 2 hours, Rs. 200

Gojal (Gulmit, Passu and Sost): Minivans, 3 hours, Rs. 400. Sometimes requires a change in Karimabad.

Chlias and Naran (via Babusar Pass): There is no direct transport to Naran – you need to change in Chilas (page 191). The journey to Chilas takes about 3 hours in a NATCO bus or local minivan and will cost about Rs. 600. From Chilas, onward transport to Naran is in a jeep or minivan. It costs about Rs. 500 and takes about 2 hours 30 minutes. The Babusar Pass is closed every year from November to May.

Nomal (for Naltar Valley): Minivans, 30 minutes, Rs. 100

Ghizer Valley: NATCO Bus operates daily from Gilgit to Mastuj via Gakuch, Gupis, Phander and Shandur Pass. The bus departs at 6am from NATCO Bus Stand, and runs until Gakuch where passengers need to change into a larger bus for the trip through the Ghizer Valley. See details on page 194.

Yasin Valley: Minivans leave mid-morning, 3 hours 30 minutes, Rs. 330

Mastuj (Chitral): See details for Ghizer Valley above. The fare from Gilgit to Gakuch is Rs. 120, and then Rs. 600 is paid for the main section from Gakuch to Mastuj. This road is closed between mid-November and mid-May every year.

Air

Islamabad: PIA, once or twice daily, 50 minutes, from Rs. 6,500 one way. Note the boxed text on pg 88.

Skardu: PIA, weekly flights, 40 minutess, from Rs. 5,500 one way. Note the boxed text on pg 88.

Trekking in northern Pakistan

The stunning beauty of this region is all the more special because of how remote parts of it are - the "Switzerland of Asia" as it is sometimes called is home to unique cultural pockets, many with traditions and languages clearly distinct from mainstream 'Pakistan'. Mountains march all the way through the region, getting ever higher, from Gilgit in the south, to the Chinese border. Notable peaks here are Rakaposhi (7,788m), Nanga Parbat (8,126m) and K2 (8,611m). The good news is that all of these are visible from various locations on or near the highway, without having to scale isolated peaks. This guide contains basic information for travellers hiking for a day or less. For more detailed information about trekking in this area, we recommend consulting one of the trekking agencies listed for each town or city.

Around Gilgit

NALTAR VALLEY

Population: nomadic/seasonal, Elevation: 3,000m (average). Telephone code: 05811
Pine forests, alpine lakes and snowcapped mountains make the Naltar Valley a visually stunning day trip or overnight trip from Gilgit *(map pg. 195)*. The valley, accessed from the village of Nomal north of Gilgit, used to be a favoured getaway for the British administration before 1947. From Nomal the gradually deteriorating road takes you past the village of Lower Naltar before ending at Upper Naltar. The beautiful Naltar Lake is a three and a half hour hike beyond that. Visitors to the Naltar Valley are advised to seek expert advice in Gilgit before setting out and come prepared with enough food and water to last them. Recommended travel agencies in Gilgit are listed on page 188, and the Hunza-based Hunza Treks and Tours (page 203) also comes highly recommended. A guide costs about Rs. 3000 per day, while an all-inclusive trek or tour will cost Rs. 50,000 for three days.

For public transport, a van from Gilgit to Nomal will cost Rs. 100 (30 minutes), and then a jeep beyond that will cost Rs. 200 to Lower Naltar village (1 hour), and Rs. 200 more to Upper Naltar village (1 hour more).

FAIRY MEADOWS and NANGA PARBAT

At 8,126 metres Nanga Parbat ("Naked Mountain") is the ninth highest mountain in the world, and is a highlight for many trekking enthusiasts travelling through Pakistan *(map pg. 193)*. The notoriously unforgiving ascent has claimed lives in the past, and is a rare undertaking. More common are treks to one of two points on the way to the mountain; beautiful Fairy Meadows, or the lofty Nanga Parbat Base Camp.

Fairy Meadows (3,300m) is an exceptionally stunning natural glade replete with pine trees and a picture perfect view of Nanga Parbat reflected in a lake. Nearby it is possible to view the Raikot Glacier which tumbles down from the mountains above. An overnight visit to Fairy Meadows is the most popular option for travelers who are more interested in natural beauty than serious trekking. Fairy Meadows' beauty is famed throughout Pakistan; the name is something of a byword for Pakistan's natural blessings. Equally, Nanga Parbat is known throughout the world of trekking for its serene environs.

Anyone who wants to go all the way to Nanga Parbat Base Camp (4,300m) should come prepared; it's a two day climb to the camp, then an eight-hour descent back to Fairy Point/Jhel, but the views are simply unrivalled. This trek requires proper planning and should not be done without expert local advice.

Fairy Meadows and Nanga Parbat are closed from late November to mid-May every year.

Staying and eating at Fairy Meadows

There are a couple of basic accommodation options at Fairy Meadows, or you can pitch a tent in the lodge grounds. Carry as much water, food and money as you think you'll need – Fairy Meadows is a stop on a trail, not a fully-stocked town or a village. One night in one of the lodges costs about Rs. 2,000 per night. There's a small fee for pitching your tent in the grounds of one of the lodges.

Higher up the mountain, you will only be able to camp, so come prepared with your own food and cooking supplies. Trekking companies in Gilgit are able to organize supplies if you need; see page 188.

Getting to Fairy Meadows
Public transport
Getting to Fairy Meadows is a three-step process; transport to Raikot, then a jeep to Fairy Point/Jhel, then a moderate, but occasionally strenuous three hour climb to the meadows.

From Chilas or Gilgit, take a minivan to Raikot on the Karakoram Highway *(map pg. 193)*. From Chilas this is 24 kilometres, 30 minutes, and costs about Rs. 100. From Gilgit it's 110 kilometres, 2 hrs 30 mins, and Rs. 200. There's not much at Raikot – it's a highway junction, but you can pick up food and water here.

From Raikot, jeeps leave for Fairy Point/Jhel. They cost about Rs. 7,000; in theory this could be divided among as many passengers as can fit in the jeep, but the drivers try their hardest to discourage random groups from banding together and splitting the cost. In any case it's not a busy route, so you should just count on paying the Rs. 7,000, and consider yourself lucky if you meet someone else to share the cost with. From Raikot onwards you'll have a police escort – a 2013 terrorist attack at the Nanga Parbat Base Camp has left local authorities jumpy. Because of this, you will also have to note down your details at a police checkpoint every time you change transport. The drive is very rough; the road is narrow and rocky, and several times the jeeps seem to teeter on the edges of the cliffs.

The jeep driver will drop you at Fairy Point/Jhel and arrange a pick-up date and time – get the driver's contact details, in case you need to change your timings. The lodge at Fairy Meadows will be able to contact Raikot to arrange this for you. In Fairy Point/Jhel you can buy any further basic supplies that you might need (packaged biscuits, bottled water), before setting out on the trek. You can also hire a porter with a donkey to carry your things – this will cost about Rs. 1,200.

Tours
A popular option for visiting Fairy Meadows is on a tour. These could either be a private tour or a group tour. A private tour would be negotiated in Gilgit with a travel agency – count on paying Rs. 35,000 for 3 days, all inclusive, to Base Camp and back. It would normally include a van to Raikot, a jeep to Fairy Point/Jhel, accommodation at Fairy Meadows and a guide/porter. Some tours include meals, but this is not common – check when you book. See page 188 about travel agencies in Gilgit who can organize this. Hunza Treks and Tours (page 203) also comes highly recommended. The advantage with a private tour is personalized service and ease of travel – the drawback is the high cost.

A group tour may leave from Gilgit, but in the summer months there are numerous group tours from Islamabad, Lahore and even Karachi. These are usually populated by large numbers of enthusiastic young Pakistanis, and include basic meals, transport on minibuses and simple accommodation. Group tours allow you to visit this area cheaply and without having to organize things yourself. Additionally, you will meet lots of friendly locals who will probably want to catch up when you get back to Lahore or wherever they're from. The disadvantage is the size of the group – in a group of 30, 40 or even 50 you may start to lose some of the serenity for which Fairy Meadows is famed. Some group tours are also aimed at travellers with little time; "Lahore to Fairy Meadows in 5 days" is only possible with long overnight trips on uncomfortable buses. These tours usually cost about Rs. 26,000 for 5 days from Lahore, Rs. 23,000 from Islamabad.

CHILAS
Population: 50,000, Elevation: 1,150m, Telephone code: 05812
Chilas *(map pg. 193)* is one of those towns that does little to smash the prevailing stereotype of Pakistan as a lawless country hostile to foreigners. It's not that Chilas is an entirely bad place, and many Chilasi folk are indeed very welcoming. However there's no denying some simple facts; that the Taliban enjoy significantly higher levels of support here than in

anywhere else in Gilgit-Baltistan (you'll see politically-charged posters and graffiti in the town), and several terrorist attacks are believed to have been planned from here, including a shooting attack on a bus at Babusar Pass in 2012 and another on a group of foreign trekkers at Nanga Parbat Base Camp in 2013. A local police guard accompanies any foreigners in Chilas, and only two hotels in the town are considered "safe enough" for foreigners to stay in.

That said, they *are* considered "safe enough" – if things were *really* bad, foreigners would just be sent away for their own protection, as happens in places like Peshawar. Recently, travelers have reported the police guard being a mere formality, and that often they were left to their own devices while in Chilas. This suggests that perhaps the security situation has significantly improved since the early 2010s.

In any case, the only reason to come to Chilas is to change transport. If you're going from Gilgit to Naran or vice-versa, this is where you break your journey. And if you're heading Fairy Meadows, this is the main population centre in the region. Stay the night if you need, dress conservatively, try not to stand out and take heed of your guard's advice.

Sleeping and eating in Chilas
The hotels you can stay in are the Panorama Hotel and the Shangrila Hotel. Both charge around Rs. 2,500 per night for a double, but are comfortable. There's no need to book – your guard will negotiate things.

Getting to and from Chilas
Naran (via Babusar Pass): Jeep or minivan, 2 hours and 30 minutes, Rs. 500. The Babusar Pass is closed every year from November to May.
Gilgit: NATCO Bus or local minivan, 3 hours, Rs. 600.
Rawalpindi/Islamabad (via Karakoram Highway): NATCO, 8 hours, Rs. 1,300
Abbottabad (via Karakoram Highway): NATCO buses, 7 hours, Rs. 1,800
Mansehra (via Karakoram Highway): NATCO buses, 6 hours, Rs. 1,700

Which mountains are these?
There is a point near the town of Jaglot, between Chilas and Gilgit, where three major mountain ranges meet at the confluence of the Indus and Gilgit Rivers. The mountains to the north of this, extending up through Hunza to China, are the Karakoram Range, including peaks such as K2, Masherbrum and Rakaposhi. East and south of this is the tip of the mighty Himalayas which extend all the way eastwards through Kashmir, India, Nepal and Bhutan, including Nanga Parbat. West and southwest of Jaglot is the Hindu Kush which continues through Chitral (including Tirich Mir) and into northern Afghanistan.

A small turnout on the road includes a platform from which to view the "Three Ranges" and the rivers *(map pg. 184)*.

ASTORE VALLEY
Population: 110,000 (throughout various villages), Elevation: 2,600m (Astore village), Telephone code: 05817
Between Nanga Parbat and Deosai is the very beautiful Astore Valley *(map pg. 193)* with the village of Astore at its centre. Numerous trekking options are available from Astore village, including the strenuous two and a half hour climb to Rama Lake, or longer trips into the Upper Astore Valley. It's also possible to trek over the mountains to Deosai National Park from here (page 200).

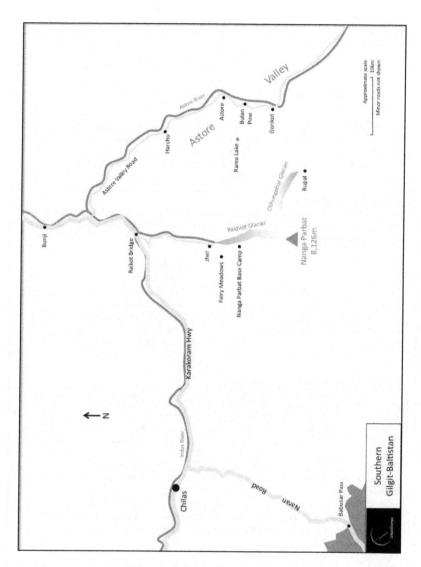

Accommodation options exist in Astore Valley, and some public transport operates from the Karakoram Highway to Astore village, but the remoteness of this region and trekking necessitates proper planning. Recommended travel/trekking agencies in Gilgit are listed on page 188, and the Hunza-based Hunza Treks and Tours (page 203) also comes highly recommended. A guide costs about Rs. 3000 per day, while an all-inclusive trek or tour will cost Rs. 65,000 for four days.

West of Gilgit

The Gilgit River cuts a narrow path through rugged terrain as it flows eastwards, forming the Ghizer Valley. Ghizer, and the nearby Yasin Valley, are often picturesque and often dramatically rocky. The region doesn't see a lot of tourists, and those who do come here are usually on their way to Chitral - except for when the Shandur Pass Polo Tournament is on (see page 196). There are very limited services in these areas; larger places like Gakuch and Gupis have internet access and small medical posts, while places like Shandur and Yasin are the definition of 'remote'.

The handful of towns throughout the valley each have their own individual drawcards, but are probably best visited as part of a wider tour; no village here is quite big or interesting enough to warrant a trip of its own. The area occupies a cultural-linguistic collision zone, and as you travel west the Gilgiti Shina tongue begins to melt away and Khowar, the language of Chitral, becomes more common.

The bus from Gilgit to Mastuj

The bus from Gilgit to Mastuj leaves at 6am daily between mid-May and mid-November, and stops throughout the Ghizer Valley. Below are sample bus timetables and their approximate stopping patterns;

To Mastuj
Depart Gilgit: 6am
Gakuch: 8:30am (change buses)
Gupis: 10:30am (stop for morning tea)
Phander: 1:30pm
Shandur Pass: 4pm (stop for tea)
Arrive Mastuj: 7pm

To Gilgit
Depart Mastuj: 5am
Shandur Pass: 8am (short break for tea)
Phander: 10:30am
Gupis: 1pm (lunch)
Gakuch: 3pm (change buses)
Arrive Gilgit: 5:30pm

Fares (in rupees) are given on the below table:

	Gakuch	Gupis	Phander	Shandur Pass	Mastuj
Gakuch		60	170	430	620
Gupis	60		100	300	560
Phander	170	100		160	360
Shandur Pass	430	300	160		250
Mastuj	620	560	360	250	

The fare from Gakuch to Gilgit is Rs. 120, and is paid separately to any of the above fares to/from Gakuch.

The road is sealed (with varying conditions of upkeep) between Gilgit and Phander - but from Phander to Mastuj the bus jolts its way along a sometimes smooth, but often rocky unsealed track.

At the time of writing there were nine checkpoints between Gilgit and Mastuj. Foreigners bound for Mastuj must register with the police once they arrive in Mastuj (see page 172 for more details). Foreigners travelling from Mastuj to Gilgit are given a registration card at the checkpoint at Barsat (see page 185 for more info about this registration card).

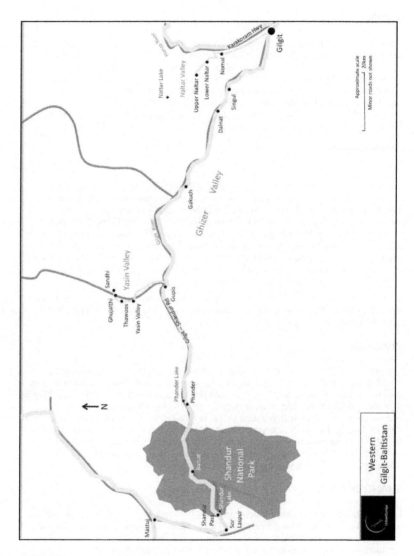

GAKUCH

Population: 12,000, Elevation: 1,850m, Telephone code: 05814

Gakuch *(map pg. 195)* is an important transport interchange, from which NATCO buses run out to the Yasin Valley. There's not much reason to stop here unless you're required to change buses, but if you do need to spend the night, NATCO has cheap retiring rooms at the bus station. Alternatively, the Hotel Green Palace Gakuch is recommended. For information about leaving Gakuch for the Ghizer Valley, Mastuj, or Gilgit, see the boxed text on page 190. For the Yasin Valley (Rs. 100, 2 hours), a Hi-Aces stops at NATCO's station at about 12:30pm each day.

GUPIS

Population: 15,000, Elevation: 2,300m, Telephone code: 05814
Gupis *(map pg. 195)* is one of the larger towns in the Ghizer Valley. Like Gakuch, it acts as a service town for much of the transport which passes through the valley. The road divides here; one fork heads north to the Yasin Valley, while the main road continues west to Phander and the Shandur Pass. NATCO buses often pull in to the Al-Falah Hotel and Restaurant here - they serve Pakistani staples and have some passable rooms if you need to stay the night. For information about leaving Gupis for elsewhere in the Ghizer Valley, Mastuj or Gilgit, see the boxed text on page 194. From Gupis, Hi-Aces travel to the Yasin Valley (Rs. 50, 30 minutes) at about 2pm.

YASIN VALLEY

Population: 45,000 (in villages throughout valley), Elevation: 2,400m (average), Telephone code: 05814
Yasin *(map pg. 195)* is a pretty, high valley to the north of Gupis, home to various small villages in relatively close proximity. This area sees few foreign travellers each year, and most of the people who visit do so to trek. There are various wild treks possible throughout and beyond the valley, the details of which are beyond the scope of this book. Consult a trekking service or tourist information in Gilgit (see page 188) before setting out. It's best to arrange accommodation before you set out - speak to a travel agency in Gilgit (page 188). If you arrive here without accommodation booked, go to the hotel in Raja Goharaman Bazaar in the village of Yasin - ask the driver of your Hi-Ace to drop you there, or alternatively, negotiate a lift in a jeep from wherever in the valley he drops you.

To get out of Yasin, a Hi-Ace picks up passengers from around the valley at about 6am, stopping at Gupis (Rs. 50, 30 minutes), Gakuch (Rs. 100, 2 hours) and Gilgit (Rs. 330, 3 hours 30 minutes).

PHANDER

Population: 30,000, Elevation: 2,930m, Telephone code: 05814
Phander *(map pg. 195)* is known for its lake which is a striking shade of turquoise in the bright alpine sunlight. Truth be told, the road between Gupis and Phander is home to many such lakes, but none as accessible as Phander Lake. Occasionally you'll see locals fishing in for trout, and the whole valley is an opportunity to go hiking - but never alone, and never without proper preparation. If you want to stay in Phander, the PTDC Motel overlooks Phander Lake, but is not the cheapest in town. Alternatively the Phander Paradise Hotel on the main road has basic rooms and breakfast. For information about leaving Phander for elsewhere in the Ghizer Valley, Mastuj or Gilgit, see the boxed text on page 194. For the Yasin Valley, you'll need to change buses in Gupis.

SHANDUR PASS

Population: nomadic/seasonal, Elevation: 3,810m, Telephone code: 05814
For 51 weeks of the year, the Shandur Pass *(map pg. 195)* is a high, lonely encampment near a placid lake. While the Shandur Pass Polo Tournament is on in July, it gets transformed into a temporary town as thousands of competitors, officials, local spectators and curious outsiders descend on the area to watch the most famous polo match on earth.

Whether you're here for the polo match or not really dictates what kind of experience you'll have in Shandur; if the match is on, then it will be social, exciting and culturally engaging; if not, then it will be eerie in its remote silence and pristine beauty. Shandur is at 3810 metres above sea level. The Shandur Pass is closed from mid-November to mid-May every year.

Either way, accommodation will take the form either of a local inn, or staying over in one of the large white tents that are erected across the plain by local graziers who are often happy to take in a paying guest. During the polo festival the number of tents increases to house the increased number of visitors.

For information about leaving the Shandur Pass for elsewhere in the Ghizer Valley, Mastuj or Gilgit, see the boxed text on page 194. For the Yasin Valley, you'll need to change buses in Gupis.

SKARDU

Population: 200,000, Elevation: 2,226m, Telephone code: 05815

Skardu is not like Gilgit; spread across a wide, flat valley, amid piles of brown mountains, it almost resembles a high altitude desert. Indeed, there are sand dunes around here, and the dust blows around the near-uncanny surroundings. It is in the heart of Baltistan, the highland region which stretches over into Tibet. In fact, the local language in Skardu, Balti, is a relative of Tibetan, and pre-Islamic history in the region is traced to the Tibetan highlands. A popular base for mountaineers, and now a base for the Pakistan Army (near Kargil, on the line of control with India), Skardu is more significant than it first appears.

Nearly everything you need can be found along the main street. It's known as Naya Bazaar (New Bazaar), and becomes Kazmi Bazaar, then Hamid Ghar Road further east, and then Hospital Road.

What to see in Skardu

Many visitors to Skardu come here with a plan to go trekking.

K2 Museum

map pg. 198, Free

At 8,611m, K2 is the second tallest mountain in the world, but its sheer cliffs have proved more deadly than those of Everest. Skardu is the usual departure point for treks to K2, Baltoro Glacier, and other lofty peaks. However don't come to Skardu expecting views of this monster mountain - it's still another 90kms trek to base camp Concordia, from where K2 is at its most dramatically beautiful.

Alternatively, you can visit the K2 Museum, commemorating the peak's first successful climbing in 1954 by an Italian team. The K2 Museum is in a tent in the garden of the PTDC K2 Motel.

Polo Ground

map pg. 198, Officially opens for tournaments, Entry: ticket price

The game of kings is played in Skardu - ask your hotel if there are any games on while you are there. Baltistan's annual tournament takes place in the first half of August each year.

Karpochu

map pg. 198, Fort open sunrise to sunset daily, Entry: Rs. 50

Karpochu is a ruined then partially reconstructed fort on the slopes above Skardu. Dating back to the 1600s, it is believed to have been built by a local king, Ali Sher Khan. To reach the fort, it's a three hour scramble up a track which starts behind Skardu's polo ground - ask around if you can't find it. The fort affords incredible views across the Skardu Valley. Take care while walking up and around here - there are lots of unmarked edges.

Staying in Skardu

Backpacker

Indus Motel: College Road; (+92) 05831-52608

map pg. 198, Dbl Rs. 500

A bit better than basic, but good value. The only issue is the location, which isn't right in the centre.

Economy

PTDC K2 Motel: Hamid Ghar Road; (+92) 05815-450291; www.tourism.gov.pk

map pg. 198, Dbl Rs. 3,800, Suite Rs. 5,700

Pleasant, airy mid-range option with a restaurant and TVs in each room.

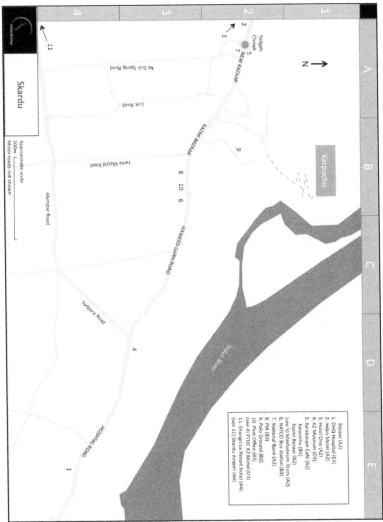

Skardu

Approximate scale
500m
Minor roads not shown

N →

Bazaar (A2)
1. DHQ Hospital (E4)
2. Indus Motel (A2)
3. Hotel One (A2)
4. K2 Museum (D3)
5. Karakoram Café (A2)
Karpochu (B1)
Kazmi Bazaar (B2)
(see 5) Mashabrum Tours (A2)
6. NATCO Bus station (B3)
7. National Bank (A2)
8. Polo Ground (B2)
9. PIA (B3)
10. Post Office (B3)
(see 4) PTDC K2 Motel (D3)
11. Shangri La Resort Hotel (A4)
(see 11) Skardu Airport (A4)

Yadgah Chowk
NEW BAZAAR
Na Guli Spong Road
Link Road
KAZMI BAZAAR
Jama Masjid Road
HAMEED GAIRI ROAD
Alamdar Road
Sadpara Road
HOSPITAL ROAD
Indus River
Karpochu

Hotel One: Airport Road; (+92) 0341-220111; www.hotelone.com.pk
map pg. 198, Dbl US$82
Pakistan's business chain has taken over an old building to create Skardu's best mid-range option.

Luxury

Shangri La Resort Hotel: Kachura Lake; (+92) 05815-454941; shangrilaresorts.com.pk
map pg. 198, Cost: US$161, Suite US$228
This luxurious location is reason enough to come to Skardu! Lakeside cottages, complimentary breakfast, three restaurants and a coffee shop. It's 28 kilometres from the centre of Skardu, lending itself to a quiet weekend away from Islamabad, but not a base for exploring the town by foot.

Eating in Skardu
Like Gilgit, the best food is to be found in the hotels. The PTDC K2 Motel, Indus Motel and Karakoram Cafe are all recommended. All are in the bazaar, where there is plenty of street food available too.

Services in Skardu
Airlines
Pakistan International: Khusho Bagh, Skardu (+92) 111-786-786 *(map pg. 198)*.

Banks
No international banks have representation in Skardu.

Internet Cafe
There are a couple of internet cafes in Kazmi Bazaar *(map pg. 198)*.

Money Exchange
National Bank at Yadgah Chowk *(map pg. 198)* can change major currencies (US Dollars, UK Pounds, Euros), but check the rate against what your hotel offers.

Post Office
The GPO is at the eastern end of Kazmi Bazaar *(map pg. 198)*.

Travel Agency
Mashabrum Tours can organise treks, tours and jeeps. Yadgah Chowk; (+92) 05815-450473; www.mashabrum.com *(map pg. 198)*.

Help in Skardu
Safety
Skardu is a fairly safe town and the usual precautions apply here - try to avoid walking alone at night if possible. Be careful of altitude sickness if you are venturing into the surrounding mountains.

Medical Services
DHQ Hospital: Hospital Road *(map pg. 198)*.
Pharmacy: is associated with the DHQ Hospital *(map pg. 198)*.

Getting around Skardu
A Suzuki around town costs no more than Rs. 100, while to the airport will cost around Rs. 300.

Leaving Skardu
The NATCO bus station is in the centre *(map pg. 198)*. The airport is 14 kms west of the centre *(map pg. 198)*.

Bus
Gilgit: NATCO buses and minivans, 7 hours, Rs. 500. Sit on the left for views, on the right if you're not good with heights. About an hour's drive out of Gilgit, before joining the Karakoram Highway, there is a great view of the sheer face of Nanga Parbat from the left side of the road.

Air
Islamabad: PIA, daily flights, 50 minutes, from Rs. 6,500 one way. Note the boxed text on page 88.
Gilgit: PIA, weekly flights, 40 minutes, from Rs. 5,500 one way. Note the boxed text on page 88.

Around Skardu

There are several day trips that can be taken in the valleys around Skardu. The nearest attraction is Satpara Lake, 9 kilometres south, whose brilliant turquoise-hued waters contrast stunningly with the dramatic, barren mountain slopes. Kachura Lake, home to the Shangri-La Resort (see page 198) is also stunning.

KHAPLU

Population: 120,000, Elevation: 2,500m, Telephone code: 05813

Khaplu *(map pg. 184)* is a pretty riverside village with a historic royal palace, about 35 kilometres from Skardu. Sometimes access to Khaplu is restricted, as the same road continues 70 kilometres on to the Siachen Glacier and the Line of Control with India. About ten kilometers past Khaplu, near the village of Yuching, there is a viewpoint offering a glimpse of the majestic Masherbrum (7,821m). The walk along the road to the viewpoint is easy, but carry water as it's hot, dusty and exposed. Across the river, between the viewpoint and the mountain, lies the Hushe Valley, the trekking base for Masherbrum. For excursions or treks into the Hushe Valley consult an agency in Skardu.

It's possible to stay the night at the PTDC Motel in Khaplu, or you can see it on a day trip from Skardu. Excursions to Khaplu can be organised through hotels or travel agencies in Skardu (page 199). Public transport from Skardu to Khaplu costs Rs. 270 in a minivan.

DEOSAI NATIONAL PARK

The Deosai Plains in the Deosai National Park *(map pg. 184)* is a high altitude plateau with a grassy carpet. Four wheel drives venture across here in the summer months only, with options to trek. Recommended travel/trekking agencies in Skardu are listed on page 199, and the Hunza-based Hunza Treks and Tours (page 203) is also highly recommended. A guide costs about Rs. 3,000 per day, while an all-inclusive trek or tour will cost Rs 65,000 for four days from Skardu or Gilgit. Deosai is closed due to heavy snowfall from late November to mid-May every year.

HUNZA VALLEY

Population: 120,000 (throughout villages in the valley), Elevation: 2,500m
Telephone code: 05813

Heading north from Gilgit the mountain gorges narrow before opening up to the wide Hunza Valley. Here, heaven meets Earth; below the snow-capped peaks, among the pine-covered hills lies a region locked away like treasure, preserved for those who seek it. Between the stone-terraced gardens lined with sunflowers and fruit orchards, visitors will uncover a gentle culture which values peace and time. Religiously, the valley is mostly Ismaili, a noticeably relaxed breakaway sect of Islam, and most locals' mother tongue is Burushashki, a language isolate (i.e. - with no related dialect anywhere in the world).

From the valley's district capital, Karimabad, it's almost unbelievable; you look back down the road towards Gilgit where a few hours earlier you were being harangued by samosa- and jeep-wallahs, and the air hung with the pungent smell of diesel. Then you look across to the Baltit Fort, past the apricots being dried on the terraced roofs, and past the rows of wild roses growing amongst the cherry orchards, riddled with the streams of crystal clear water from natural springs, and wonder if you'll ever be able to leave.

The Hunza is a large valley about 20 kilometres long and of varying breadth. The Hunza River travels along the valley floor, while settlements are perched on the slopes above it. Travelling north from Gilgit, the road passes several villages but the first significant stop is Aliabad, where many of the minivans start and end their journeys. Another seven kilometres along a winding road is Karimabad, where most visitors stay. There are countless other villages around the valley, and if you have time, they make perfect destinations for walking trips.

While it's more open than much of the rest of Pakistan, the Hunza Valley is still a traditional society. Always ask before pointing your camera at someone or walking into someone's garden (many gardens are very photogenic and have no fences). If someone indicates that they don't want their photo taken, respect that decision – several tourists have become engaged in heated exchanges over this issue.

Your hotel will be able to recommend a reputable local agent to organise jeeps, guides, or equipment for treks to the mountains around the Hunza Valley. Alternatively, contact Hunza Treks and Tours (page 203).

What to see in the Hunza Valley
Baltit Fort
map pg. 198, Open 9am – 1pm and 2 – 5:30pm in summer, 9:30am – 4pm in winter, Entry: Rs. 800 (including guide)
The undisputed focal point for tourism in the Hunza Valley is the Baltit Fort, a microcosm of the history of dynasties and splendour of the region. Dating back to the 1200s, It was added to over the centuries, taking on a Baltistani style, from where it takes its name.

Part of entry to the Baltit Fort is an introductory tour by a local guide - they will show you around a bit and point out the highlights. Remarkably, the fort underwent major renovation works in the 1990s, but this is almost undetectable, so subtle is the restoration.

The fort has three floors including the rooftop terrace. The first floor contains many prison chambers, bedrooms and storage rooms, the second floor houses and abundance of living quarters, while the rooftop has space for drying and storing fruit, and a small mosque. As you approach Baltit Fort there are lots of tourist shops with carpets, hats, carvings and jewellery.

Altit Fort
map pg. 202, Open 9am – 1pm and 2 – 5:30pm in summer, 9:30am – 4pm in winter, Entry: Rs. 700 (including guide)
Less tourists make it to Altit, although it is an easy 2km walk downhill from Karimabad (a taxi back is Rs. 500) and entertaining tour. See the execution ledge where prisoners were pushed off for an almost 1,000 foot drop into the river below.

Two and a half hours climb from Altit is Melishkar, a tiny village which, at 3000 metres, affords incredible views across the valley.

Walks and hikes in the Hunza Valley
There are several pleasant walks and climbs around the Hunza Valley which are easily accessed by the casual visitor. Walking in the mountains, through the orchards on the hillside behind Karimabad, is a nice way to take in the spectacular views across the valley while getting an insight into local life.

One hour walk uphill from Baltit Fort is a monument in honour of Queen Victoria, known as Malika Shikar or Victoria Shikar *(map pg. 202)*. It's not difficult or dangerous to reach, but ask for clear directions before you set out. Make sure you climb up the 'face' of the hill on the left side, before crossing along the ridge top – the cliff face is sheer and slippery. Further up the hill and in the canyon behind lies the Ultar Glacier. The hike there can be done in a day, but it is essential to get local advice in Karimabad before setting out.

Ganish Village
map pg. 202, 24 hours, but visit in daylight hours, Entry: Rs. 200 (including guide)
With its traditional architecture, Ganish is a highlight. You can walk to Ganish by taking the steep roads down from Karimabad, or alternatively get in a jeep for about Rs. 30. The entry to the old village is just out of the centre of modern Ganish – continue along the Karakoram highway away from Karimabad, and there's a sign marking the entrance on the left. Walk past the mosque on the right and the man-made lake on the left, then go through the small gate and follow the laneways through. You'll eventually enter the historic town centre with its mosque, traditional architecture with carved wooden doors, and laneways shaded by

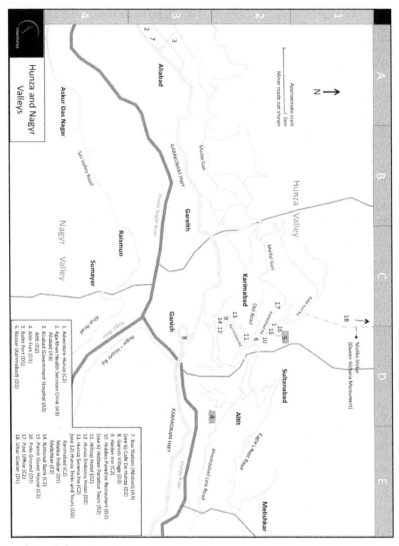

Hunza and Nagyr Valleys

N →

Approximate scale
1km
Minor roads not shown

1. Adventure Hunza (C2)
2. Aga Khan Health Services Clinic (A3)
3. Aliabad Government Hospital (A3)
4. Altit Fort (D3)
5. Altit (D2)
6. Baltit Fort (D1)
6. Bazaar (Karimabad) (D2)

7. Bus Station (Aliabad) (A3)
8. Ganish Village (D3)
(see 6) Café De Hunza (D2)
9. Haider Inn (C2)
10. Hidden Paradise Restaurant (D2)
(see 6) Hidden Paradise Tours (D2)
11. Hilltop Hotel (D2)
12. Hunza Embassy Hotel (D2)
13. Hunza Serena Inn (C2)
(see 12) Hunza Treks and Tours (D2)
Karimabad (C2)
14. National Bank (C2)
Melishkar (E2)
Malika Shikar (D1)
15. Pamir Guest House (C2)
16. Polo Ground (D2)
17. Post Office (C2)
18. Ultar Glacier (D1)

apricot and cherry trees.
A small shop on the left of the entrance to the village asks for Rs. 200 as an entrance fee. This looks rather unofficial, but the guide it buys might be helpful in guiding you around the pokey laneways and obscure corners of the village.

Staying in Karimabad
Backpacker
Pamir Guest House: Fort Chowk; (+92) 0343-9893203
map pg. 202, Dbl Rs. 1,400
Higher up the mountain than many other hotels, this is clean and central.

Haider Inn: Zero Point; (+92) 05813-457209
map pg. 202, Dorm Rs. 300, Dbl Rs. 500
One of the first hotels in Hunza. Some rooms are much cleaner than others – the dorms seem to be better than the private rooms. Good view from the restaurant, even better from the rooftop, all managed by the kind, rambling Mr Haider!

Economy
Hilltop Hotel: Old Road; (+92) 05813-57145; www.hilltophunza.com
map pg. 202, Sgl, US$35, Dbl US$54
The rooms are comfortably appointed and have awesome views. The food is good too, and the garden is very pretty.

Hunza Embassy Hotel: Karimabad Rd; (+92) 05813-457001
map pg. 202, Dbl Rs. 4,000
Dark rooms, but really quiet with great views of mountains. Excellent dhal and chapati in the restaurant.

Luxury
Hunza Serena Inn: Old Road; (+92) 05813-457660; www.serenahotels.com/serenahunza
map pg. 202, Deluxe Tents US$144, Dbl US$144, Suite US$172
A restaurant, coffee lounge, business centre and complimentary wifi - everything you would expect from this top-end chain, although in a distinct mountain lodge setting. Great views across the valley and pretty grounds. There are also permanent marquee-style tents for the true Silk Road caravan experience.

Eating in Karimabad
The best food is to be found in hotel restaurants, and it's pretty good here too. There is also a lot of fresh fruit and vegetables, and fried snacks available in the bazaar. For some traditional Hunzai food, try the restaurant **Hidden Paradise** whose terrace affords views over Altit. For a real espresso the **Café de Hunza** is an institution around these parts *(all map pg. 202)*.

Services in Karimabad
Banks
No international banks have representation in the Hunza Valley.

Internet Cafe
There are internet cafes in the main bazaar *(map pg. 202)*, and most hotels offer internet access.

Money Exchange
The National Bank on Old Ganish Road *(map pg. 202)* can change US dollars and UK pounds, but check the rates with your hotel too.

Post Office
The post office is along the bazaar road towards Aliabad, past the fort *(map pg. 202)*.

Travel Agency
Hunza Treks and Tours: Zero Point, Karimabad (+92) 05813-457209; www.trekkinginhunza.blogspot.com *(map pg. 202)*
Adventure Hunza: Baltit Fort Road; (+92) 3454865707; www.adventurehunza.com *(map pg. 202)*.
Hidden Paradise Tours: Near Hilltop Hotel; (+92) 05813-480950 *(map pg. 202)*.

Help in the Hunza Valley
Safety
The Hunza Valley is one of the safest parts of Pakistan. Petty theft exists, and you should still keep your wits about you, and avoid unnecessary walks alone at night. Take care when walking around the mountains - loose ground has been known to give way, and you don't

want to tread on the edge of a cliff when that happens, nor be on the receiving end of a falling rock.

Altitude sickness is a real threat for hikers and climbers to the mountains around the Hunza Valley, although you probably won't be affected if you're staying around the settled areas.

Medical Services

Karimabad has a small hospital at the bottom end of the bazaar, but Aliabad has a better serviced government hospital and Aga Khan Health Services clinic *(both map pg. 202)*. A pharmacy is associated with the Aga Khan Health Services clinic *(map pg. 202)*.

Getting around the Hunza Valley

A van or hi-ace (a utility vehicle fitted out for passengers) around either Aliabad or Karimabad costs no more than Rs. 30, while further out into the valley will cost a couple of hundred rupees. Suzuki minivans also run around the valley, most frequently between Aliabad and Karimabad, for about Rs. 30 a ride. Ask at your hotel for more information about the nearest pickup point, and cost.

Leaving the Hunza Valley

The bus station is at Aliabad *(map pg. 202)*. Minivans stop at the turnoff to Karimabad on the Karakoram Highway, but they're often full by then.

Gilgit: Minivans from Aliabad's bus station hang around (sometimes driving around) until they're full; the fare is about Rs. 200 and the journey takes two hours. Be aware the day's last departure is often at 3pm.

NATCO also run this route - ask at the NATCO office at the bus station, as it depends on demand and availability.

Gulmit: Minivans, 1 hour, Rs. 90
Passu and Hussaini: Minivans, 1 hour 30 mins, Rs. 100
Sost: Minivans, 2 hours 30 mins, Rs. 170

Around the Hunza Valley
NAGYR VALLEY

The Nagyr Valley *(map pg. 202)* is the leafy collection of villages on the hill across from Karimabad, to the south. Traditionally a separate local kingdom to Hunza, it is pleasantly quiet and untouristed. The villages are interesting and quaint to stroll through. Few jeeps run specifically from Karimabad to Sumayar or Askur Das Nagar but if you hire one it will cost around Rs. 2,000 for the round trip. Most visitors walk from Karimabad in about 2 hours.

HOPPA GLACIER

A half day trip will bring you to the majestic Hoppa Glacier in valley above Nagyr *(map pg. 184)*. Once the jeep parks it's a short walk to the spectacular viewpoint. You can walk on the glacier itself, but beware of deadly crevasses. Hire a jeep with driver through your hotel or travel agency in Karimabad (Rs. 3,500 for half a day).

GHULMET and RAKAPOSHI VIEWPOINT

About 30 kilometres from Karimabad, back along the highway towards Gilgit, in the village of Ghulmet is the "Rakaposhi Viewpoint" *(map pg. 184)*. Just a few metres off the highway near a stream stands a collection of drink and snack stalls; sip a cold drink in Rakaposhi's shadow while dangling your feet in the glacial melt running off the mammoth mountain. To get here take any van headed towards Gilgit along the Karakoram Highway – it will take about 20 minutes and costs about Rs. 50.

GOJAL (UPPER HUNZA)

North of the Hunza Valley, the gorges become narrower again and the road begins to climb. You pass waterfalls, suspension bridges over the Hunza River, and even a glacier up in the peaks.

23 kilometres from Karimabad, the road climbs towards the end of the Attabad Lake. Here, on 4th January 2010, a massive landslide buried the village of Attabad killing 20 people, blocking the valley, and plugging the Hunza River. The resulting lake is a stunning shade of turquoise in the sunlight, but is equally horrific when one considers what lies beneath it.

At the northern end of the Attabad Lake is the partially-rebuilt village of Gulmit, and further north lies the startlingly dramatic Cathedral Range and four major glaciers, best seen from the village of Passu. Passu is a small place, with only a handful of streets and services.

As the road continues past Passu the mountains seem to close in, creating ever-tighter gorges. End-of-the-world Sost is a small village which serves as the last main settlement before the Chinese border. Sost really is a one-street town - nearly everything happens on the Karakoram Highway. The crossing to China is at the Khunjerab Pass, 84 kilometres northeast of Sost.

This area is known as Gojal or Upper Hunza, and the locals speak Wakhi, a linguistic relative of Tajik. Despite being on the way to a major international border crossing, the region is isolated and services and comforts are minimal. At the time of writing, there are no internet cafes in the Gojal region. Much of the area shuts down between November and May due to snow drifts - the exact date depends on the conditions. Plan your travel here wisely.

Where you stay here depends on what you're planning to do. Try to base yourself in Passu - the scenery is stunning and there are plenty of walks to keep you busy. Meanwhile if you're planning to cross the border to China, you'll probably end up spending a night in Sost as well so you can set off early for the journey towards the border.

GULMIT

Population: 5,000, Elevation: 2,460m, Telephone code: 05813

Gulmit is the place to stay if you're interested in seeing the Attabad Lake. If they're around, local boatmen can take you for a punt on the lake for 15 minutes for about Rs. 150, but sometimes the boatyard is eerily deserted. There are a few small hotels in town, the Gulmit Tourist Inn *(map pg. 206)* is recommended. Gulmit is also home to Gojal's most important polo ground *(map pg. 206)*, Gojal's best-equipped (but still limited) hospital – the Agha Khan Health Centre *(map pg. 206)* – and a trailhead for the Borit Lake hike (see pg. 207).

From Gulmit minivans go to **Passu** (45 minutes, Rs. 70), **Hussaini** (30 minutes, Rs. 50), **Karimabad** (1 hour, Rs. 90) and **Sost** (1 hour 30 mins, Rs. 120). Vans are most frequent in the morning, decreasingly so through the afternoon – flag them down from the intersection just south of the Gulmit Tourist Inn.

HUSSAINI

Population: 700, Elevation: 2,500m, Telephone code: 05813

Hussaini is remarkable for two things; the breathtaking panorama from the small tea shop *(map pg. 206)* just southeast of town, and the "Hussaini Bridge" *(map pg. 206)*, a precarious rope bridge which crosses the Hunza River to a scattering of villages on the other side.

The rope bridge is an easy 25-minute downhill walk from the town centre. Misshapen planks with a sheer drop between the gaps into the river below make this a thrilling experience. Take care and hold on, as the bridge also sways like crazy if someone else is on it! Even if you don't cross the bridge, this is a highly photogenic spot.

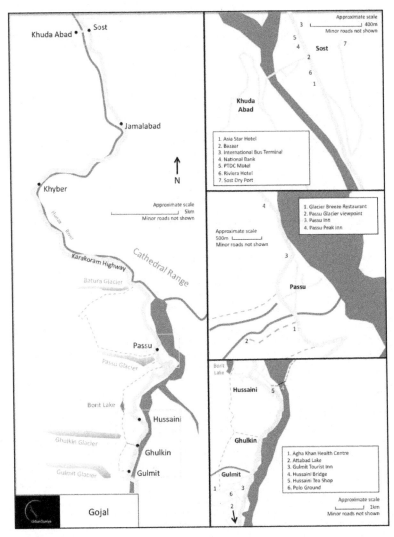

From the main highway in the centre of Hussaini minivans go to **Passu** (15 minutes, Rs. 50), **Gulmit** (30 minutes, Rs. 50), **Karimabad** (1 hour 30 minutes, Rs. 100) and **Sost** (1 hour, Rs. 100). Vans are most frequent in the morning, decreasingly so through the afternoon.

PASSU

Population: 978, Elevation: 2,400m, Telephone code: 05813

Passu isn't as important as Gulmit or Sost, but for the casual traveller it's possibly the most spectacular place along the Karakoram Highway, and a great place to chill out. There's nothing to do here, but that's the point – could you ever get bored of gazing at the Cathedral Range?

What to see around Passu

Cathedral Range

You don't need to look far to find the dramatic Cathedral Range *(map pg. 206)* - dominating Passu's panorama like a theatre backdrop, these incredible jagged peaks are beautiful and forbidding. Reaching for the sky, up to 6100m high, they make amazing photography subjects during the day, and especially in the afternoon when the sun's rays set their glistening walls alight.

Passu Glacier

There are several walks and hikes which start from Passu *(map pg. 206)*, some as short as a few hours, some take all day. Shorter trips include walks to the spectacular frozen environs of the Passu and Batura Glaciers.

The gleaming white Passu Glacier is to the south of Passu, and is an easy 20 minute walk along a dusty trail to the viewing point, just before the glacial lake. The trail leaves the highway just north of the Glacier Breeze restaurant *(map pg. 206)* – it's about 20 minutes walk from the centre of Passu.

The Passu Glacier is a focus for environmentalists as it is retreating at a tremendous rate due to the increase in temperatures here. It is possible to walk around the lake and up to the glacier itself. It is a long and dangerous climb to the glacier, or take a more leisurely half-day walk to the 'snout' where ice melts into crystal clear water. Either way, it's not an easy walk, and you should come prepared.

At the snout you can bring a snack or fill your water bottle from the pure water. Listen and watch as parts of the glacier break off and crash down with tremendous echoes from the valley walls; mesmerising and unforgettable. A guide from one of the local hotels is Rs. 2,000 for half a day. Do not attempt on your own; there is sinking sand near the glacier, and close to the stream crossings, which you could easily be lost in.

Batura Glacier

The Batura Glacier *(map pg. 206)* cuts a swathe through the rock north of Passu. It is called a 'black glacier', but in reality it's brown – it collects mud and dust as it descends. The walk there is a bit tougher than the one to the Passu Glacier, but still manageable in about 30 to 40 miuntes from the highway. The trailhead for the Batura Glacier is not as close as the Passu Glacier – it's an hour-long walk along the highway for several kilometers (consider getting a lift here). The trail begins south of the stream, before the bridge.

Walks and hikes

The Passu and Gulmit Glacier walks *(map pg. 206)* continue past the viewpoints, past their respective glaciers. They eventually curve around to meet in a pretty mountain glen in the valley behind Passu village. While this trail can be approached from either side, it's more popular to start from the Passu Glacier and end with the Batura Glacier. It's a moderate, all-day hike with little or no services along the way – you'll only see nomadic farmers if you're lucky. While it's a 'local' hike, it should not be undertaken without advice from the hotels in Passu – many travelers have been rescued here after underestimating the conditions.

Serious hikers can go for nearby Borit Lake (which can also be accessed from Gulmit). None of these walks should be attempted alone, or without consulting a guide in Passu, Gulmit or another local town.

For treks into the mountains around Passu, you would be best advised to contact one of the travel agencies in Karimabad (page 203). Otherwise your local accommodation should be able to recommend something.

Staying in Passu

Backpacker
Passu Peak Inn: Karakoram Highway; (+92) 03449876547
map pg. 206, Dorm Rs. 400, Sgl Rs. 900, Dbl Rs. 1,100
A very friendly manager makes up for the basic facilities and distance from the main town.

Economy
Passu Inn: Karakoram Highway; (+92) 03555310183
map pg. 206, Dbl Rs. 1,200
In the centre of town – hot showers, comfortable rooms and a pleasant restaurant.

Eating in Passu
There aren't a lot of places to eat in Passu, and most travellers end up eating two or three meals a day at their hotel. You can buy fresh produce in the small bazaars. One great option just out of Passu is the **Glacier Breeze Restaurant** *(map pg. 206)*; Tanveer Ahmad's business is known for its moist apricot cake.

Services in Passu
There are no international banks or internet facilities in Passu; ask at your hotel for advice. Your hotel in Passu might be able to change money, but don't count on it.

Help in Passu
Safety
The dangers in Passu are more of the environmental kind - freezing temperatures, rockfall, unmarked walking trails, and landslides or avalanches are all possible. Plan accordingly, and take due care when travelling in this region.

Altitude sickness is also a major concern for anyone heading over 2,500 metres. At 2,400m, Passu is close to, but not really *in* the danger zone. Give yourself time to acclimatise, and don't attempt any strenuous activities until your body has adjusted. If you experience symptoms such as headaches, dizziness, difficulty in breathing or nausea, you would be advised to move to lower altitudes as quickly as possible.

The advice provided in this book is general advice only, and cannot replace the advice of a trained health professional. If you are travelling to high altitudes, you are advised to speak with your doctor or another expert about the dangers of altitude sickness.

Medical Services
Passu has a local clinic with a dispensary, but it's not well equipped. If you require medical assistance, ask at your hotel, and consider travelling to Gulmit, Karimabad (in the Hunza Valley) or Gilgit for treatment.

Getting around Passu
You can really only walk or ask someone for a lift around Passu. Minivans headed northbound for Sost, or southbound for Gulmit can give you a ride to places further out of town.

Leaving Passu
Minivans leave from outside the Passu Inn to **Hussaini** (15 minutes, Rs. 50), **Gulmit** (45 minutes, Rs. 70), **Karimabad** (1 hour 30 minutes, Rs. 100) and **Sost** (1 hour, Rs. 70). Vans are most frequent in the morning, decreasingly so through the afternoon.

My favourite place in the world?
Passu is one of my favourite places in the world. Want to know why? Read my blog, here; www.urbanduniya.com/traveller/introducing-passu/

SOST

Population: 520, Elevation: 2,700m, Telephone code: 05813
Sost is a border town, and not really worth your time unless you are travelling to China or the border; it's much better to stay in Passu and get a transfer. Sost is the old name for what is properly called Affyitabad, but everyone still calls it Sost.

What to see and do in Sost
Not a lot. If you're stuck here, there are a handful of pleasant, easy walks to take; ask at your hotel for directions to Khuda Abad Road across the suspension bridge west of town. Khuda Abad is a small village with apricot and apple trees, and views back across the valley. On the other side of the valley is a steep climb up to the uninteresting 'Sost Dry Port' at Hussainabad; here, cargo waits to be sent towards China.

The Chapursan Valley is a little-touristed valley that stretches northwest from Sost, out towards Afghanistan's Wakhan Corridor. It's a wonderland of high-altitude treks and tiny villages with apricot and cherry orchards, but is only accesed through a series of jeep traks and strenuous hiking trails. Contact a travel agency in Karimabad, Hunza Valley (page 203) to arrange a trek - Hunza Treks and Tours is highly recommended. An all-inclusive trek will cost Rs 35,000 for three days from Hunza.

Staying in Sost
Backpacker
Asia Star Hotel Sost: Karakoram Highway; (+92) 03453461502
map pg. 206, Rs. 500
Nothing fancy here, but friendly service and tasty meals at the restaurant.

Economy
PTDC Motel Sost: Karakoram Highway; (+92) 05823-51030; www.tourism.gov.pk
map pg. 206, Dbl US$48
Sost's best option. Comfortable, clean but basic rooms with temperamental hot water, and a pleasant eatery.

Riviera Hotel: Karakoram Highway; (+92) 3115994279
map pg. 206, Cost: Dbl Rs. 3,000
If only it was on the Riviera. Not the cleanest hotel, and its restaurant leaves a lot to be desired.

Eating in Sost
There are few nice places to eat in Sost – fresh fruit in the bazaar, dhal from a handful of restaurants and maybe the odd hotel restaurant are the best options.

Services in Sost
There are few facilities in Sost other than those required at a national border crossing.

Money Exchange
Being a gateway town, moneychangers are dotted around the bazaar in Sost; ask around for the best rate. Alternatively, there is the National Bank *(map pg. 206)*, about halfway through town.

Help in Sost
Safety
The danger in Sost is the environmental kind - freezing temperatures, rockfall, unmarked walking trails, and landslides or avalanches are all possible. Plan accordingly, and take care when travelling in this region.

Altitude sickness is a concern for anyone heading over 2500 metres; Sost is at 2700m. Give yourself time to acclimatise; don't attempt strenuous activities until you have adjusted. If you experience symptoms such as headaches, dizziness, difficulty in breathing or nausea, you are advised to move to lower altitudes as quickly as possible.

The advice provided in this book is general advice only, and cannot replace the advice of a trained health professional. If you are travelling to high altitudes, you are advised to speak with your doctor or another expert about the dangers of altitude sickness.

Medical Services

Sost has a local clinic with a dispensary, but it's not well equipped. If you require medical assistance, ask at your hotel, and consider travelling to Gulmit, Karimabad (in the Hunza Valley) or Gilgit for treatment.

Getting around Sost

You can only walk or ask someone for a lift around Sost. Minivans headed southbound for Passu or Gulmit can give you a ride to places further out of town.

Leaving Sost

Minivans leave from the bazaar to **Passu** (1 hr, Rs. 70), **Hussaini** (1 hr 15 mins, Rs. 100), **Gulmit** (1.5 hrs, Rs. 120), **Karimabad** (2.5 hrs, Rs. 170). Vans are frequent in the morning, decreasingly in the afternoon.

From Sost it's possible to take a van up to the top of the Khunjerab Pass for a morning's joy ride. You'll need to hire a van for yourself; plan on paying around Rs. 2,000.

Going to China

If you are headed to China, you must begin your journey at Sost. Buy a ticket on one of the bus companies (NATCO or a Chinese company - about PKR 2,600) at the international bus terminus at the northern end of town, past the PTDC Motel on the opposite side of the road. Buses depart when demand warrants it, so they could run daily in peak times, or you could wait up to a week during slow periods. The journey takes approximately nine hours if everything runs smoothly - but has been known to take twelve or more.

Try to change money in Sost before you leave – Pakistani Rupees aren't easy to change in China (although if you don't there is a "Pakistan Street" near the bazaar in Tashkurgan where you can change money).

In Sost, the Pakistani customs post is part of the bus terminal. Before boarding the bus your bags will be searched, visa checked and passport stamped. You must have a valid Chinese visa before boarding. The nearest Chinese embassy is in Islamabad – so plan ahead.

The bus pulls out of Sost at 7:30am and one or two hours later drives into the Khunjerab National Park at the tiny hamlet of Dih. Here it stops for a security check, and foreigners have to pay US$8 as a national park fee. Officially this has to be paid in US dollars, although travellers often pay in Pakistani Rupees.

Dih is the only stop before the Chinese border (unless nature intervenes in the form of a toilet stop or a road blockage - equally likely). A Pakistan army guard is on board the bus, and makes sure that everyone who boarded in Sost leaves the country - passengers' passports have, after all, been stamped out of Pakistan. Through the national park the bus continues for another hour or two, gradually climbing towards the Khunjerab Pass. If you're *really* lucky, you might spot a snow leopard or a Marco Polo sheep.

Khunjerab means "valley of blood" in the local Wakhi dialect, and is supposedly named after the bloody raids on caravans which took place in the days of the silk road. The highway switchbacks its way up the pass before a few kilometres of relative flat, then the border. A couple of hundred metres before the border the bus will stop to let the Pakistani guard off - passengers also disembark for a photo with the arch at the frontier. Take care - you are 4,693 metres above sea level and there is a lack of oxygen. You mightn't have noticed it sitting placidly on the bus, but a brisk walk will have you gasping for air.

Arriving at the border proper, a security check is conducted by Chinese officials. Every photograph on every phone and camera is checked by the Chinese authorities, and every part of every bag is searched and unpacked. All passengers pass through a full-body x-ray scanner. Buses generally take 3 - 4 hours to clear every passenger. Don't take photos here.

The bus collects you from the other side of the border post and you will be joined by a Chinese soldier; he stays on the bus to make sure no-one disembarks before border control at Tashkurgan. After 30 minutes there's a security check point at Pirali. Again, no photos please.

Finally, after Pirali, it's a two and a half hour drive to Tashkurgan, where the bus is fumigated, and passengers are herded into an arrivals hall. Luggage is searched, visas checked and passports stamped.

The process from China into Pakistan via the Khunjerab Pass is roughly the same but in reverse. Make sure you have a valid Pakistani visa before booking the bus ticket from Tashkurgan.

BALOCHISTAN
PESHAWAR AND CENTRAL KHYBER PUKHTOONKHWA
THE SWAT VALLEY
FEDERALLY ADMINISTERED TRIBAL AREAS (FATA)
AZAD JAMMU AND KASHMIR

Due to a variety of security concerns these areas have not been covered in this edition of Pakistan Traveller, but may appear in future editions as conditions allow. If you choose to travel to these regions you are advised to check your country's travel advisory (see 'safety', page 32) and the nearest branch of PTDC (see individual city sections).

Balochistan and Peshawar are both accessible to tourists, however doing so is reportedly highly dangerous. That said, several tourists report crossing from Iran into Pakistan (or vice versa) and travelling via Quetta, Balochistan. Usually they are not prevented from proceeding, but assigned an individual armoured van with at least one or two guards per passenger.

Casual visitors to Peshawar are normally approached by guards upon arrival and told that they can't stay, due to security reasons. They're usually put straight back on the first bus back to Islamabad. People who are staying with relatives or friends in Peshawar and surrounds do not seem to be subject to this rule.

The Swat Valley reopened to tourism, albeit with an armed guard, shortly before the publication of this book. For details on how to travel here, speak to PTDC in Islamabad.

At the time of publishing it was in fact illegal for foreigners to enter FATA and AJ&K, a rule enforced by the Pakistan Army at roadblocks. FATA has been off limits to non-locals for at least a decade, while entry to AJ&K is occasionally permitted with possession of a No Objection Certificate (NOC) from the Interior Ministry in Islamabad - again, speak to the nearest PTDC office for details.

Credits

Thanks to:
Aehsun Hafeez, Yassar Shahbaz and the whole family for making much of this possible, Anas Wahab and Ruqayya Hafeez, Faizan Choudhary, Tazeem Razi and the whole family, Muhammad Umer, Shoaib Khalid, Aaqib Hussain, Ali Shayan, Awais Ahmed, Ghluam Mustafa, Saadi Hussain, Shahbaz Kunwar, Shahid Ismail, Syed Sohaib, Nawaz Khan, Waqas Ahmad, Junaid Shah, Munib Shah and everyone at the village, Asad-ur-Rehman Abbasi, Imran Ali, Huma Bhalli, Ahsan Bhatti, Ahsan Khan, Naveed ur-Rehman, Dilawar "Peter" Masih, Chand Abbas, Ghalib Khalil, Hassan Mirza, Cez Krol, Agness Walewinder, Garry Farmer, Amit Bose, Kashif Hassan Bukhari, Asim Zafar and Naheed Asim, Farah Hassan, Muhammad Sajid, Farah and Adeel, Taha, Mohid and the family for being there from the start

Special thanks for this edition:
Usman Anwar, Zeerak, Abraiz and Sheraiz and the whole family for your help and support, Abdul Rehman (Sehwan Sharif), Simon Proudman (Karakoram Highway), Essakhan and Mansoor Hunzai (Karimabad), Iqrar Din and Shahzad Ahmad (Chitral), Amjad Ali (Chitral), Fateh Aman (Mastuj and Gilgit), Ghulam Mahmad (Ghizer Valley), Raja Jehangeer Khoshwaqt (Yasin and Naltar Valleys), Umar Jan (Gilgit), Awais Khan (Gilgit), Tanveer Ahmad (Passu), Akhtar Hussain (Passu), Naseeruddin (Passu), Saleem and Muhammad Ali Musofer (Gojal), Ali Raza (Faisalabad and Jhang), Shakeeb Illyas (Sargodha), Valeed Hussain (Soon Valley), Zeeshan Arain (Sukkur), Umar Abbasi (Pakpattan), Sana Saeed and Sara Gill (Karachi), Khani Zaman Mughal (Karachi), Syed Waji (Abbottabad), Danish Qadeer (Sheikhupura), Mian Haider Ali, Fahad Khan Kakar and everyone at the haveli (Lahore) and Moazam Ali, my travelling companion, fixer and partner in crime all over Pakistan.

And of course my own family, without whom I couldn't have realised any of these dreams.

We would love your feedback! Please contact us via our website and tell us about what you thought of this book, how it could be improved, any corrections to be made, or simply tell us about your Pakistan experience – we may even publish your piece online!

UrbanDuniya and the author did not receive remuneration or compensation of any kind for inclusion or coverage of a particular business or service in this book.

Cover image: Mountains near Mastuj

About the Author

Tim Blight fell in love with
Pakistan on its first visit
in 2006. Since then it has
been a roller-coaster ride of
perilous mountain roads,
getting caught up in religious
processions in crowded streets,
learning a lesson about
the effects of eating spicy street
food, standing awestruck
by beautiful architecture and
meeting more than a few friends
for life.

Since his first visit, Tim has visited Pakistan ten times,
criss-crossing the country and visiting almost every
(accessible) corner of the land. He is the author of
Pakistan Traveller, a project of his website UrbanDuniya.
He has also authored Recipes for Ramadan, a collection of recipes from around the world,
and contributed to an eBook about Creative Urbanism in Melbourne, authored by Agness
Walewinder of eTramping.com.

About UrbanDuniya

UrbanDuniya is my blog, featuring travel, photography, food, coffee, entertainment,
opinions and more. Since 2013 I've published from four continents, sharing my adventures
with the world

Urban denotes a local sensibility, seeking the best that our communities have to offer.
Duniya is an Arabic word for 'world'. We're all neighbours, the world is our city – and
we're going to experience it together!

UrbanDuniya

UrbanDuniya.com
UrbanDuniya.com/PakistanTraveller

Basic Urdu

To teach Urdu is beyond the scope of both this book, and most casual visitors to Pakistan. This is a basic guide to some useful Urdu phrases which are adaptable to several different situations. For example, "do you have bottled water?" could also be used to ask for biryani, time or even flight tickets. Where there is a slash, such as in *chata/i*, the *-a* ending is used by men, the *-i* ending by women.

Greeting and practicalities
hello - *asalamu aleikum* (literally "peace be upon you")
how are you? - *aap kaise hai?*
I'm fine - *mae thik hoong* (pronounced 'teak')
thank you - *shukriya*
goodbye - *Allah hafiz*
please - there is no word in Urdu for 'please' - politeness is implied with tone and manner. Sometimes *meherbani* is used - it literally means "kindly".
sorry - *maaf ki-ji-ye* (but often just 'sorry' is used)
yes - *jee haa* (sometimes *haa jee*)
no - *jee nahi* (often just *nahi* or *nai*)
ok - *thik hai* (pronounced 'teak')
good – *acha*
what's your name? – *aapka naam kya hai?*
my name is John - *mera naam John hai*
I'm from Australia - *mae Australia se hoong*
where are you from? - *aap kahaa se hai?*
where is the Shalimar Hotel? - *Shalimar Hotel kahaa hai?*
do you have bottled water? - *kya aapka pas pani bottle?*
I want to go to Islamabad - *mae Islamabad jana chata/i hoong*
I would like biryani - *mujhe biryani chaaiye*
I don't want chicken - *mujhe murgh nahi chaaiye*
how much is it? - *kitne paise hai?*
do you speak English? - *aap Angrez bolte hai?*
do you have rooms available? - *aapka pas kamra hai?*
when is the next bus? - *agla bus kab hai?*
five o'clock - *panch baje*
is this the train to Lahore? - *is Lahore ka train hai?*
it's not a problem - *ko-ee masla nahi*
is it safe? - *kya woh mehfooz hai?*
what's the time? - *waqt kya huwa hai?*
just a minute! - *ek minute!*

Places and objects
bus - *bus*
train - *train*
car - *gari*
aeroplane/flight - *hawai jahaz* (literally 'air ship')
boat - *kashti*
ship – *jahaz*

hotel – *hotel*
shop - *dukaan*
bathroom - *washroom*
laundry - *dhobi*

restaurant - usually the word 'hotel' is used to describe a low-to-middle range eatery
station - *station*
street - *sarak*
airport - *airport*
pharmacy - *dawakhana*
hospital - *hospital*
mosque - *masjid*
Shia mosque and mourning hall - *imambargah*

---

temple - *mandir* (usually used for a Hindu temple)
church - *girja*
shrine / tomb - *darbar / mazar*
post office - *post office*
internet cafe - *internet cafe*
doctor – *doctor*
police - *police*
security guard - *chowkidaar*

shop keeper - *dukaanwala*
rickshaw driver - *rickshaw-wala*
luggage – *samaan*

phone - *phone*
map - *naksha*
key - *chaabi*
hot water - *garam pani*
blanket - *kumble*

Numbers and time
today - *aaj*
tomorrow - kal (be aware that '*kal*' also means 'yesterday' - the correct meaning is understood from context)
morning - *subah*
afternoon - *do pehar*
evening - *shaam*
night - *raat*
tonight - *aaj ki raat*

Numbers in Urdu are complicated. 1.5 and 2.5 have their own names, but from 3.5 and above the 'half' is added as '*saare*' before the number - see below. Similarly, there is no obvious pattern for numbers between 13 and 99 - each one has to be individually learnt. For the purpose of telling the time, we have included numbers up to twelve. Half hours are expressed using the number and 'baje', so 2:30 is *dai-ee baje*. After 100, a pattern develops where *do* means 'two', *sor* means 'hundred', so *do sor* means 'two hundred' and so on. 'Million' and 'billion' do not exist in Urdu; instead, a comma is added after every two digits over 10,000; e.g. 2,000,000 (two million) is written as 20,00,000 and known as *bees lakh* (twenty *lakh*).

1 - *ek*	11 - *gyara*
1.5 - *der*	12 - *bara*
2 - *do*	20 - *bees*
2.5 - *dai-ee*	25 - *pachees*
3 - *teen*	30 - *tees*
3.5 - *saare teen*	40 - *charlis*
4 - *char*	50 - *pachaas*
4.5 - *saare char*	100 - *sor*
5 - *panch*	200 - *do sor*
6 - *che*	1,000 - *hezar*
7 - *saat*	2,000 - *do hezar*
8 - *art*	1,00,000 - *lakh* (one hundred thousand)
9 - *noh*	1,00,00,000 - *crore* (ten million)
10 - *das*	

Health
I feel sick – *mujhe lagta hai meri tabiyat kharab hai*
My arm hurts – *mera bazoo me dard hai*
I broke my leg - *mera tung toota hai*
I have a headache - *mujhe saar dard hai*
I have a cold (common cold) – *mujhe zukhaam hua hai*
I feel dizzy – *mujhe chakkar aa raha hai*
I have diarrhoea – *mera pet kharab hai*
I have been vomiting – *me ulti kar raha/i hoong*
I ate some bad food – *mene kuch kharab khaya*

I have a fever – *mujhe bukhar hua hai*
I am allergic to aspirin - *mujhe aspirin bardasht nahi hota*
It's itchy – *mujhe khoojli ho raha hai*
I have insurance – *mera pas insurance hai*

leg - *tung*
arm - *bazoo*
ankle – *takhne* (but often just the word for "foot" is used - see below)
foot - *pear*
knee – *gootni*
back - *kammar*
neck – *gar-dan*
finger - *oongli*
throat – *gala*
chest - *sina*
stomach - *pet*
eye - *aankh*
ear - *kaan*
nose - *naak*
teeth - *daant*

Emergencies
quickly - *jaldi*
hurry up - *jaldi karo!*
stop (as in "stop the bus") - *rukhye!*
stop (as in "enough, leave me alone") - *bas!*
I'm lost - *mae kho gaya hoong*
I'm sick - *mae bimar hoong*
I've been in an accident – *mera accident hua hai*
I'm not from here - *mae mehmaan hoong* (literally "I'm a guest")
I don't understand - *mae nahi samjaa*
I've lost my phone – *mera phone kho gaya*
I've been robbed - *mujhe loota gaya hai*
my passport has been stolen - *mera passport chori hogaya hai*
call the police - *police call karo!*
call a doctor - *doctor call karo!*
it's an emergency! – *emergency hai!*

QUICK REFERENCE GUIDE
Important telephone numbers

Police – 15
Fire – 16
Ambulance – 115
Rescue – 1122
Traffic police – 1915

List of foreign embassies in Pakistan
Pages 42 - 46

———

Made in the USA
Middletown, DE
03 January 2020

82464433R00126